Advances in Complex Analysis and Applications

Edited by Francisco Bulnes and Olga Hachay

Published in London, United Kingdom

IntechOpen

Supporting open minds since 2005

Advances in Complex Analysis and Applications
http://dx.doi.org/10.5772/intechopen.79799
Edited by Francisco Bulnes and Olga Hachay

Contributors
José Trinidad Guillen Bonilla, Verónica María Rodríguez-Betancourtt, Alex Guillén-Bonilla, Gustavo Adolfo Vega Gómez, Héctor Guillén-Bonilla, María Susana Ruiz-Palacios, Martin Javier Martínez-Silva, Mario Alberto Garcia-Ramirez, Zitouna Bessem, Ben Hadj Slama Jaleleddine, Mozhgan (Nora) Entekhabi, Vyacheslav O Vakhnenko, Dmitri Vengrovich, Alexandre Michtchenko, Robson Pires, Gerardo R. Chacón, Gerardo A. Chacón, Xiao Huang, Peng Du, Haibao Hu, Francisco Bulnes

First published in London, United Kingdom, 2020 by IntechOpen
IntechOpen is the global imprint of INTECHOPEN LIMITED, registered in England and Wales, registration number: 11086078, 5 Princes Gate Court, London, SW7 2QJ, United Kingdom
Printed in Croatia

British Library Cataloguing-in-Publication Data
A catalogue record for this book is available from the British Library

Additional hard and PDF copies can be obtained from orders@intechopen.com

Advances in Complex Analysis and Applications
Edited by Francisco Bulnes and Olga Hachay
p. cm.
Print ISBN 978-1-83968-360-2
Online ISBN 978-1-83968-361-9
eBook (PDF) ISBN 978-1-83968-362-6

For EU product safety concerns:
IN TECH d.o.o., Prolaz Marije Krucifikse Kozulić 3, 51000 Rijeka, Croatia, info@intechopen.com or visit our website at intechopen.com.

Meet the editors

Dr. Francisco Bulnes, PhD, PostDocs, Doctor H. C., HonDSc, zbMATH, MathSci PhD in Mathematical Sciences, IM/UNAM. IINAMEI Director, Mathematics Research Centre in Mexico, 2015-present. Editor-in-Chief of Journals of Mathematics, in USA, and India, 2015-present. Member of various international committees of science. Reviewer of British journals of Mathematics and Physics in SCOPUS; Head of Research Department, GI-TESCHA. Numerous papers (more than 100) in mathematics and physics research journals, and author of several books of mathematics and physics. Recognized in East Europe, Asia, Arab continents. He has many theories, theorems, and math objects with his name. He has received various honors and awards (Doctorates Honoris Causa) by universities and NGOs, likewise GOs. He received the Doctor Honoris Causa in Education Philosophy and Peace Ambassador by ODAEE in Frankfurt, Germany. He is also a Czech Republic Mathematics Society distinguished member (JCFM). He has two post-doctorates in Cuba and Russia in mathematics. Many international awards and badges (more than 50) as Publons badge, SCOPUS, ZbMath, Thomsom Reuters, ORCID, Peace Ambassador and others. In addition, he has undertaken advanced research in electronics, micro-electronics and spintronics. He is an author, reviewer, book editor, and collaborator with IntechOpen from 2010.

Dr. Olga A. Hachay graduated with a degree in Astrophysics from Ural State University in 1969. She obtained her PhD from the Pushkov Institute of Terrestrial Magnetism, Ionosphere and Radiowave Propagation of the Russian Academy of Sciences (IZMIRAN) in 1979 with her thesis "The inverse problem for electromagnetic research of one-dimensional medium." Since 1969, she has been a scientific member of the Institute of Geophysics Ural Branch of Russian Academy of Sciences (UB RAS), Ekaterinburg, Russia. From 1995 to 2004, she served as chief of the group of seismic and electromagnetic research. Her research interests include developing new methods for searching the structure and the state of the Earth's upper crust, as well as elaborating a new theory of interpretation of electromagnetic and seismic fields. From 2002, she has been the main scientific researcher of the Institute of geophysics UB RAS. Since 2008, she has been a lead scientific researcher for UB RAS in the laboratory of borehole geophysics. Dr. Hachay is a member of various organizations and societies, including the American Mathematical Society, Mathematical Association of America, International Association of Geomechanics, and the European Geosciences Union, among others. Dr. Hachay is fluent in Russian, English and German language.

Contents

Preface

The complex analysis is known as the theory of functions of complex variables inside of the mathematical analysis having extensions in arithmetic and algebraic geometry, number theory, and other sophisticated theories as the Nevanlinna theory to the meromorphic functions study, the Morse theory and complex projective geometry, where this last arises from the hyperbolic geometry and their extensions. The present book is centered on the advances in holomorphicity, analyticity of complex functions of one or several variables, their integration and evaluation. From the point of view of their geometry, we discuss the conformal mappings of surfaces and complex Riemannian surfaces, considering their singularities and their treatment through diverse tools that offer the complex analysis theory. Also we focus on the topology relationships between geometrical manifolds considering the integration invariants and their cohomology. In addition, diverse applications in inverse problems and ill posed problems of complex functions in engineering fields will be important.

Dr. Francisco Bulnes
IINAMEI A. C. (Investigación Internacional Avanzada
en Matemáticas e Ingeniería),
Research Department in Mathematics and Engineering,
TESCHA,
Chalco, Mexico

Olga A. Hachay
Ural Branch of the Russian Academy of Sciences,
Yekaterinburg, Russian Federation

Section 1

Introductory Section

Chapter 1

Introductory Chapter: Frontiers and Future Developments of the Complex Analysis

Francisco Bulnes

1. Introduction

The complex analysis development can establish three fundamental ways of modern research with the goal to solve certain conjectures and complete certain theories as the Lie groups representation theory, obtaining of a general cohomology for certain integral operators in the differential equations solution and extend these solutions to the meromorphic context [1].

The three ways are defined for the relations between the complex analysis, with the cohomology with coefficients in holomorphic vector bundles, the hyper-complex analysis in a quaternionic algebra and the unitary representations in the Lie group theory [2].

Likewise, some objects as modular forms can be the key for the multidisciplinary investigations in complex functions without the condition that $f(z)$, be holomorphic in the upper half-plane. Then the modular forms are meromorphic functions [3]. The before, can be reflected in the satisfying of the certain functional equation $\mathrm{Tf}(z) = \xi$, in which the conditions of the complex function $f(z)$, respect to the transformation T, can be relaxed and the corresponding modular groups can be smaller groups. Such is the case, for example for the functional equation of the homographic transformation.

The transcendence goes more beyond of the analyticity problems in complex analysis. The study of the complex Riemannian manifolds results relevant in algebraic geometry and strings theories, where complex Riemann surfaces as complex submanifolds can be useful in the determination of integration invariants. Also in the Fröbenius distribution for the determination of integral submanifolds as cycles, whose values are co-cycles in a spectrum of the category Spec_k, of the category of the complex vector spaces Vec_C.

The theory of Riemann surfaces can be applied to the space $G \setminus H*$, to obtain further information about modular forms and functions. Likewise, the modular and cusp forms spaces $M_k(G)$, and $S_k(G)$, for a group G, are of finite dimension, and [4] their dimensions can be computed thanks to the Riemann-Roch theorem in terms of the geometry of the G−action on H. For example to the Lie group $SL(2, \mathbb{Z})$, this finite dimension is computed as[1]:

$$\dim_C M_k(\mathrm{SL}(2, Z)) = \begin{cases} \left\lfloor \frac{k}{12} \right\rfloor, & k \equiv 2(\mathrm{mod}12) \\ \left\lfloor \frac{k}{12} \right\rfloor + 1, & \mathrm{else} \end{cases} \tag{1}$$

[1] Here $\lfloor , \rfloor$, is a floor function.

IntechOpen

In projective spaces, the functions are homogeneous polynomials. These algebro-geometric objects are the sections of a sheaf (one could also say a line bundle in this case). Precisely here arises the re-interpretation of the differential operators through the homogeneous polynomials of the corresponding lines bundles sections of their respective connections [5] (**Figure 1**).

However, there is other conjecture established years ago, which establish the sentence.

Conjecture 1.1. All complex function (analytic function) $f(z)$, can be determined for hypercomplex functions [6].

This could be obtained in a clear way, without pass for the holomorphicity.

This represents all a joint research program between the hypercomplex analysis and the integral operators cohomology, and for it is established determine an integral operators theory that establish equivalences between cohomology classes on different complex base spaces and the cycles and co-cycles of these under the corresponding integral operators.

Likewise, can be obtained integral representations that are realizations of certain unitary representations of Lie groups such as $U(n)$, $\mathrm{SU}(2)$, $\mathrm{SU}(n)$, $\mathrm{SU}(2,2)$, $\mathrm{SU}(p,q)$, and $U(p,q)$, for the obtaining of the general solution of a partial differential equations in contexts of the quaternion algebra. And not only that, also are contemplated the equivalences of the corresponding cohomology classes obtained through the restricted objects to a space of certain dimension, for example, the hypercomplex analysis in $\mathbb{R}^4 \cong \mathbb{C}^2$, and in $\mathbb{C}^4$, is a quaternion analysis. Other example we can find in the integrals of the integral geometry of $G_{2,4}(\mathbb{C})$, through the space $\mathbb{P}^3(\mathbb{C})$, which establishes a twistor geometry [2, 7].

However, the isomorphism relations in homogeneous vector bundles are equivalent to the followed in cohomology developed in vector tomography. Likewise, the intertwining integral operators between cohomological classes of both contexts (respective cycles) result be cohomological classes in contexts of lines bundles (or equivalent co-cycles). In this sense a conjecture that can be proved is: "the Penrose transform is a vector Radon transform on homogeneous vector bundles sections in a Riemannian manifold" And considering the re-construction of a Riemannian manifold through cycles, we can consider the following conjecture also.

Conjecture 1.2. [2] The twistor transform is the generalization of the Radon transform on lines bundles and the Penrose transform is a specialization of the twistor transform in S^4.

Of fact, the twistor transform can be determined for the Penrose transforms pair on $G-$orbits of projective spaces $\mathbb{P}^-$, and $\mathbb{P}^+$. Then here arises the mentioned before in modular forms, the use of the lines bundles restricted to the polynomial rings corresponding to the subjacent operators on the complex vector spaces. In a more general sense, the vector bundles which refer us, are the seated in the homogeneous spaces $G^{\mathbb{C}}/L$, with homogeneous subspaces $G^{\mathbb{C}}/Q$, where is subjacent a

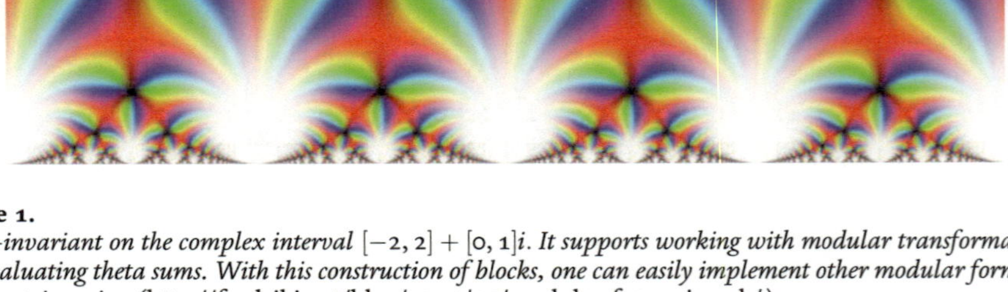

Figure 1.
The j*−invariant on the complex interval* $[-2, 2] + [0, 1]i$. *It supports working with modular transformations and evaluating theta sums. With this construction of blocks, one can easily implement other modular forms such as Eisenstein series.* (http://fredrikj.net/blog/2014/10/modular-forms-in-arb/).

holomorphic manifold with $G-$ orbits (parabolic orbits) of $G^{\mathbb{C}}/L$, which have an induced Haar measure in each closed submanifold given for the flags of the corresponding holomorphic vector $G-$ bundle. Then their orbital integrals are calculated on said orbits, obtaining invariants applicable to whole the homogeneous space in question, $G^{\mathbb{C}}/L$. This process called of orbitalization of the homogeneous space $G^{\mathbb{C}}/L$, is based in major part in the inclusion of homogeneous spaces obtained for reduction of $G^{\mathbb{C}}/L$, through its holonomy [7].

The spaces or cohomology groups of the complex corresponding of sheaves $H^s(G/H, \nu_n)$, result be fine representations of $G^{\mathbb{C}}/L$, through of the flags bundle corresponding to the complex holomorphic $G-$ bundle in $G^{\mathbb{C}}/L$. The realizations of these unitary representations are the orbital integrals on the flags that are the $K-$ orbits of the corresponding vector $G-$ bundle. This is precisely used in representations of $G-$ (a complex Lie group) constructed on spaces of holomorphic sections of vector bundles and generalizations as the studied for the modular forms. The problem that here arise (in the unitary representations) is the verifying of the Hermitian forms calculated through the diverse integral realizations with the corresponding representations choosing the smooth and minimal globalizing, adequate. For it is used in a general version of the complex cohomology known as $\bar{\partial}-$ cohomology called Serre generalization [7].

However, this is not reduced to the obtaining of representations of complex groups. Also the obtaining of an analytic function $f(z)$, of a space to other is realized accord to the integral cohomology $(n-1-q)-\bar{\partial}-$ cohomology $H^{n-1,q}(\mathbb{C}^n/D, V)$, where D, is a linearly concave domain on $\mathbb{C}^2$. Likewise, for example, if we consider the space $\mathbb{C}^2$, the integral operator that obtains a harmonic function in $\mathbb{R}^4$, through calculated functions of $C^\infty(\mathbb{C}^3)$, on lines S^1, in $\mathbb{C}^2$, comes given for [8, 9]:

$$\varphi(w, x, y, z) = \int_{S^1} f[(w + x) + (y + \mathrm{i}z)\zeta, (y - \mathrm{i}z) + (w - x)\zeta, \zeta]d\zeta, \tag{2}$$

which represents a transformation in cycles (lines) of a flag manifold $\mathbb{F} = (L|L \subset \mathbb{R}^4)$. Likewise complex functions in certain complex manifolds can be obtained through complex or hypercomplex functions defined in complex subspaces (or submanifolds) which could be varieties in an algebraic context, for certain conditions of its cohomology. For example in a complex sheaves cohomology, results interesting for problems of differential equations whose operators are germs of these sheaves.

Other study is the singularities study through varieties considering newly the complex varieties, in a pure algebraic treatment, or using the analyticity as a concept required for contour integrals to define a singularity as a pole of an analytic function.

Likewise in concrete, through an analytic functions study, can be extended and generalized the Cauchy integral as through integrals of contour can be generalized functional in a cohomology of contours (cohomological functional). The Morera's and Cauchy-Goursat's theorems can be applied in a sense geometrical more general as cohomological functional of contours whose residue value can be modulo $l(S^1) = 2\pi$. For example, two singularities or poles. This could represent the surface of the real part of the function $g(z) = \frac{z^2}{z^2+2z+2}$. The moduli space of these points are less than 2 and thus lie inside one contour. Likewise, the contour integral can be split into two smaller integrals using the Cauchy-Goursat theorem having finally the contour integral [10] $\oint_C g(z)\mathrm{d}z = \oint_C \left(1 - \frac{1}{z-z_1} - \frac{1}{z-z_2}\right)\mathrm{d}z = 0 - 2\pi\mathrm{i} - 2\pi i = -4\pi i$. This is a good example of traditional cohomological functional element of $\mathrm{H}^f(\Pi - \ell', \Omega^r) = \mathbb{C}$.

As a way to extend the meromorphic functions, the Nevanlinna theory searches generalizations of extensions of analytic functions to algebroid functions, holomorphic curves [10], holomorphic maps between complex manifolds of arbitrary dimension, quasi-regular mappings and minimal surfaces [11]. This is being applicable in moduli problems and Shimura varieties.

2. Future research

Finally, the future researches in complex analysis will be centered on major research of meromorphicity, in the automorphicity [12, 13], bi-holomorphicity, Riemann-Zeta function, Hodge theory and the complex ideals for improve methods of homogeneous polynomials in the complex vector bundles studied in complex Riemaniann manifolds and their submanifolds, involving singularities as poles or insolated singularities of rational curves. The automorphic forms generalize the Cauchy and Morera's theorems in an arithmetic sense inside the analytic functions theory and their probable holomorphicity. The automorphic forms are the other basic operations that arise inside the mathematics in the modular forms.

Author details

Francisco Bulnes
IINAMEI, Research Department in Mathematics and Engineering, TESCHA, Mexico

*Address all correspondence to: francisco.bulnes@tesch.edu.mx

References

[1] F. Bulnes, Integral Geometry Methods in the Geometrical Langlands Program, Scientific Research Publishing, Inc. USA, 8 jun. 2016.

[2] Bulnes, F. and Shapiro, M. (2007) Sobre una Teoría General de Operadores Integrales para Análisis y Geometría, Appliedmath 3 (Pure Mathematics Section) IPN, IM-UNAM, CINVESTAV, COFFA, ESIME-IMPN, ESFM-IPN Ciudad de México, Mexico.

[3] Kichoon Y. (1999) Meromorphic Functions and Projective Curves, Kluwer Academic Publishers, Netherlands.

[4] Shimura, Goro, An Introduction to the Arithmetic Theory of Automorphic Functions, Princeton University Press, 1994.

[5] Available from: http://fredrikj.net/blog/2014/10/modular-forms-in-arb/

[6] Sorin D. Gal (2004) Introduction to the Geometric Function theory of Hypercomplex variables, Nova Science Publishers. New York, USA.

[7] Francisco Bulnes, Integral Geometry and Cohomology in Field Theory on the Space-Time as Complex Riemannian Manifold, Book Chapter of Advances in Complex Analysis, Intech, July 2020. doi: 10.5772/intechopen.92969

[8] Francisco Bulnes. Mathematical Electrodynamics: Groups, Cohomology Classes, Unitary Representations, Orbits and Integral Transforms in Electro-Physics, American Journal of Electromagnetics and Applications. Vol.3, No. 6, 2015, pp. 43-52. doi: 10.11648/j.ajea.20150306.12

[9] Francisco Bulnes, Ronin Goborov, Integral Geometry and Complex Space-Time Cohomology in Field Theory, Pure and Applied Mathematics Journal. Special Issue: Integral Geometry Methods on Derived Categories in the Geometrical Langlands Program. Vol. 3, No. 6-2, 2014, pp. 30-37. doi: 10.11648/j.pamj.s.2014030602.16

[10] H. Weyl (1943). Meromorphic functions and analytic curves. Princeton University Press. New Jersey, USA.

[11] Drasin, D. (1976). "The inverse problem of the Nevanlinna theory". Acta Math. 138 (1): 83–151. doi: 10.1007/BF02392314

[12] Shimura, Goro (1971), Introduction to the arithmetic theory of automorphic functions, Publications of the Mathematical Society of Japan, 11, Tokyo: Iwanami Shoten, Theorem 2.33, Proposition 2.26.

[13] H. Iwaniec, Spectral Methods of Automorphic Forms, Second Edition, (2002) (Volume 53 in Graduate Studies in Mathematics), American Mathematical Society, Providence, RI, USA.

Section 2

Complex Functions and Some of Their Functional Transforms

Chapter 2

Interference Pattern Representation on the Complex s-Plane

José Trinidad Guillen Bonilla, Alex Guillen Bonilla, Mario Alberto García Ramírez, Gustavo Adolfo Vega Gómez, Héctor Guillen Bonilla, María Susana Ruiz Palacio, Martín Javier Martínez Silva and Verónica María Bettancourt Rodriguez

Abstract

In this work, the normalized interference pattern produced by a coherence interferometer system was represented as a complex function. The Laplace transform was applied for the transformation. Poles and zeros were determined from this complex function, and then, its pole-zero map and its Bode diagram were proposed. Both graphical representations were implemented numerically. From our numerical results, pole location and zero location depend on the optical path difference (OPD), while the Bode diagram gives us information about the OPD parameter. Based on the results obtained from the graphical representations, the coherence interferometer systems, the low-coherence interferometer systems, the interferometric sensing systems, and the fiber optic sensors can be analyze on the complex s-plane.

Keywords: coherence interferometer system, Laplace transform, complex function, pole-zero map, Bode diagram, graphical representations

1. Introduction

Many coherence interferometers systems find practical applications for the physical parameter measurement, such as are temperature, strain, humidity, pressure, level, current, voltage, and vibration [1–10]. Physical implementation and signal demodulation are very important for the good measurement. Many implementations are based on the Bragg gratings, fiber optics, vacuum, mirrors, crystals, polarizer, and their combinations [11–15]; whereas in the signal demodulation, has been applied commonly the Fourier transform [16–20]. This transform permits us to know all frequency components of any interference pattern, doing possible the signal demodulation for the interferometer systems.

The Laplace transform has many practical applications in topics such as control systems, electronic circuit analysis, mechanic systems, electric circuit system, pure mathematics, and communications. The linear transformation permits us to transform any time function into a complex function whose variable is $s = i\omega + \sigma$, where i is the complex operator, ω is the angular frequency, and σ is a real value. The complex function can represent in the complex s-plane, where their axes represent the real and imaginary parts of the complex variable s. This complex plane does feasible the study of dynamic systems, and some applications are the tuning closed-loop, stability, mathematical methods, fault detection, optimization, and filter design [21–23]. In addition, the s-plane permits graphical methods such as pole-zero map, Bode diagrams, root locus, polar plots, gain margin and phase margin, Nichols charts, and N circles [24].

In dynamic system analysis, pole-zero map and Bode diagrams are two graphical methods which have many practical applications. Both methods require a complex function, where the frequency response plays a very important role. In the pole-zero map, poles and zeros have been calculated from the complex function, and then, their locations are represented on the complex s-plane. It is usual to mark a zero location by a circle ($\circ$) and a pole location a cross ($\times$) [24]. In the Bode diagram, the magnitude and phase are calculated from the complex function, and then, both parameters are graphed. The graphic is logarithmic, and it shows the frequency response of our system under study.

Under our knowledge, the coherence interferometer system was not studied on the s-plane, and as a consequence, its interference pattern was not represented over the pole-zero map or Bode diagrams. In this work, the complex s-plane was used to represent the output signal of an interferometer system. Applying two graphical methods, such as pole-zero plot and Bode plot, the optical signal was represented. Numerically was verified that the pole location and the zero location depend directly on the optical path difference, while a Bode diagram shows the stability/ instability of the interferometer.

2. Interference pattern

Figure 1 shows a schematic example of a Michelson interferometer [25]. The interferometer consists of a coherent source, an oscilloscope, a generator function, a beam splitter 50/50 and a PZT optical element. This interferometric system has

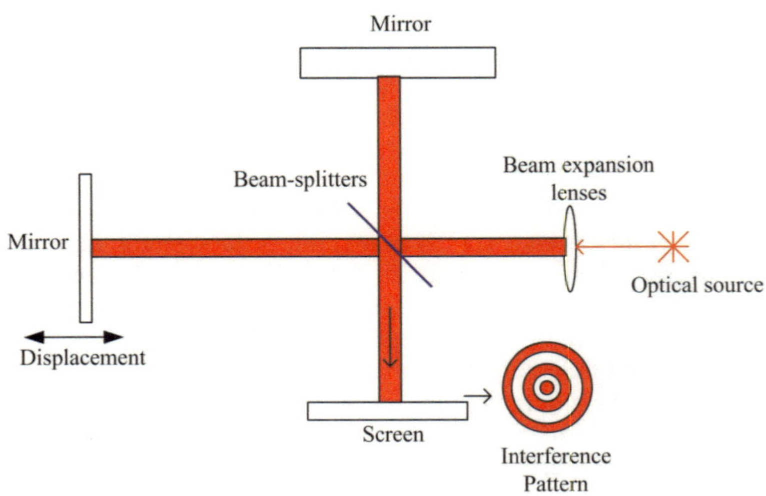

Figure 1.
Michelson interometer system.

two ways and its difference produces the optical path difference. The first one will be the reference. Its electrical field is

$$E_R(t) = A_R e^{i(\omega t + \varphi_R)}. \quad (1)$$

The second one is the signal measurement and its electrical field is

$$E_D(t) = A_D e^{i(\omega t + \varphi_D)}. \quad (2)$$

A_R and A_D are amplitudes, ω is the angular frequency, t is the time, and φ_R and φ_D are given by

$$\varphi_R = 2kx_R, \quad (3)$$

and

$$\varphi_D = 2kx_D. \quad (4)$$

x_R and x_D are the distances traveled by both beams and $k = \frac{2\pi n}{\lambda}$ is the wavenumber: λ is the wavelength and n is the refraction index.

From **Figure 1**, when the photodetector detects the total field, its signal is

$$E_T(t) = A_R e^{i(\omega t + \varphi_R)} + A_D e^{i(\omega t + \varphi_D)}. \quad (5)$$

Following, the irradiance E_T^2 will be

$$E_T^2 = \left[A_R e^{i(\omega t + \varphi_R)} + A_D e^{i(\omega t + \varphi_D)}\right]\left[A_R e^{-i(\omega t + \varphi_R)} + A_D e^{-i(\omega t + \varphi_D)}\right]. \quad (6)$$

Developing, we will obtain

$$E_T^2 = E_R^2 + E_D^2 + E_R E_D\left[e^{i(\omega t + \varphi_R)} e^{-i(\omega t + \varphi_D)} + e^{i(\omega t + \varphi_D)} e^{-i(\omega t + \varphi_R)}\right] \quad (7)$$

or

$$E_T^2 = E_R^2 + E_D^2 + E_R E_D\left[e^{i(\varphi_R - \varphi_D)} + e^{-i(\varphi_R - \varphi_D)}\right]. \quad (8)$$

Using the identity $cos\,(\theta) = \frac{e^{i\theta} + e^{-i\theta}}{2}$, Eq. (8) takes the form

$$E_T^2 = E_R^2 + E_D^2 + 2E_R E_D \cos(\varphi_R - \varphi_D). \quad (9)$$

In terms of intensity, the interferometer system produces the next interference pattern

$$I_T = I_R + I_D + 2\sqrt{I_R I_D} \cos(\varphi_R - \varphi_D). \quad (10)$$

If both beams have the same intensity $I_R = I_D = I_o$, the total intensity will take the form

$$I_T = 2I_o[1 + \cos(\varphi_R - \varphi_D)]. \quad (11)$$

As seen in Eq. (11), the phase difference is due to the optical path difference between the two beams. Substituting Eqs. (3) and (4) into Eq. (11), the interference pattern in terms of intensity can be written as

$$I_T(t) = 2I_o\left[1 + \cos\left(\frac{4\pi n}{\lambda}\Delta x(t)\right)\right], \tag{12}$$

where $\Delta x = x_R - x_D$ is the length difference between the distances x_R and x_D. Basically, the irradiance is an interference pattern which is formed by two functions: enveloped and modulate. The enveloped function is $f_{env} = 2I_o\left[\frac{W}{m^2}\right]$ and this function contains information from the optical source. The modulate function is given by $f_{mod} = 1 + \cos\left(\frac{4\pi n}{\lambda}\Delta x(t)\right)$ and it contains information about the interference pattern. The modulate function consist of a constant (direct component) and a trigonometric function (cosine function) whose frequency depends on the optical path difference.

3. Complex function

Observing **Figure 1** and Eq. (11), the phase difference $\varphi_R - \varphi_D$ is a time-varying function, and as a consequence, the phase $\frac{4\pi n}{\lambda}\Delta x(t)$ is also a time-varying function. In this case, the instantaneous output voltage (or current) of our photodector is proportional to the normalized optical intensity $\frac{I_T(t)}{I_o}$, where I_o is the LASER intensity $\left[\frac{W}{m^2}\right]$ [25]. Mathematically, the normalized interference pattern can be written as

$$I_n(t) = \frac{I_T(t)}{I_o} = 2[1 + \cos(\omega_m t)]. \tag{13}$$

Here, the angular frequency ω_m was proposed from the phase $\frac{4\pi n}{\lambda}\Delta x(t)$ and the interferometer system has not external perturbations.

To determinate the complex function $I_n(s)$, we calculate the unilateral Laplace transform for our last expression

$$I_n(s) = \int_0^\infty I_n(t)e^{-st}dt = 2\int_0^\infty e^{-st}dt + 2\int_0^\infty \cos(\omega_m t)e^{-st}dt. \tag{14}$$

Substituting the trigonometric identity $\cos(\omega_m t) = \frac{e^{i\omega_m t} + e^{-i\omega_m t}}{2}$ into Eq. (14), the complex function can be estimated through

$$I_n(s) = 2\int_0^\infty e^{-st}dt + 2\int_0^\infty \left(\frac{e^{i\omega_m t} + e^{-i\omega_m t}}{2}\right)e^{-st}dt, \tag{15}$$

or

$$I_n(s) = 2\int_0^\infty e^{-st}dt + \int_0^\infty e^{i\omega_m t}e^{-st}dt + \int_0^\infty e^{-i\omega_m t}e^{-st}dt. \tag{16}$$

Solving the integrals, the complex function will be

$$I_n(s) = -\frac{2}{s}e^{-st}\bigg|_0^\infty + \frac{e^{-(-i\omega_m t+s)t}}{-(-i\omega_m t + s)}\bigg|_0^\infty + \frac{e^{-(i\omega_m+s)t}}{-(i\omega_m + s)}\bigg|_0^\infty. \tag{17}$$

Evaluating the limits,

$$I_n(s) = \frac{2}{s} + \frac{1}{s - i\omega_m} + \frac{1}{s + i\omega_m}. \tag{18}$$

Using the algebraic procedure, we obtain

$$I_n(s) = \frac{2}{s} + \frac{s + i\omega_m + s - i\omega_m}{s^2 - i^2\omega_m^2} = \frac{2}{s} + \frac{2s}{s^2 + \omega_m^2}. \tag{19}$$

As seen in Eq. (19), the first term was produced by the direct component and the second term was produced by cosine function. Now, let us represent the complex function as

$$I_n(s) = \frac{4s^2 + 2\omega_m^2}{s\left(s^2 + \omega_m^2\right)}. \tag{20}$$

Because the Laplace transform was used for the transformation, the normalized interference pattern can be studied in the time domain and on a complex s-plane. It is possible since both Eqs. (13) and (20) contain the same information.

4. Graphical representation

In mathematics and engineering, the s-plane is the complex plane which Laplace transform is graphed. It is a mathematical domain where, instead of view processes in the time domain modeled with time-based functions, they are viewed as equations in the frequency domain. Then, the function $I_n(s)$ can be graphed using the pole-zero map and the Bode diagrams. These graphical representations provide a basis for determining important system response characteristics.

4.1 Pole-zero plot

In general, the poles and zeros of a complex function may be complex, and the system dynamics may be represented graphically by plotting their locations on the complex s-plane, whose axes represent the real and imaginary parts of the complex variable s. Such graphics are known as pole-zero plots. It is usual to mark a zero location by a circle ($\diamond$) and a pole location a cross ($\times$). In this study, it is convenient to factor the polynomials in the numerator and denominator and to write the complex function in terms of those factors

$$I_n(s) = \frac{P_N(s)}{P_D(s)} = \frac{4s^2 + 2\omega_m^2}{s\left(s^2 + \omega_m^2\right)}, \tag{21}$$

where the numerator and denominator polynomials, $P_N(s)$ and $P_D(s)$, have real coefficient defined by the system's characteristic. To calculate the zeros, we require

$$P_N(s) = 0 = 4s^2 + 2\omega_m^2. \tag{22}$$

Solving last polynomial function, the roots (zeros) are localized at

$$s^2 = \frac{-\omega_m^2}{2} \to s = \sqrt{-\frac{\omega_m^2}{2}}. \tag{23}$$

From our last results, the zeros are imaginary values

$$\begin{aligned} s_1 &= i\frac{\omega_m}{\sqrt{2}} \\ s_2 &= -i\frac{\omega_m}{\sqrt{2}} \end{aligned}. \tag{24}$$

By the similar way,

$$P_D(s) = 0 = s\left(s^2 + \omega_m^2\right). \tag{25}$$

To calculate the roots,

$$\begin{aligned} s_1 &= 0 \\ s_2 &= i\omega_m \\ s_3 &= -i\omega_m \end{aligned}. \tag{26}$$

Using our previous results presented at Eq. (24) and Eq. (26), we represent a pole-zero plot for the interference pattern, see **Figure 2**.

From **Figure 2**, the interference pattern produces two zeros and three poles. Both zeros (s_1 and s_2) and two poles (s_2 and s_3) are over the imaginary axes and their locations depend on the angular frequency. The pole (s_1) was obtained by the direct component; our normalized interference pattern and the location are over the origin.

4.2 Bode diagram

Based on the system theory and system graphic representation, the complex interference pattern can be represented through the Bode diagram. The graphical representation permits us to graph the frequency response of our interferometer system. It combines a Bode magnitude plot, expressing the magnitude (decibels) of the frequency response, and a Bode phase plot, expressing the phase shift.

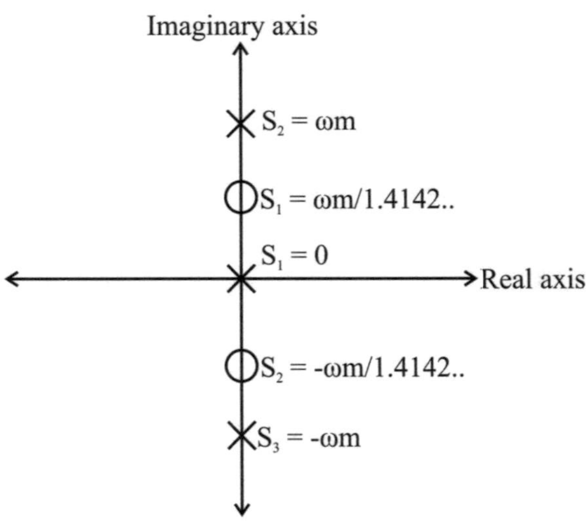

Figure 2.
Polo-zero map obtained from the interference pattern.

As was mentioned, the complex interference pattern can be represented through the Bode diagram. To represent it, the term s is substituted by the term $i\omega$: i is the complex number and ω is the angular frequency. Such that, Eq. (20) takes the form

$$I_n(i\omega) = I_n(\omega) = \frac{2\left[2(i\omega)^2 + \omega_m^2\right]}{i\omega\left[(i\omega)^2 + \omega_m^2\right]}. \tag{27}$$

The magnitude (in decibels) of the transference function above is given by decibels gain expression:

$$A_{vdB} = 20\ log\ |I_n(i\omega)|. \tag{28}$$

Substituting Eq. (27) into Eq. (28), the magnitude will be

$$A_{vdB} = 20\ log\left|\frac{2\left[2(i\omega)^2 + \omega_m^2\right]}{i\omega\left[(i\omega)^2 + \omega_m^2\right]}\right|. \tag{29}$$

Applying the logarithm rules, Eq. (29) can express as

$$\begin{aligned} \mathrm{A_{vdB}} &= 20\ log\ (2) + 20\ log\ \left(\left|2(\mathrm{i}\omega)^2 + \omega_\mathrm{m}^2\right|\right) - 20\ log\ (|\mathrm{i}\omega|) \\ &-20\ log\ \left(\left|(i\omega)^2 + \omega_m^2\right|\right). \end{aligned} \tag{30}$$

To determine the phase, Eq. (27) will express as

$$I_n(i\omega) = \frac{-4\omega^2 + 2\omega_m^2}{i\left[-\omega^3 + \omega\omega_m^2\right]}. \tag{31}$$

Here, $i^2 = -1$ was used. Last expression can be written as

$$I_n(i\omega) = -i\frac{-4\omega^2 + 2\omega_m^2}{\left[-\omega^3 + \omega\omega_m^2\right]}. \tag{32}$$

From Eq. (32), the phase can also be determined.

5. $I_n(t)$ retrieval

As the Laplace transform is a linear transformation, during the transformation: $I_n(t) \to I_n(s)$ and $I_n(s) \to I_n(t)$, the information is not lost and then the interference pattern can be studied in the time domain and on the complex s-plane. In Section 2, it was explained the transformation $I_n(t) \to I_n(s)$, and their poles and zeros were graphed over the pole-zero map. In addition, we developed interference pattern on the frequency plane, being possible to implement the Bode plot. Following, we recover the time function from the complex function $I_n(s) \to I_n(t)$. This section is didactic since the objective is to verify that the complex function's information can also be represented in the time domain.

To recover the time function, we calculate the inverse Laplace transform through

$$I_n(t) = \frac{1}{2\pi i} \lim_{T\to\infty} \int_{\gamma-iT}^{\gamma+iT} I_n(s) e^{st} ds = \mathcal{L}^{-1}\{I_n(s)\}. \tag{33}$$

The integral complex is in the s-plane; their limits are $\gamma - iT$ and $\gamma + iT$; the symbol $\mathcal{L}^{-1}\{\cdot\} = \frac{1}{2\pi i} \lim_{T\to\infty} \int_{\gamma-iT}^{\gamma+iT} \{\cdot\} e^{st} ds$ indicates the inverse Laplace transform. Substituting Eq. (21) into Eq. (33), the normalized interference pattern can be obtained by

$$I_n(t) = \frac{1}{2\pi i} \lim_{T\to\infty} \int_{\gamma-iT}^{\gamma+iT} \frac{4s^2 + 2\omega_m^2}{s(s^2 + \omega_m^2)} e^{st} ds = \mathcal{L}^{-1}\left\{\frac{4s^2 + 2\omega_m^2}{s(s^2 + \omega_m^2)}\right\}. \tag{34}$$

Applying the partial fraction, Eq. (34) can be expressed as

$$I_n(t) = \frac{1}{2\pi i} \lim_{T\to\infty} \int_{\gamma-iT}^{\gamma+iT} \left(\frac{A}{s} + \frac{Bs + C}{s^2 + \omega_m^2}\right) e^{st} ds = \mathcal{L}^{-1}\left\{\frac{A}{s} + \frac{Bs + C}{s^2 + \omega_m^2}\right\}. \tag{35}$$

Here, A, B, and C are constants. To calculate the constant, we use next equality

$$\frac{4s^2 + 2\omega_m^2}{s(s^2 + \omega_m^2)} = \frac{A}{s} + \frac{Bs + C}{s^2 + \omega_m^2} \to 4s^2 + 2\omega_m^2 = As^2 + A\omega_m^2 + Bs^2 + Cs \tag{36}$$

Using Eq. (36), we obtain the next equation system and their solutions as

$$\begin{aligned} (A + B)s^2 &= 4s^2 & & A = 2 \\ Cs &= 0 & \to \quad & B = 2\,. \\ A\omega_m^2 &= 2\omega_m^2 & & C = 0 \end{aligned} \tag{37}$$

Substituting all constants into Eq. (37), the time function will be

$$I_n(t) = \mathcal{L}^{-1}\left\{\frac{2}{s}\right\} + \mathcal{L}^{-1}\left\{\frac{2s}{s^2 + \omega_m^2}\right\}. \tag{38}$$

Laplace transform	**Inverse Laplace transform**		
Time function	**Complex function**	**Complex function**	**Time function**
$f(t) = ku(t)$	$F(s) = \frac{k}{s}$	$F(s) = \frac{k}{s}$	$f(t) = ku(t)$
$f(t) = tu(t)$	$F(s) = \frac{1}{s^2}$	$F(s) = \frac{k}{s}$	$f(t) = tu(t)$
$f(t) = t^n u(t)$	$F(s) = \frac{n!}{s^{n+1}}$	$F(s) = \frac{n!}{s^{n+1}}$	$f(t) = t^n u(t)$
$f(t) = cos\ (\omega t)u(t)$	$F(s) = \frac{s}{s^2 + \omega^2}$	$F(s) = \frac{s}{s^2 + \omega^2}$	$f(t) = cos\ (\omega)u(t)$
$f(t) = sen\ (\omega t)u(t)$	$F(s) = \frac{\omega}{s^2 + \omega^2}$	$F(s) = \frac{\omega}{s^2 + \omega^2}$	$f(t) = sen\ (\omega t)u(t)$
$f(t) = cosh\ (\omega t)u(t)$	$F(s) = \frac{s}{s^2 - \omega^2}$	$F(s) = \frac{s}{s^2 - \omega^2}$	$f(t) = cosh\ (\omega)u(t)$
$f(t) = senh\ (\omega t)u(t)$	$F(s) = \frac{\omega}{s^2 - \omega^2}$	$F(s) = \frac{\omega}{s^2 - \omega^2}$	$f(t) = senh\ (\omega t)u(t)$

Note: $u(t)$ is the Heaviside function.

Table 1.
Fundamental Laplace transform [24].

Applying **Table 1**, the solved inverse Laplace transform is

$$I_n(t) = 2[1 + \cos(\omega_m t)]. \tag{39}$$

Observing both Eq. (13) and Eq. (39), we recover the time function from the complex function. Thus, we confirm that the complex s-plane permits us to study the interferometer system through the complex s-plane, using the pole-zero map and Bode diagrams.

6. Numerical results and discussion

6.1 Results

To verify our proposal, we consider the next interference pattern

$$I_T(t) = 2e^{t^2}[1 + \cos(10t)]. \tag{40}$$

From Eq. (40), the enveloped f_{env} is a Gaussian function $\left(f_{env} = 2I_o = 2e^{t^2}\right)$ and the modulate function is $f_{mod} = 1 + \cos(10t)$, where the angular frequency is $\omega_m = 10\ \left[\frac{radians}{se}\right]$. If the interference pattern is normalized as Eq. (12), we obtain

$$I_n(t) = \frac{I_T(t)}{I_o} = 2[1 + \cos(10t)]. \tag{41}$$

Figure 3 shows the interference pattern and the modulate function. Calculating the Laplace transform,

$$I_n(s) = \frac{P_N(s)}{P_D(s)} = \frac{4s^2 + 200}{s(s^2 + 100)}. \tag{42}$$

Using Expressions (24) and (42), the zeros are localized at the points

$$\begin{aligned} s_1 &= i\frac{10}{\sqrt{2}} \\ s_2 &= -i\frac{10}{\sqrt{2}} \end{aligned}. \tag{43}$$

Now, using Eqs. (26) and (42), the poles are

$$\begin{aligned} s_1 &= 0 \\ s_2 &= i10 \\ s_3 &= -i10. \end{aligned} \tag{44}$$

Finally, its pole-zero map can observe in **Figure 4**.

As seen in **Figure 4**, the zeros (s_1 and s_2) and the poles (s_2 and s_3) are over the imaginary axis. Their positions depend on the angular frequency, and therefore, their positions change due to the variations of the optical path difference. The pole s_1 is over the origin (of the complex s-plane), and it was generated by the direct component of our interference pattern.

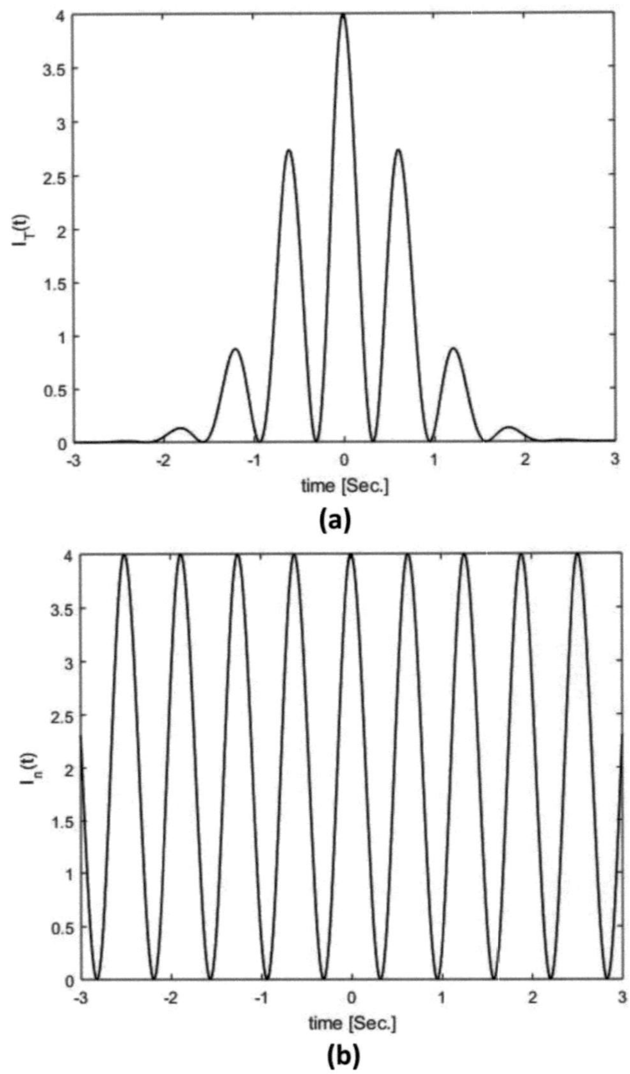

Figure 3.
(a) The simulated interference pattern. (b) The modulate function.

To generate the Bode diagram, we consider the next complex function

$$I_n(s) = \frac{4(i\omega)^2 + 200}{i\omega\left[(i\omega)^2 + 100\right]}. \tag{45}$$

Combining Eqs. (28) and (45), the magnitude (in decibels) is

$$A_{vdB} = 20\ log\left|\frac{4(i\omega)^2 + 200}{i\omega\left[(i\omega)^2 + 100\right]}\right|, \tag{46}$$

where $s = i\omega$ was used. Applying the logarithm rules, the magnitude can calculate as

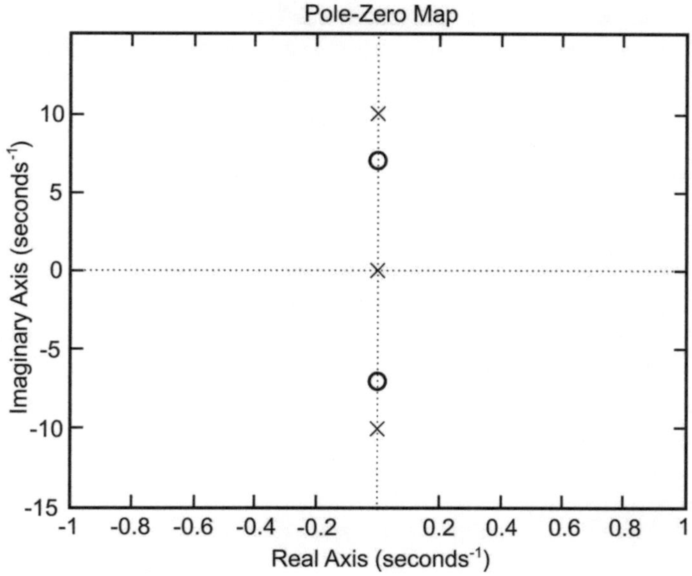

Figure 4.
Pole-zero plot determined from the complex modulate function (42).

$$A_{vdB} = 20\ log\left(\left|4(i\omega)^2 + 200\right|\right) - 20\ log\ (|i\omega|) - 20\ log\left(\left|(i\omega)^2 + 100\right|\right). \quad (47)$$

Using the Scientific MatLab software, we represent its Bode plot, see **Figure 5**. Observing **Figure 5**, the magnitude has a small variation between the intervals of 10^0 to $10^{0.7}$ and from 10^1 to 10^2 while the phase is -90^0. These results confirm the integrative action indicated by Eq. (47). The interferometric system produces two asymptotics for the magnitude. First asymptotic is negative, its location is at the point $10^{0.7}$ and the phase has transition from $-90°$ to 90^0. Second asymptotic

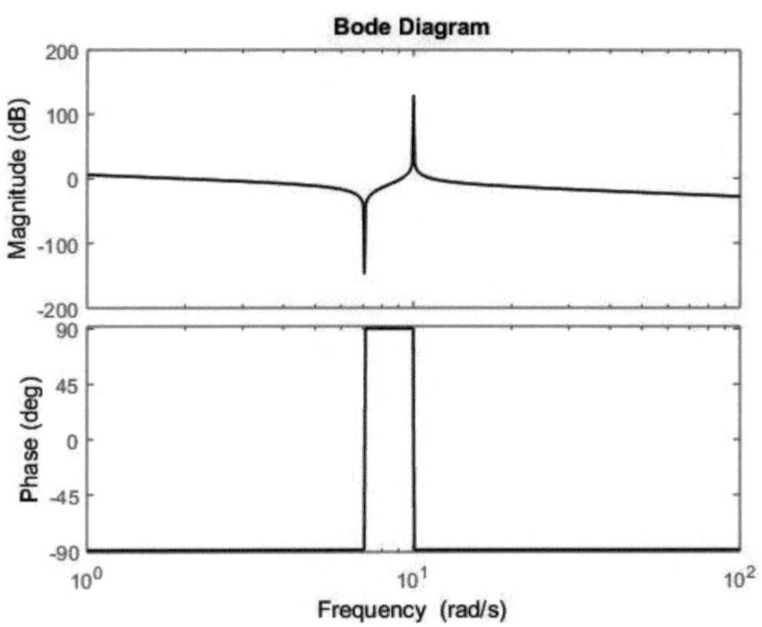

Figure 5.
Bode diagram obtained from the interference pattern.

is positive, its location is 10^1 and the phase has transition from 90^0 to -90°. Last interval is between $10^{0.7}$ and 10^1. In this case, the magnitude has small variation again but the phase is constant to 90°. These results confirm that the interferometer system will have integrative action and derivative action.

6.2 Discussion

Here, a complex function was obtained from the interference pattern produced by a coherence interferometer. Considering the pole-zero map, poles and zeros depend directly on the optical path difference of an interferometer. The interference pattern generates three poles and two zeros. A pole is over the origin and two poles are over the points $\pm i\omega_m$. The zeros are over the points $\pm i\frac{\omega_m}{\sqrt{2}}$. Now, considering the Bode plot, the interferometer can act as an integrator and as a derivator since the phase can take the value of -90° or 90°, see **Figure 5**. Both graphical representations permit to know the optical path difference through the angular frequency and its dynamic response.

From our analysis and results, it is possible to infer a few key point of our novel method.

- The complex s-plane permits us to study the interferometric systems.
- The interference pattern can represent as a complex function whose poles are three and zeros are two.
- Pole-zero map gives information about the optical path difference.
- The pole s_1 is over the origin and it was generated by the direct component of the interference pattern.
- s_2 and s_3 poles are over the imaginary axis and their position are $\pm i\omega_m$, where ω_m is the angular frequency.
- s_1 and s_2 zeros are over the imaginary axes and their locations depend on the angular frequency, see **Figure 4**.
- Bode diagram gives us information about the dynamic response of any interference pattern.
- Based on the Bode diagram (Phase information), the interferometer can act as an integrative action and as a derivative action.

Based on our results, the interference pattern can be studied by both graphical methods. Those graphical representations can be applied to low-coherence interferometric systems, optical fiber sensors, communication systems, and optical source characterization.

7. Conclusion

In this work, applying the Laplace transform and inverse Laplace transform, we confirm that the interference pattern produced by an Interferometer, can study in the time domain and on the complex s-plane. The pole-zero plot and the Bode diagram were obtained from the complex interference pattern. Both graphical representations give us information about the interferometer. The optical Path Difference (OPD) information can measure through the pole-zero map and the behavior of interferometer can understand through the Bode diagram. Therefore, the interferometers can be studied on the complex s-plane, being possible measures physical parameters when those interferometers were disturbed. Also, the signal demodulation can be implemented for the quasi-distributed fiber sensor when the local sensors are interferometers. Some measurable parameters are temperature, string, displacement, voltage and pressure.

If a low-coherence interferometer is studied on the s-plane, then the fringe visibility and the magnitude of coherence grade can be measured.

Acknowledgements

Authors thank the Mexico's National Council for Science and Technology (CONACyT) and university of Guadalajara for the support.

Conflict of interest

The authors declare no conflict of interest.

Author details

José Trinidad Guillen Bonilla[1,2*], Alex Guillen Bonilla[3], Mario Alberto García Ramírez[1], Gustavo Adolfo Vega Gómez[1], Héctor Guillen Bonilla[4], María Susana Ruiz Palacio[1], Martín Javier Martínez Silva[1] and Verónica María Bettancourt Rodriguez[5]

1 Electronic Department, CUCEI, University of Guadalajara, Guadalajara, Jaliscos, Mexico

2 Mathematic Department, CUCEI, University of Guadalajara, Guadalajara, Jaliscos, Mexico

3 Department of Computer Science and Engineering, CUVAlles, University of Guadalajara, Ameca, Jalisco, Mexico

4 Department of Engineering Projects, CUCEI, University of Guadalajara, Guadalajara, Jaliscos, Mexico

5 Chemical Department, CUCEI, University of Guadalajara, Guadalajara, Jaliscos, Mexico

*Address all correspondence to: trinidad.guillen@academicos.udg.mx

References

[1] Zhao N, Lin Q, Jiang Z, Yao K, Tian B, Fang X, et al. High temperature high sensitivity multipoint sensing system based on three cascade Mach-Zehnder interferometers. Sensors. 2018; **18**(8):2688. DOI: 10.3390/s18082688

[2] Jia X, Liu Z, Deng Z, Deng W, Wzng Z, Zhen Z. Dynamic absolute distance measurement by frequency sweeping interferometry based Doppler beat frequency tracking model. Optics Communication. 2019;**430**:163-169

[3] Peng J, Lyu D, Huang Q, Qu Y, Wang W, Sun T, et al. Dielectric film based optical fiber sensor using Fabry-Perot resonator structure. Optics Communication. 2019;**430**:63-69

[4] Vigneswaran D, Ayyanar VN, Sharma M, Sumahí M, Mani Rajan MS, Porsezian K. Salinity sensor using photonic crystral fiber. Sensors and Actuors A: Physical. 2018;**269**(1):22-28. DOI: 10.1016/j.sna2017.10.052

[5] Kamenev O, Kulchin YN, Petrov YS, Khiznyak RV, Romashko RV. Fiber-optic seismometer on the basis of Mach-Zehnder interfometer. Sensors and Actuors A: Physical. 2016;**244**:133-137. DOI: 10.1016/j.sna.2016.04.006

[6] Li L, Xia L, Xie Z, Liu D. All-fiber Mach-Zehnder interferometers for sensing applications. Optic Express. 2012;**20**(10):11109-11120. DOI: 10.1364/OE.20.011109

[7] Yu Q, Zhou X. Pressure sensor based on the fiber-optic extrinsic Fabry-Perot interferometer. Photonic Sensors. 2011; **1**(1):72-83. DOI: 10.1007/s13320-010-0017-9

[8] Yeo TL, Sun T, Grattan KTV. Fibre-optic sensor technologies for humidity and moisture measurement. Sensors and Actuators: Physical. 2008;**144**(2): 280-295. DOI: 10.1016/j.sna.2008.01.017

[9] Dong C, Li K, Jiang Y, Arola D, Zhang D. Evaluation of thermal expansion coefficient carbon fiber reinforced composites using electronic speckle interferometry. Optics Express. 2018;**26**(1):531. DOI: 10.1364/OE.26.000531

[10] Wang S, Gao Z, Li G, Feng Z, Feng Q. Continual mechanical vibration trajectory tracking based on electro-optical heterodyne interferometric. Optics Express. 2014;**22**(7):7799. DOI: 10.1364/OE.22.007799

[11] Wan X, Ge J, Chen Z. Development of stable monolithic wide-field Michelson interferometers. Applied Optics. 2011;**50**(21):4105-4114. DOI: 10-1364/AO.50.004105

[12] Hassan MA, Martin H, Jiang X. Development of a spatially dispersed short-coherence interferometry sensor using diffraction grating orders: Publisher's note. Applied Optics. 2018; **57**(1):5. DOI: 10.1364/AO.57.000005

[13] Guillen Bonilla JT, Guillen Bonilla A, Rodríguez Betancourtt VM, Guillen Bonilla H, Casillas Zamora A. A theoretical study and numerical simulation of a quasi-distributed sensor based on the low-finesse Fabry-Perot interferometer: Frequency-division multiplexing. Sensors. 2017;**17**(4):859. DOI: 10.3390/s17040859

[14] Liang Y, Zhao M, Wu Z, Morthier G. Investigation of grating-assisted trimodal interferometer biosensors based on a polymer platform. Sensors. 2018;**18**(5):1502. DOI: 10.3390/s.18052502

[15] Guillen Bonilla JT, Guillen Bonilla H, Casillas Zamora A, Vega Gómez GA, Franco Rodríguez NE, Guillen Bonilla A, et al. Twin-grating fiber optic sensors applied on wavelength-division multiplexing and its numerical

simulation. In: Rao SP, editor. Book of Numerical Simulation in Engineering and Science. 1st ed. IntechOpen. DOI: 10.5772/intechopen.75586

[16] de SAuza JC, Oliveira ME, Dos Santos PAM. Brach-cut algorithm for optical phase unwrapping. Optics Letters. 2015;**40**(15):3456-3459. DOI: 10.1364OL.40.003456

[17] Mizuno T, Kitoh T, Oguma M, Inoue Y, Shibata T, Hiroshi T. Mach-Zehnder interferometer with uniform wavelength period. Optics Letters. 2004;**29**(5):454-456. DOI: 10.1364/OL.29.000454

[18] Miridonov SV, Shlyagin M, Tentori D. Twin-grating fiber optic sensor demodulation. Optics Communication. 2001;**191**(3–6): 253-362. DOI: 10.1016/S0030-4018(01) 01160-9

[19] Kin JA, Kim JW, Kang CS, Jin J, Eom TB. Interferometric profile scanning system for measuring large planar mirror surface based on single-interferogram analysis using Fourier transform. Measurements. 2018;**118**: 113-119. DOI: 10.1016/j.measurement.2018.01.023

[20] Perea J, Libbey B, Nehmetallah G. Multiaxis heterodyne vibrometer for simultaneous observation of 5 degrees of dynamic freedom from a single beam. Optics Letters. 2018;**43**(13):3120-2123. DOI: 10.1364/OL.43.003120

[21] Davoodi M, Mezkin N, Khorasani K. A single dynamic observer-based module for design of simultaneous fault detection, isolation and tracking control scheme. International Journal of Control. 2018;**91**(3):508-523. DOI: 10.1080/00207179.2017.1286041

[22] Ordóñez Hurtado RH, Crisostomi E, Shorten RN. An assessment on the use of stationary vehicles to support cooperative positioning systems. International Journal of Control. 2018; **91**(3):608-621. DOI: 10.1080/00207179.2017.1286537

[23] Xu S, Sun G, Li Z. Finite frequency vibration suppression for space flexible structures in tip position control. International Journal of Control, Automation and Systems. 2018;**16**(3): 1021-1029. DOI: 10.1007/s12555-0160343-9

[24] Wolovich WA. Automatic Control Systems: Basic Analysis and Design. 1st ed. Sounders College Pub.; 1994. 450 p. ISBN: 0030237734, 9780030237737

[25] Andrade Barbosa FA, Nader G, Tokio Higuti R, Kitano C, Nelli Silva E. A simple interferometric method to measure the calibration factor and displacement amplification in piezoelectric flextensional actuators. Revista Controle & Automação. 2010; **21**(6):577-587

Chapter 3

Inverse Scattering Source Problems

Mozhgan "Nora" Entekhabi

Abstract

The purpose of this chapter is to discuss some of the highlights of the mathematical theory of direct and inverse scattering and inverse source scattering problem for acoustic, elastic and electromagnetic waves. We also briefly explain the uniqueness of the external source for acoustic, elastic and electromagnetic waves equation. However, we must first issue a caveat to the reader. We will also present the recent results for inverse source problems. The resents results including a logarithmic estimate consists of two parts: the Lipschitz part data discrepancy and the high frequency tail of the source function. In general, it is known that due to the existence of non-radiation source, there is no uniqueness for the inverse source problems at a fixed frequency.

Keywords: scattering theory, inverse scattering theory, Helmholtz equation, Bessel functions

1. Introduction

This chapter tries to provide some results and materials on inverse scattering, direct scattering theory and inverse source scattering problems. There have been many scientists who have contributed to the different components of this field, such as linearity or non-linearity of the inverse source problem, computational and numerical solution to the inverse source problem and analytical aspects of the problem, which have their own interests. We obviously cannot give a complete account of inverse scattering here from all angles. Hence, instead of attempting the impossible, we have chosen to present inverse scattering theory from the of our own interests and research program. Particularly, we will focus on inverse source problems for acoustic, elastics and electromagnetic waves. In other words, certain areas of inverse scattering theory are either ignored.

Scattering theory has played a central role in twentieth century mathematical physics and applied mathematics. Indeed, from Rayleigh's explanation of why the sky is blue, to Rutherford's discovery of the atomic nucleus, through the modern medical and clinical applications of computerized tomography, scattering phenomena have attracted scientists and mathematicians for over a hundred years. Broadly speaking, scattering theory is concerned with the effect an inhomogeneous medium has on an incident particle or wave. In particular, if the total field is viewed as the sum of an incident field u^i and a scattered field u^s then the direct scattering problem is to determine u^s form a knowledge of u^i and the differential equation governing the wave motion. There are even more in the inverse scattering problem of determining the nature of the inhomogeneity from a knowledge of the asymptotic behavior of u^s, i.e., to reconstruct the differential equation or its domain or source functions of definition from the behavior of solutions of the direct problems. In this chapter, we are following this notation; C denote generic constants depending on the domain Ω or domain D, which is different in different results, and $\|u\|_{(l)}(\Omega)$ denotes the standard norm in Sobolev space $H^l(\Omega)$.

2. The direct and inverse scattering problem

The stationary incoming wave u of frequency k is a solution to the perturbed Helmholtz equation (scattering by medium)

$$Au - k^2u = 0\, in\, \mathbb{R}^3 \tag{1}$$

(A is the elliptic operator $A = -\nabla(a\nabla) + b.\nabla + c$ with $\Re e b = 0, \nabla b = 0$, and $\Im m c \leq 0$, which coincides with the Laplace operator outside a ball B and which possesses the uniqueness of continuation property) or to the Helmholtz equation (scattering by an obstacle D for acoustic waves)

$$\Delta u + k^2u = 0\, in\, \mathbb{R}^3 \backslash \overline{D}, \tag{2}$$

with the Dirichlet boundary data

$$u = 0\, on\, \partial D \quad (soft\, obsacle\, D). \tag{3}$$

or the Neumann boundary data

$$\partial_\nu u = 0\, on\, \partial D \quad (hardo\ bsacle\, D). \tag{4}$$

The function u is assumed to be the sum of the so-called incident plane wave $u^i(x) = \exp(ik\xi \cdot x)$ and a scattered wave u^s satisfying the Sommerfeld radiation condition

$$\lim_{r\to\infty} r\left(\frac{\partial u^s}{\partial r} - iku^s\right) = 0, \tag{5}$$

where $\xi \in \mathbb{R}^3$, $|\xi| = 1$, is the so-called incident direction and

$$u(x) = \exp(ik\xi \cdot x) + u^s(x). \tag{6}$$

The electromagnetic scattering problem corresponding to the electric field E and magnetic field H such as

$$curlE - ikH = 0, \quad curlH + ikE = 0\, in\, \mathbb{R}^3 \backslash \overline{D}, \tag{7}$$

$$E(x) = \frac{i}{k} curl\, curl \exp(ik\xi \cdot x) + E^s(x), \tag{8}$$

$$H(x) = curl \exp(ik\xi \cdot x) + H^s(x), \tag{9}$$

$$\nu \times E = 0 \quad on \quad \partial D, \tag{10}$$

with the Silver- Muller radiation condition;

$$\lim_{r\to\infty}(H^s \times x - rE^s) = 0 \tag{11}$$

where (7) are the time-harmonic Maxwell equations and ν is again the unit outward normal to ∂D. As in previous case more general boundary condition can also be considered, for example the impedance boundary condition

$$\nu \times curlE - i\lambda(\nu \times E) \times \nu = 0, \tag{12}$$

where λ is a positive constant. The mathematical technique used to investigate the direct scattering problems for and electromagnetic waves depends heavily on the frequency of the wave motion. The first question about direct scattering is about uniqueness of a solution. The basic tools used to prove the uniqueness are Green's theorems and the unique continuation property of solutions to elliptic equations. Since Eqs. (2)–(5) for exterior problem have constant coefficients, the uniqueness question is much easier to handle. Similar argument can be applied on the Maxwell equations. The first result being given by Sommerfeld in 1912 for the case of acoustic case [1]. His work was generalized by Rellich [2] and Vekua [3], all under the assumption $\Im\mathfrak{m}k \geq 0$. The uniqueness of a solution to the exterior scattering problems for acoustic and electromagnetic is more difficult since use must now be made of the unique continuation principle for elliptic equations with non-analytic coefficients. After uniqueness, the most important questions would be the existence and numerical approximation of the solution. The most common technique to existence has been through the method of integral equation. For example for Eqs. (2)–(5), it is easy to see that for all positive values of wave number k the field u is the unique solution of the Lippman-Schwinger equation

$$u(x) = u^i + u^s \tag{13}$$

$$= exp\,(ik\xi \cdot x) + \frac{1}{r}\,exp\,(ikr)\mathcal{A}\left(\frac{x}{r}, \xi, k\right) + O\left(\frac{1}{r^2}\right) \tag{14}$$

where $r = |x|$ and the function $\mathcal{A}$ is called the scattering amplitude (or the scattering pattern or far field pattern).

The representation (14) follows from the fact that any solution u^s to the Helmholtz equation satisfying the radiation condition (5) has the representation by a single layer potential

$$u^i(x) = \int_{\partial B} g(y)K(x - y; k)d\Gamma(y), \tag{15}$$

where $K(x;k) = e^{ik|x|}/(4\pi|x|$ and B is some large ball (i.e., see [4]).

As showed above, the direct scattering problem has been thoroughly investigated and a considerable amount of information is available concerning its solution. In contrast, the inverse scattering problem has only recently progressed. It is worth to mention that the inverse problem is inherently nonlinear. In areas such as radar, sonar, geophysical exploration, medical imaging and nondestructive testing. As in with direct problem, the first question in inverse scattering problem is, how about uniqueness?. The first result in uniqueness brought up to the attention by Schiffer [5] who showed for the problem (2)–(5) the far field pattern $\mathcal{A}\left(\frac{x}{r}, \xi, k\right)$ with fixed wave number k uniquely determines the scattering obstacle D. And result for corresponding exterior problem obtained by Nachman [6], Novikov [7, 8]. Uniqueness theorems for electromagnetic problems were obtained by Colton and Päivärinta [9]. The next step will be the question of existence of the to the inverse scattering problem. The mathematically speaking, the solution of the inverse scattering problem does not exist, but we can speak about stabilization and approximation of the solutions. The earliest efforts in this direction attempted to linearize the problem by reducing it to the problem of solving a linear integral equation of the first kind. The initial attempts to treat the inverse scattering problem without linearizing were investigated by Imbriale and Mittra [10]. Their techniques were based on analytic continuation. In 1980's a number of methods were given to solving the inverse scattering problem which explicitly acknowledged the nonlinear and ill-posed nature of the problem. The two-dimensional case can be used as an approximation for the scattering from finitely long cylinders. In the next sections, we will discuss Helmholtz equation and two and three dimensional inverse source scattering problems for acoustic, elastic and electromagnetic waves. The following lemma is establishing the uniqueness for the direct solution(1) in $\mathbf{R}^3$. The following lemma is stated in [4].

Theorem 1.1. If u solves Eq. (1) in $\mathbb{R}^3$ and satisfies the radiation condition (5), then $u = 0$.

Proof. There is a weak solution to Eq. (1) in B with the test function $\phi = u$ we have

$$\int_{\partial B} \partial_\nu u\overline{u} = \int_B \left(a\nabla u \cdot \nabla\overline{u} + b \cdot \nabla u\overline{u} + \left(c - k^2\right)u\overline{u}\right) \tag{16}$$

$$= \int_B \left(a\nabla u \cdot \nabla\overline{u} + \overline{b \cdot \nabla uu} + \left(c - k^2\right)u\overline{u}\right) \tag{17}$$

using the condition $\mathfrak{Re}b = 0, \nabla b = 0$ and integration by part over ∂B the internal is a sum of two part; one involving ∇u and another $cu\overline{u}$. The first term coincides with its complex conjugate, so its imaginary part is zero, and the second one has a non-positive imaginary part due to the condition on c, hence

$$\mathfrak{Im}\int_{\partial B} \partial_\nu u\overline{u} \leq 0. \tag{18}$$

since u satisfied the Helmholtz equation and the radiation condition, the known results imply that $u = 0$ outside B. By uniqueness of the continuation for the elliptic operator $A - k^2$ we obtain that $u = 0$ in $\mathbb{R}^3$, so the proof is complete.

2.1 Helmholtz equation

Studying an inverse problem always requires a solid knowledge of the theory for the corresponding direct problem. Therefore in this section is devoted to presenting the foundations of obstacle scattering problems for time harmonic acoustic waves. The Helmholtz equation often arises in the study of physical problems involving partial differential equations (PDEs) in both space and time. The Helmholtz equation, which represents a time-independent form of the wave equation, results from applying the technique of separation of variables to reduce the complexity of the analysis. Colton and Kress showed that [11] how one can derived the Helmholtz equation from the Euler's equation. Then the domain of the solution is outside a bounded open set $D \in \mathbb{R}^d$, describing the scatterer. The equation is

$$\Delta u + k^2 u = 0 \tag{19}$$

where the wave number k is given by the positive constant $k = \omega/c$, with inhomogeneous boundary conditions on D of Dirichlet or Neumann type:

$$u(x) = g(x) \quad (Dirichlet), \quad \frac{\partial u(x)}{\partial \nu} = h(x), x \in \partial D, \quad (Neumann) \tag{20}$$

and it is a well-posed problem if

$$\lim_{r \to \infty} r^{\frac{d-1}{2}} \left(\frac{\partial u}{\partial r} - iku \right) = 0. \tag{21}$$

Let $G(x)$ be the Green's function for Helmholtz in d dimensions, e.g.

$$G(x-y) = \begin{cases} \frac{i}{4} H_0^1(k|x-y|), & d=2, \quad x \neq y \\ \frac{e^{ik(x-y)}}{4\pi|x-y|}, & d=3, \quad x \neq y \end{cases}$$

where $H_0^1(z) = \frac{1}{\pi i} \int_{1+i\infty}^{1} e^{izs} (s^2-1)^{-1/2} ds$, for $Rez > 0$, is the Hankel function of the first kind [12]. It is also can be defined as

$$H_0^{(1)}(z) = J_0(z) + iY_0(z), \tag{22}$$

where

$$\begin{aligned} J_0(z) &= \sum_{m=0}^{\infty} \frac{(-1)^m \left(\frac{1}{2}z\right)^{2m}}{(m!)^2}, \\ Y_0(z) &= 2\left\{\gamma + \log\left(\frac{1}{2}z\right)\right\} J_0(z) - 2\sum_{m=1}^{\infty} \frac{(-1)^m \left(\frac{1}{2}z\right)^{2m}}{(m!)^2} \left\{1 + \frac{1}{2} + \dots + \frac{1}{m}\right\}, \end{aligned} \tag{23}$$

and $\gamma = 0.5772157 \dots$ is the Euler's constant.
Then, we can solve the single layer potential integral equation

$$u(x,k) = \int_{\partial D} G(x-y)\psi(y)dy, \qquad x \in \overline{D}^c. \tag{24}$$

Alternatively, we can solve the double layer potential integral equation

$$-u^i(x,k) = \frac{1}{2}\psi(x) - \int_{\partial D} \frac{\partial G(x-y)}{\partial n} \psi(y)dy, \qquad x \in \partial D. \tag{25}$$

In this case the scattered solution outside D is given by

$$u(x) = -\int_{\partial D} \frac{\partial G(x-y)}{\partial n} \psi(y)dy, \qquad x \in \overline{D}^c. \tag{26}$$

2.2 Inverse source scattering problem

Motivated by the significant applications, the inverse source problems, as an important research subject in inverse scattering theory, have continuously attracted much attention by many researchers. Consequently, a great deal of mathematical and numerical results are available. In general, it is known that there is no uniqueness for the inverse source problem at a fixed frequency due to the existence of non-radiation sources. Hence, additional information is required for the source in order to obtain a unique solution, such as to seek the minimum energy solution. From the numerical and computational point of view, a more challenging issue is lack of stability. A small variation of the data might lead to a huge error in the reconstruction. Recently, it has been realized that the use of multi-frequency data is an effective approach to overcome the difficulties of non- uniqueness and instability which are encountered at a single frequency. An attempt was made in [13] to extend the stability results to the inverse random source of the one-dimensional stochastic Helmholtz equation. The inverse source problem seeks for the right hand side of a partial differential equation from boundary data. The inverse source problems are also considered as a basic mathematical tool for solving many imaging problems including reflection tomography, diffusion-based optical tomography, lidar imaging for chemical and biological threat detection, and fluorescence microscopy. In general, a feature of inverse problems for elliptic equations is a logarithmic type stability estimate which results in a robust recovery of only few parameters describing the source and hence yields very low resolution numerically.

For the Helmholtz equations, the results have shown increasing (getting nearly Lipschitz) stability when the Dirichlet data or Cauchy data are given on the whole boundary and K is getting large. Similar results are obtained for the time periodic solutions of the more complicated dynamical elasticity system. For elastic waves, the inverse source problem is to determine the external force that produces the measured displacement. The inverse source scattering problem for Maxwell equation arises in many scientific areas such as medical imaging. More specifically, Magnetoencephalography (MEG), the imaging modality is a non-invasive neurophysiological technique that measures the electric or magnetic fields generated by neuronal activity of the brain. For electromagnetic waves, the inverse source problem is to reconstruct the electric current density from tangential trace of electric field. As we know in [14], the inverse source problem does not have a unique solution at a single or at finitely many wave numbers. On the other hand, if we use all wave numbers in $(0, K)$ one can regain uniqueness. Another purpose of this chapter is to establish uniqueness for the source from the Cauchy data on any open non empty part of the boundary for arbitrary positive K. For uniqueness, we will show two different techniques. The first technique is to use the stability estimate for the source functions and the second technique is a direct proof.

First increasing stability results were obtained in [15] by using the spatial Fourier transform. In [16, 17] more general and sharp results were obtained in sub-domain of $\mathbb{R}^3$ *and* $\mathbb{R}^2$ in an arbitrary domains with C^2 boundary by the temporal Fourier transform, with a possibility of handling spatially variable coefficients. The recent results showed that the estimate for source functions is a logarithmic type. The right hand-side of the estimate consists of two parts: data discrepancy and the high frequency tail. In the papers [15, 18], Li, Bao and others showed the similar results for disc and ball. For instance, the results by Entekhabi and Isakov are as follows;

Let the radiated wave field $u(x, k)$ solve the scattering problem in $\mathbb{R}^2$ with the source term $-f_1 - ikf_0$ and the radiation condition

$$(\Delta + k^2)u = -f_1 - ikf_0 \text{ in } \mathbb{R}^2, \tag{27}$$

$$\lim r^{1/2}(\partial_r u - iku) = 0 \text{ as } r = |x| \to +\infty. \tag{28}$$

Both $f_0, f_1 \in L^2(\Omega)$ are assumed having $suppf_0, suppf_1 \subset \Omega$ where Ω is a bounded domain with the boundary $\partial\Omega \in C^2$.

The stability of functions f_0, f_1 from the data

$$u = u_0, \partial_\nu u = u_1 \text{ on } \Gamma, \text{ when } K_* < k < K, \tag{29}$$

where Γ is an non empty open subset of $\partial\Omega$ with outer unit normal ν and $0 < K_* < K$, was the following theorem;

Theorem 1.2. Let $\|f_0\|^2_{(4)}(\Omega) + \|f_1\|^2_{(3)}(\Omega) \le M$, $1 \le M$, and $\delta < |x - y|, x \in \partial\Omega$, $y \in supp f_0 \cup supp f_1$ for some positive δ.

Then there exist a constant $C = C(\Omega, \delta)$ such that

$$\|f_1\|^2_{(0)}(\Omega) + \|f_0\|^2_{(1)}(\Omega) \le C\left(\varepsilon^2 + \frac{M^2}{1 + K^{\frac{2}{3}}E^{\frac{1}{4}}}\right) \tag{30}$$

for all $u \in H^2(\Omega)$ solving (27) and (28) with $1 < K$. Here

$$\epsilon^2 = \int_0^K \left(\omega^2 \|u(,\omega)\|^2_{(0)}(\partial\Omega) + \|\nabla u(,\omega)\|^2_{(0)}(\partial\Omega)\right) d\omega, \quad 0 < E = -\ln\epsilon. \tag{31}$$

While Bao, Li and Lu used Dirichlet to Neumann map to simplify the boundary conditions for two dimensional and three dimensional domains (disks and balls), Isakov, Lu, Chang and Entekhabi used the Fourier transform and observability bound for corresponding hyperbolic initial value boundary problem (wave equation) for two and three dimensional domain with C^2-boundary. In papers [19, 20], authors considered inverse source scattering problems with damping factor for two and three dimensional domains, that is, they considered the following equation:

$$(\Delta + k^2 + ikb)u = -f_1 - bf_0 + ikf_0 \tag{32}$$

where $b > 0$ is the damping factor. In particular attenuation can have various reasons and in application, one of the fundamental reasons of poor resolution in inverse problems is a spatial decay of the signal due in part to the damping factor. The results was the following theorem:

Theorem 1.3. There exists a generic constant C depending on the domain Ω such that

$$\|f_0\|^2_{(1)}(\Omega) + \|f_1\|^2_{(1)}(\Omega) \le Ce^{Cb^2}\left(\varepsilon^2 + \frac{(b^2+1)M_3^2}{1 + K^{\frac{2}{3}}E^{\frac{1}{4}} + b}\right) \tag{33}$$

for all $u \in H^2(\Omega)$ solving (1), with $1 < K$ and $M_3 = \max\left\{\|f_0\|_{(4)}(\Omega) + \|f_1\|_{(3)}(\Omega), 1\right\}$. As you can see, the results showed a deterioration of stability with growing attenuation/damping constant b.

In papers [21, 22], authors considered inverse source scattering problems for double layers medium. The results in the papers [23, 24] showed an stability estimate for elastic and electromagnetic waves. Also authors in [23] proved a stability estimate using just Dirichlet data. Increasing stability for the Schrodinger potential from the complete set of the boundary data (the Dirichlet-to Neumann map) was demonstrated in [25, 26]. They showed that the boundary condition for elastic waves they considered the following equation

$$\sigma(\mathbf{u}) + k^2\mathbf{u} = -\mathbf{f}_1 - ik\mathbf{f}_0 \; in \; \mathbb{R}^n, \tag{34}$$

$$\mathbf{u} = \mathbf{u}_0 \text{ in } \Gamma, \tag{35}$$

where $\sigma = (\mu\Delta + (\mu + \lambda)\nabla \cdot \nabla)$, where μ, λ are Lame constants satisfying $\mu > 0$ and $\mu + \lambda > 0$, functions $\mathbf{f_1}, \mathbf{f_0} \in L^2(\Omega)$ are the external force are assumed to be compactly supported in a C^2-boundary domain $\Omega \subset \mathbb{R}^n$ and $\Gamma \subset \partial\Omega$ is an open non-void set. By the Helmholtz decomposition, the displacement filed $\mathbf{u}$ can be written as

$$\mathbf{u} = \mathbf{u}_p + \mathbf{u}_s \text{ in } \mathbb{R}^n \backslash \overline{\Omega}, \tag{36}$$

where $\mathbf{u}_p$ and the sheer part $\mathbf{u}_s$ which satisfy Sommerfeld radiation conditions

$$\lim_{r \to \infty} r\left(\partial_r \mathbf{u}_p - ik_p \mathbf{u}_p\right) = 0, \quad \lim_{r \to \infty} r(\partial_r \mathbf{u}_s - ik_s \mathbf{u}_s) = 0, \quad r = |\mathbf{x}|, \tag{37}$$

To achieve the result, authors used Helmholtz decomposition. The decomposition was allowed them to break the Navier-Lame equation to two elliptic equations.

The results for discrete data for inverse source problem which was obtained in [27] are as follows:

Theorem 1.4. Let $\mathbf{u}$ be the solution of the following scattering problem corresponding source $\mathbf{f} \in F_M(\mathbb{B}_\mathbb{R})$,

$$(\mu\Delta + (\mu + \lambda)\nabla \cdot \nabla)(\mathbf{u}) + \omega^2 \mathbf{u} = \mathbf{f} \ in \ \mathbb{R}^n, \tag{38}$$

with radiation condition (37),

Then

$$\|\mathbf{f}\|^2_{(0)}(B_R) \leq C\left(\epsilon_2^2 + \frac{M^2}{\left(\frac{N^{\frac{5}{8}} |ln\, \epsilon_3|^{\frac{1}{9}}}{(6m-3n+3)^3}\right)^{2m-n+1}}\right) \tag{39}$$

where

$$\epsilon_2 = \left(\sum_{n=1}^{N} \|\mathbf{u}(., \omega_{p,n})\|_0^2(\Gamma_R) + \|\mathbf{u}(., \omega_{s,n})\|_0^2(\Gamma_R)\right)^{\frac{1}{2}},$$

$$\epsilon_3 = \sup_{\omega \in \left(0, \frac{\pi}{c_p R},\right]\right)} \|\mathbf{u}(., \omega)\|_0^2(\Gamma_R),$$

and

$$F_M(\mathbb{B}_\mathbb{R}) = \left\{\mathbf{f} \in H^{m+1}(B_R) : \|\mathbf{f}\|_{(m+1)}(B_R) \leq M\right\}.$$

The stability increases as N increases, i.e., the inverse problem is more stable when higher frequency data is used.

2.2.1 Uniqueness of source function

To achieve the uniqueness, we introduced two different approaches. The first approach is using the estimate for the source function. Letting the norm of the boundary data goes to zero, then the proof is complete. For instance, consider Theorem 1.2 and let $\epsilon \to 0$. The second approach is the result has proved by Isakov, Chang and Lu. They used classical result of the hyperbolic initial value boundary problem indirectly. The following theorem is the result of [16]. In the following theorem $\Omega \subset \mathbb{R}^n$ with $n = 2, 3$ and $\Gamma \subset \partial\Omega$.

Theorem 1.5. Let u be a solution to the scattering problem (27) and (28) with $f_0 \in H^1(\Omega), f_1 \in L^2(\Omega)$. If the Cauchy data $u_0 = u_1 = 0$ on Γ when $k \in (K_*, K)$, then $f_0 = f_1 = 0$ in Ω.

Proof. Denote by U_0 the solution to the following hyperbolic problem

$$\begin{aligned} &\partial_t^2 U_0 - \Delta U_0 = 0 \quad \text{on} \quad \Omega \times (0, \infty), \\ &U_0 = -f_0, \partial_t U_0 = f_1 \quad \text{on} \quad \Omega \times \{0\}, U_0 = 0 \quad \text{on} \quad \partial\Omega \times (0, +\infty). \end{aligned} \tag{40}$$

Under their assumptions, there is a unique solution to the problem (40) with $\|U_0(,t)\|_{(1)}(\Omega) + \|\partial_t U_0(,t)\|_{(0)}(\Omega) \le C\left(\|f_0\|_{(1)}(\Omega) + \|f_1\|_{(0)}(\Omega)\right)$.

Now let

$$u^*(x,k) = \frac{1}{\sqrt{2\pi}} \int_0^\infty U_0(x,t) e^{ikt} dt$$

Due to the properties of U_0, in particular to the conservation of the energy, the function $u^*(x,k)$ is well defined and analytic with respect to $k = k_1 + ik_2, k_2 > 0$. Applying the integration by parts and using standard properties of the Fourier-Laplace transform we conclude that

$$(\Delta + k^2) u^* = -f_1 - ikf_0 \quad \text{in} \quad \Omega, \quad u^* = 0 \quad \text{on} \quad \partial\Omega. \tag{41}$$

Due to the assumption, the function u solves the same Dirichlet problem for $\Delta + k^2$ when $0 < k_1, 0 < k_2$. Indeed, u solves the homogeneous Helmholtz equation in $\mathbb{R}^n \backslash \overline{\Omega}$ and has zero Cauchy data on Γ. By the uniqueness in the Cauchy problem for elliptic equations, $u = 0$ on $\mathbb{R}^n \backslash \overline{\Omega}$ and hence on $\partial\Omega$ provided $K_* < k < K$. As follows from the integral representation of solution (27), the function $u(;k)$ is (complex) analytic when $0 < \Re ek$, hence $u(;k) = 0$ on $\partial\Omega$ provided $0 < \Re ek$. Since $k_2 > 0$, the solution of (41) is unique, hence $u = u^*$ on Ω (see Section 4). Consequently, we obtain $u^* = u = 0$, $\partial_\nu u^* = \partial_\nu u = 0$ on Γ. Since u^* is an analytic function, we can conclude that $u^* = 0, \partial_\nu u^* = 0$ on Γ for all $k = k_1 + ik_2$ with $k_2 > 0$. Due to the uniqueness of the inversion of the Fourier-Laplace transform we will obtain

$$\partial_\nu U_0 = 0 \quad \text{on} \quad \Gamma \times (0, \infty).$$

Due to the uniqueness in the lateral Cauchy problem for the wave equation (40) with the Cauchy data on $\Gamma \times (0, +\infty)$ [Holmgren-John theorem ([28], Section 3.4)], we can conclude that $U_0 = 0$ on $\Omega \times (T, +\infty)$ for some positive T. Hence from the uniqueness in the backward initial boundary value problem for the hyperbolic equation (39) in $\Omega \times (0, T)$ with zero boundary data on $\partial\Omega \times (0, T)$ and initial data at $\Omega \times \{T\}$ we conclude that $U_0 = 0$ on $\Omega \times (0, T)$. So $-U_0(,0) = f_0 = 0, \partial_t U(,0) = f_1 = 0$ on Ω which finishes the proof of uniqueness.

3. Conclusions

In this section, the scattering and inverse scattering theory, inverse source scattering problem were considered briefly. The recent results such stability estimates for external source and electric current density from boundary measurements of radiated wave field and uniqueness for source function for Helmholtz equation, Elasticity and Maxwell system have showed. We also show some result for discrete data. In addition, we also showed some results of using just Dirichlet data for improving stability which was a big improvement. There are still many challenges remain in this field. For instance, studying the stability in the inverse source problems for inhomogeneous media where the analytical Green tensors are not available and the present method may not be directly applicable. Another interesting topic in stability of the external source is to consider the governing equation in the time domain. The non-linear case is also is a very challenging problem. The direct and inverse scattering problems when both the source and the linear load are random is also an open problem. Another challenging problem is to study the random source scattering problem for three dimensional elastic wave equation. As I mentioned before, there are many scientist and researcher have been working on inverse scattering and more specifically on inverse source problems. To expand your knowledge and further mathematical development in this field of research, please see the result authors in [29–41], which were discussed different aspects of the problems.

Acknowledgements

Without doubt, our world is a beautiful place full of questions and challenges thanks to people who want to develop and overcome these challenges who share the gift of their time and passion to mentor future generation. Thank you to everyone who strives to grow and help others grow. To all the individuals I have had the opportunity to lead, be led by, or watch their leadership and mentoring from afar, I want to say thank you for being the inspiration.

I am grateful to all of those with whom I have had the pleasure to work and those who help me to grow and learn. I would especially like to thank Dr. Victor Isakov, my PhD adviser who has provided me extensive personal and professional guidance and taught me a great deal about both scientific research and life in general. He has taught me more than I could ever give him credit for here. He has shown me, by his example, what a good scientist (and person) should be. I also would like to thank Professor Alexander Bukhgeym and Professor Thomas K. DeLillo for their help and advice.

I would like to thank my mother and belated father, whose love and guidance are with me in whatever I pursue. Many thanks to my sisters Marjan, Mona and Mina and my brother Jamshid for their constant support and unending inspiration.

This chapter is supported in part by NSF Award HRD-1824267.

Author details

Mozhgan “Nora” Entekhabi
Florida Agricultural and Mechanical University, Tallahassee, USA

*Address all correspondence to: mozhgan.entekhabi@famu.edu

References

[1] Sommerfeld A. Die Greensche Funktion der Schwingungsgleichung. Jahresbericht der Deutschen Mathematiker-Vereinigung. 1912;**21**: 309-353

[2] Rellich F. Uber des asymptotiche Verhalten der Losungen von $\Delta u + \lambda u = 0$ in unendlichen Gebieten. Deutsche Mathematiker-Vereinigung. 1943;**5**: 57-65

[3] Vekua IN. Metaharmonic functions. Trudy Belinskogo Matematicheskoe Instituta. 1943;**12**:105-174

[4] Isakov V. Inverse Problems for Partial Differential Equations. 2nd ed. New York: Springer International Publishing, Verlag; 2017. pp. 173-177. DOI: 10.1007/978-3-319-51658-5

[5] Lax PD, Phillips RS. Scattering Theory. New York: Academic Press; 1967. ISBN 10: 0124400507

[6] Nachman A. Reconstructions from boundary measurements. Annals of Mathematics. 1988;**128**:531-576

[7] Novikov R. Multidimensional inverse spectral problems for the equation $-\Delta\psi + (v(x) - Eu(x))\psi = 0$. Functional Analysis and Its Applications. 1988;**22**: 263-272

[8] Ramm AG. Recovery of the potential from fixed energy scattering data. Inverse Problems. 1988;**4**:877-886

[9] Colton D, Päivärinta L. The uniqueness of a solution to an inverse scattering problem for electromagnetic waves. Archive for Rational Mechanics and Analysis. 1992;**119**:59-70

[10] Imbriale WA, Mittra R. The two-dimensional inverse scattering problem. IEEE Transactions on Antennas and Propagation. 1970;**18**: 633-642

[11] Colton D, Kress R. Inverse Acoustic and Electromagnetic Scattering Theory. New York: Springer Verlag; 2013. ISBN-10: 1461449413

[12] Watson GN. A Treatise on the Theory of Bessel Functions. USA: Cambridge University Press; 1922. ISBN: 9780521483919

[13] Li P, Bao G, Chen C. Inverse random source scattering for elastic waves. SIAM Journal on Numerical Analysis. 2017;**55**:2616-2643

[14] Eller M, Valdivia N. Acoustic source identification using multiple frequency information. Inverse Problems. 2009;**25**: 115005

[15] Bao G, Lin J, Triki F. A multi-frequency inverse source problem. Journal of Difference Equations. 2010; **249**:3443-3465

[16] Cheng J, Isakov V, Lu S. Increasing stability in the inverse source problem with many frequencies. Journal of Difference Equations. 2016;**260**: 4786-4804

[17] Entekhabi MN, Isakov V. On increasing stability in the two dimensional inverse source scattering problem with many frequencies. Inverse Problems. 2017;**34**:055005

[18] Bao G, Li P. Inverse medium scattering problems in near-field optics. Journal of Computational Mathematics. 2007;**25**(3):252-265

[19] Isakov V, Lu S. Increasing stability in the inverse source problem with attenuation and many frequencies. SIAM Journal on Applied Mathematics. 2018;**18**:1-18

[20] Entekhabi MN. Increasing stability in the two dimensional inverse source

scattering problem with attenuation and many frequencies. Inverse Problems. 2018;**34**:115001

[21] Entekhabi MN, Gunaratne A. A Logarithmic Estimate for Inverse Source Scattering Problem with Attenuation in a Two-Layered Medium, to be Appeared in Journal of Inverse and Ill-Posed Problems. 2019;. Available from: https://arxiv.org/pdf/1903.03475.pdf

[22] Zhao Y, Li P. Stability on the one-dimensional inverse source scattering problem in a two-layered medium. Applicable Analysis. 2017;**98**(4): 682-692. DOI: 10.1080/00036811.2017.1399365

[23] Entekhabi MN, Isakov V. Increasing stability in acoustic and elastic inverse source problems, SIAM Journal on Mathematical Analysis. 2018. Available from: https://arxiv.org/abs/1808.10528

[24] Li P, Helin T. Inverse Random Source Problems for Time-Harmonic Acoustic and Elastic Waves, Submitted. 2018

[25] Isakov V, Lai R-Y, Wang J-N. Increasing stability for the attenuation and conductivity coefficients. SIAM Journal on Mathematical Analysis. 2016; **48**:1-18

[26] Isakov V. Increasing stability for the Schrodinger potential from the Dirichlet-to Neumann map. Discrete and Continuous Dynamical Systems. 2011;**4**:631-641

[27] Bao G, Li P, Zhao Y. Stability for the inverse source problems in elastic and electromagnetic waves. Journal de Mathématiques Pures et Appliquées. 2018

[28] John F. Partial Differential Equations, Applied Mathematical Sciences. New York/Berlin: Springer-Verlag; 1982

[29] Isakov V, Lu S. Inverse source problems without (pseudo) convexity assumptions. Inverse Problems & Imaging. 2018;**12**:955-970

[30] Isakov V, Lu S, Xu B. Linearized inverse Schrödinger potential problem at a large wave number. SIAM Journal on Applied Mathematics. arXiv: 1812.05011

[31] Isakov V. On increasing stability in the continuation for elliptic equations of second order without (pseudo) convexity assumptions. Inverse Problems & Imaging. 2019;**13**:983-1006

[32] Isakov V, Wang J-N. Increasing stability for determining the potential in the Schrödinger equation with attenuation from the Dirichlet-to Neumann map. Inverse Problems & Imaging. 2014;**8**:1139-1150

[33] Isakov V, Lai R-Y, Wang J-N. Increasing stability for conductivity and attenuation coefficients. SIAM Journal on Mathematical Analysis. 2016;**48**: 569-594

[34] Nakamura G, Saitoh S, Seo JK. Inverse Problems and Related Topics. New York; 2000. ISBN-13: 978-15848819192000

[35] Ivanov VK, Vasin VV, Tanana VP. Theory of Linear Ill-Posed Problems and its Applications. 2002. ISBN: 978-3-11-094482-2

[36] Lavrentiev R, Vasiliev. Inverse problems for second-order elliptic equations. In: Multidimensional Inverse Problems for Differential Equations. Lecture Notes in Mathematics. Vol. 167. Berlin/Heidelberg: Springer; 1970

[37] Tikhonov AN. On the regularization of ill-posed problems. SSSS Doklady Akademii Nauk SSSR. 1963;**153**:49-52

[38] Bao G, Gao J, Li P. Analysis of direct and inverse cavity scattering problems.

Numerical Mathematics: Theory, Methods and Applications. 2011;**4**: 419-442

[39] Bao G, Liu J. Numerical solution of inverse scattering problems with multi-experimental limited aperture data. SIAM Journal on Scientific Computing. 2003;**25**(3):1102-1117

[40] Isakov V. Inverse Source Problems. Vol. 34. USA: American Mathematical Society; 1990. ISBN: 978-0-8218-1532-8

[41] Bukhgeim AL. Introduction to the Theory of Inverse Problems. 2000

Chapter 4

Solution Methods of Large Complex-Valued Nonlinear System of Equations

Robson Pires

Abstract

Nonlinear systems of equations in complex plane are frequently encountered in applied mathematics, e.g., power systems, signal processing, control theory, neural networks, and biomedicine, to name a few. The solution of these problems often requires a first- or second-order approximation of nonlinear functions to generate a new step or descent direction to meet the solution iteratively. However, such methods cannot be applied to functions of complex and complex conjugate variables because they are necessarily nonanalytic. To overcome this problem, the Wirtinger calculus allows an expansion of nonlinear functions in its original complex and complex conjugate variables once they are analytic in their argument as a whole. Thus, the goal is to apply this methodology for solving nonlinear systems of equations emerged from applications in the industry. For instances, the complex-valued Jacobian matrix emerged from the power flow analysis model which is solved by Newton-Raphson method can be exactly determined. Similarly, overdetermined Jacobian matrices can be dealt, e.g., through the Gauss-Newton method in complex plane aimed to solve power system state estimation problems. Finally, the factorization method of the aforementioned Jacobian matrices is addressed through the *fast Givens transformation* algorithm which means the square root-free Givens rotations method in complex plane.

Keywords: large nonlinear system of equation solution in complex plane, complex-valued Newton-Raphson and gauss-Newton iterative algorithms, Cartesian coordinates

1. Introduction

This work is a tribute to Steinmetz's contribution [1]. The reasons and motivations are stated throughout the whole document once the numerical solutions for solving power system applications are typically carried out in the real domain. For instance, the power flow analysis and power system state estimation are well-known tools, among others. It turns out that these solutions are not well suited for modeling voltage and current phasor. To overcome this difficulty, the proposal described in this chapter aims to model the aforementioned applications in a unified system of coordinates, e.g., complex domain. Nonetheless, the solution methods of these problems often require a first- or second-order approximation of the set of power flow equations; such methods cannot be applied to nonlinear functions of complex variables because they are nonanalytic in their arguments. Consequently, for these functions Taylor series expansions do not exist. Hence, for many decades this problem has been solved redefining the nonlinear functions as separate functions of the real and imaginary parts of their complex arguments so that standard methods can be applied. Although not widely known, it is also possible to construct an extended nonlinear function that includes not only the original complex state variables but also their complex conjugates, and then the Wirtinger calculus can be applied [2]. This property lies on the fact that if a function is analytic in the space spanned by $\Re\{x\}$ and $\{x\}$ in $\mathbb{R}$, it is also analytic in the space spanned by x and x^* in $\mathbb{C}$. In complex analysis of one and several complex variables, *Wirtinger operators* are partial differential operators of the first order which behave in a very similar manner to the ordinary derivatives with respect to one real variable, when applied to *holomorphic* functions, *non-holomorphic* functions, or simply differentiable functions on complex domain. These operators allow the construction of a differential calculus for such functions that is entirely analogous to the ordinary differential calculus for functions of real variables [2, 3]. Then, taken into account the Wirtinger calculus, this chapter shows how the Jacobian matrix patterns emerge in complex plane corresponding to the steady-state models of power flow analysis and power system state estimation, respectively.

In this chapter the classical Newton-Raphson and Gauss-Newton methods in complex plane aiming the numerical solution of the power flow analysis and power system state estimation are derived, respectively. Moreover, the factorization methods addressed to deal with the Jacobian matrices emerged from these approaches are included [4].

This chapter is organized as follows. The theoretical foundation which is based on *Wirtinger calculus* is summed up in Section 2. Section 3 describes two algorithms suggested to factorize Jacobian matrix in complex plane regardless if it is exactly determined or overdetermined. In Section 4, the complex-valued static model solution by using Newton-Raphson method is derived, whereas in Section 5, the Gauss-Newton method developed in complex plane is equally presented. Finally, in Section 6 some conclusions are gathered and stated the next issues to be investigated in the near future.

2. Theoretical foundation

2.1 Complex differentiability

A complex function is defined as

$$f(x) = u(a,b) + j\,v(a,b), \tag{1}$$

where $x = a + j\,b$ and $u(a,b)$, $v(a,b)$ are real functions, u, v: $\mathbb{R}^2 \rightarrow \mathbb{R}$. Functions like Eq. (1) are in general complex but may be real-valued in special cases, e.g., squared error cost function $\mathcal{J}\left(\left|\mathbf{e}^2\right|\right)$. The definition of complex differentiability requires that the derivatives defined as the limit be independent of the direction in which Δx approaches 0 in complex plane:

$$f'(x_0) = \lim_{\Delta x \rightarrow 0} \frac{f(x+\Delta x) - f(x)}{\Delta x}. \tag{2}$$

This requires that the Cauchy-Riemann equations be satisfied, i.e.,

$$\frac{\partial u}{\partial a}=\frac{\partial v}{\partial b}, \qquad \frac{\partial v}{\partial a}=-\frac{\partial u}{\partial b}. \tag{3}$$

These conditions are necessary for $f(x)$ to be complex differentiable. If the partial derivatives of $u(a,b)$ and $v(a,b)$ are continuous on their entire domain, then they are sufficient as well. Therefore, the complex function $f(x)$ is called an analytic or holomorphic function [2]. As an example, let $f(x)=x^2$ be a complex function with $x=a+j\,b$. Then,

$$f(x)=x^2=\underbrace{a^2-b^2}_{=u}+j\,\underbrace{2ab}_{=v}=y, \tag{4}$$

which under differentiation rule leads to

$$\frac{\partial u}{\partial a}=2a=\frac{\partial v}{\partial b}=2a; \qquad \frac{\partial u}{\partial b}=-2b=-\left(\frac{\partial v}{\partial a}=2b\right). \tag{5}$$

These results show that the Cauchy-Riemann equations hold, and hence $f(x)=y=x^2$ is a holomorphic function.

2.2 *CR-Calculus* or Wirtinger calculus

Introduced by Wilhelm Wirtinger in 1927 [2], the *CR-Calculus*, also known as the Wirtinger calculus, provides a way to differentiate nonanalytic functions of complex variables. Specifically, this calculus is applicable to a function $f(x)$ given by Eq. (1) if $u(a,b)$ and $v(a,b)$ have continuous partial derivatives with respect to a and b, yielding

$$\frac{\partial f}{\partial x}=\frac{\partial f}{\partial a}\frac{\partial a}{\partial x}+\frac{\partial f}{\partial b}\frac{\partial b}{\partial x}. \tag{6}$$

Since we have

$$a=\frac{(x+x^*)}{2}, \qquad \partial a=\frac{(\partial x+\partial x^*)}{2}, \tag{7}$$

$$b=j\,\frac{(x^*-x)}{2}, \qquad \partial b=j\,\frac{(\partial x^*-\partial x)}{2}, \tag{8}$$

and by setting $\frac{\partial x^*}{\partial x}$ to zero, it follows that

$$\frac{\partial f}{\partial x}=\frac{1}{2}\left(\frac{\partial f}{\partial a}-j\,\frac{\partial f}{\partial b}\right). \tag{9}$$

Note that the Cauchy-Riemann conditions for $f(\cdot)$ to be analytic in x can be expressed compactly using the gradient as $\frac{\partial f}{\partial x^*}=0$, i.e., $f(\cdot)$ is a function of only x.
Similarly, if we take the derivative of $f(\cdot)$ with respect to x^*, that is,

$$\frac{\partial f}{\partial x^*}=\frac{\partial f}{\partial a}\frac{\partial a}{\partial x^*}+\frac{\partial f}{\partial b}\frac{\partial b}{\partial x^*}. \tag{10}$$

By setting $\frac{\partial x}{\partial x^*}$ to zero, we get

$$\frac{\partial f}{\partial x^*} = \frac{1}{2}\left(\frac{\partial f}{\partial a} + j\,\frac{\partial f}{\partial b}\right). \tag{11}$$

Again, the Cauchy-Riemann conditions for $f(\cdot)$ to be analytic in x^* can be expressed compactly using the gradient as $\frac{\partial f}{\partial x} = 0$, i.e., $f(\cdot)$ is a function only of x^*.

In other words, the gradient (respectively conjugate gradient) operator acts as a partial derivative with respect to x (respectively to x^*), treating x^* (respectively x) as a constant. Formally, we have

$$\frac{\partial f(x_c)}{\partial x} = \left.\frac{\partial f(x, x^*)}{\partial x}\right|_{x^* = Const} = \frac{1}{2}\left(\frac{\partial f}{\partial a} - j\,\frac{\partial f}{\partial b}\right), \tag{12}$$

$$\frac{\partial f(x_c)}{\partial x^*} = \left.\frac{\partial f(x, x^*)}{\partial x^*}\right|_{x = Const} = \frac{1}{2}\left(\frac{\partial f}{\partial a} + j\,\frac{\partial f}{\partial b}\right). \tag{13}$$

As an example, let $f(x_c) = f(x, x^*) = x^*x = \|x\|^2 = a^2 + b^2$ be a real function of complex variable which is the squared Euclidean distance to the origin, with $x = a + j\,b$. Then,

$$f(x_c) = f(x, x^*) = x^*x = \underbrace{a^2 + b^2}_{=u} + j\,\underbrace{(ab - ab)}_{=v} = y \tag{14}$$

as $v = 0$; clearly the Cauchy-Riemann equations do not hold, and hence $f(x_c) = f(x, x^*) = x^*x$ is not analytic and thus is non-holomorphic function. To overcome this apparent difficult, by applying the *CR-Calculus* leads to

$$\frac{\partial f(x_c)}{\partial x} = x^*; \; \frac{\partial f(x_c)}{\partial x^*} = x, \tag{15}$$

which suggests the geometric interpretation shown in **Figure 1**. Its analysis allows us to infer that the direction of maximum rate of change of the objective function is given by the conjugate gradient defined in Eq. (13). Observe that its positive direction is referred to a maximization problem (dot arrow), whereas the opposite direction concerns to the cost function minimization.

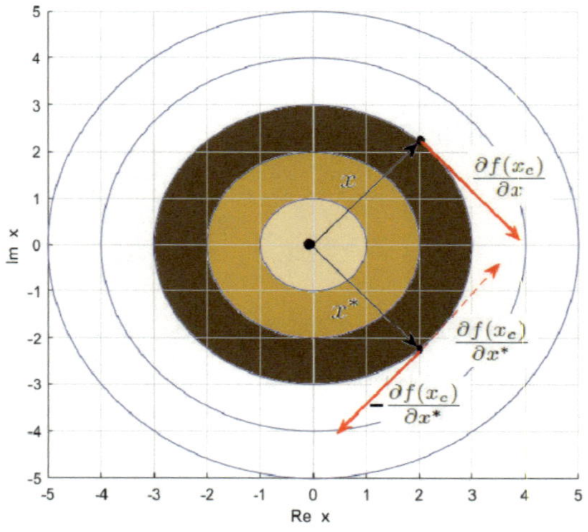

Figure 1.
Contour plot of the real function of complex variable.

Hereafter, a real-valued or complex-valued function and its argument are provided with a subscript c if it is a function in the complex conjugate coordinates, i.e., (x, x^*). Moreover, when the *CR-Calculus* is extended to the vector case, it is denoted that the multivariate *CR-Calculus* and the basic rules for the scalar case remain unchanged.

3. Solution of the problem: $\mathbf{A}_{m\times n}\, \underline{x}_{n\times 1} = \underline{y}_{m\times 1} \in \mathbb{C}^{m\times n}$

As well in the real domain, there are two classes of methods for the numerical solution of large linear system of equations in complex plane:

- Direct methods: Which produce the exact solution assuming the absence of truncation and round-off errors, by performing a finite number of *flops* in a finite known number of steps. These methods are usually recommended when most of the entries in the coefficient matrix are nonzero and the dimension of the system is not too large, for instance, the Gaussian elimination, the LU decomposition and QR factorization, to cite a few.

- Iterative methods: This class of methods is beyond of this work. Notice the solution provided by these methods is approximated and the accuracy is imposed by the user. The number of ν accomplished iterations depends on the given precision or convergence criterion. This class of methods is preferred when the majority of the coefficients are equal to zero and the number of unknowns is very large. The methods of Jacobi and Gauss-Seidel are good examples, besides the classical Conjugate gradient method [5].

3.1 Three-angle complex rotation algorithm

The first studied algorithm is the *three-angle complex rotations (TACR)*, which is derived in polar coordinates [6]. Nonetheless, the key idea behind *QR* decomposition is to eliminate the square roots needed for the computation of the cosine and sine which represent a bottleneck in real-time applications. Consequently, this algorithm is devoid of interest for the solution of large linear systems of equations.

3.2 Complex-valued fast givens rotations

On the other hand, the *fast plane rotation* [7] that is derived in complex plane and rectangular coordinates is a square root- and division-free Givens rotations [8]. In this sense, the fast plane rotation which is also referred as the complex-valued fast Givens rotations ($CV - FGR$) is a very efficient algorithm, aiming a *QR-decomposition* of matrices once the computations are performed incrementally, i.e., as the data arrives sequentially in time. Thus, it allows us to reduce the overall latency and hardware resources drastically. In the forthcoming contribution, the $CV - FGR$ performance will be compared to the well-known approaches which were successfully applied to the power system state estimation [9–11], once they are accordingly converted from real to complex domain. Further proposals in the updated state of the art will be equally considered, e.g., [12] and [13], to cite a few.

The complex fast Givens transformation $\mathbf{M}$ is computed using **Algorithm 1** such that the second component of $\mathbf{M}^H \underline{x}$ is zero and $\mathbf{M}^H\mathbf{DM}$ is a diagonal matrix, as shown below:

$$\mathbf{M} = \underbrace{\begin{bmatrix} \beta & 1 \\ 1 & \alpha \end{bmatrix}}_{type=1} \quad or \quad \underbrace{\begin{bmatrix} 1 & \alpha \\ \beta & 1 \end{bmatrix}}_{type=2} \tag{16}$$

$$\mathbf{M}^H \underline{x} = \begin{bmatrix} r \\ 0 \end{bmatrix} \quad \& \quad \mathbf{M}^H \underbrace{\begin{bmatrix} d_f & 0 \\ 0 & d_g \end{bmatrix}}_{=\mathbf{D}} \mathbf{M} = \underbrace{\begin{bmatrix} d_f^{new} & 0 \\ 0 & d_g^{new} \end{bmatrix}}_{=\mathbf{D^{new}}}. \tag{17}$$

Notice the superscript H denotes the *Hermitian* operation, i.e., complex conjugate transpose.

Algorithm 1. Complex fast Givens transform.

$[\alpha, \beta, \mathrm{r}, type, d_f^{new}, d_g^{new}]$ = **fast.givens** (f, g, d_f, d_g);
if $f = 0$ **then**
  $type = 1; \alpha = \beta = 0; r = g;$
  $d_f^{new} = d_g;\ d_g^{new} = d_f;$
else if $g = 0$ **then**
  $type = 2; \alpha = \beta = 0; r = f;$
  $d_f^{new} = d_f;\ d_g^{new} = d_g;$
else if $\|f\|^2 \leq \|g\|^2$ **then**
  $type = 1; i = f/g; s = d_g/d_f;$
  $\alpha = -i; \beta = s * i;$
  $\gamma = s * \|i\|^2; r = g * (1 + \gamma);$
  $d_f^{new} = (1 + \gamma) * d_g;\ d_g^{new} = (1 + \gamma) * d_f;$
else
  $type = 2; i = g/f; s = d_f/d_g;$
  $\alpha = -i; \beta = s * i;$
  $\gamma = s * \|i\|^2; r = f * (1 + \gamma);$
  $d_f^{new} = (1 + \gamma) * d_f;\ d_g^{new} = (1 + \gamma) * d_g;$
end if

The matrices **Q**, **M**, and **D** are connected to the following equation:

$$\mathbf{Q} = \mathbf{M}\left(\mathbf{D^{new}}\right)^{-1/2} = \mathbf{M}\, diag\left(1/sqrt\left(d_i^{new}\right)\right). \tag{18}$$

In the sequence the *QR-decomposition* using complex fast Givens transformations is presented as **Algorithm 2**.

Algorithm 2. Sequential fast Givens QRD decomposition.

$[Q_\alpha, Q_\beta, type, R]$=**fast.givens_QRD** (A);
[m,n]=size(A);
$R = zeros(n); D = I_n;$
$R(1, 1:n) = A(1, 1:n);$
for $i = 2:m$ **do**
  new$= A(i, 1:n); d_{new} = 1;$
  if $i < = n$ **then**
    $k = i;$
  else

$k = n + 1;$
end if
for $j = 1 : k - 1$ **do**
Step 1: Get *alpha* **and** *beta* **using Algorithm 1:**
$[\alpha, \beta, \mathbf{R}(j,j), type, d_f^{new}, d_g^{new}]$=**fast.givens** $(\mathbf{R}(j,j), \mathbf{new}(1,j), d_f, d_g)$;
Step 2: Update elements based on *type*
if $j < n$ and *type*=1 **then**

$$\begin{bmatrix} R(j, j+1:n) \\ new(1, j+1:n) \end{bmatrix} = \begin{bmatrix} 1 & \beta \\ \alpha & 1 \end{bmatrix}^H \begin{bmatrix} R(j, j+1:n) \\ new(1, j+1:n) \end{bmatrix}$$

else if $J < n$ and *type*=2 **then**

$$\begin{bmatrix} R(j, j+1:n) \\ new(1, j+1:n) \end{bmatrix} = \begin{bmatrix} \beta & 1 \\ 1 & \alpha \end{bmatrix}^H \begin{bmatrix} R(j, j+1:n) \\ new(1, j+1:n) \end{bmatrix}$$

end if
end for
if $k < = n$ **then**
$R(k, 1:n) = new(1, 1:n); d(k) = d_{new};$
end if
end for

Note that the complex fast Givens QRD does not require any square root operation, and during each incremental QRD-update step, the incoming input data row-vector is stored, i.e., vector **new**. In the sequence, the input data row-vector elements are zero-out (inner for loop) in order to update upper triangular matrix **R**. The **new** vector is overwritten each time till the *QRD*-algorithm has exhausted all the input data, i.e., the upper triangular matrix **R** is entirely updated.

4. Complex-valued Newton-Raphson method

Aiming the solution of any set of exactly determined equations in complex plane, the vector of unknowns is regularly taken into account in the iterative algorithm as follows:

$$\underline{x}_c = \left[x_1, x_2, \dots, x_{N-1}, x_1^*, x_2^*, \dots, x_{N-1}^*\right]^T, \tag{19}$$

and the residual vector hereafter termed as "mismatches" vector leads to

$$\underline{M}(\underline{x}_c) = \left[M_1, M_2, \dots, M_{N-1}, M_1^*, M_2^*, \dots, M_{N-1}^*\right]^T. \tag{20}$$

Nonetheless, here the goal is to calculate $\underline{x}_c$ that satisfies

$$\underline{M}(\underline{x}_c) = \underline{Y}_e(\underline{x}_c) - \underline{Y}_s = 0, \tag{21}$$

where in Eq. (21), $\underline{Y}_s$ is a vector of specified quantities, i.e., constant term; $\underline{Y}_e(\underline{x}_c) = \mathbf{J}_c\, \Delta\underline{x}_c$ is a vector of calculated quantities at each iteration. Consequently, the linearization of Eq. (21) from one step to the sequel leads to

$$\underline{M}\left(\underline{x}_c^{(\nu-1)}\right) + \mathbf{J}^{(\nu-1)}\, \Delta\underline{x}_c^{(\nu)} = 0, \tag{22}$$

or

$$\Delta \underline{x}_c^{(\nu)} = -\left(\mathbf{J}^{(\nu-1)}\right)^{-1} \underline{M}\left(\underline{x}_c^{(\nu-1)}\right), \tag{23}$$

where $\mathbf{J}$ is the complex-valued Jacobian matrix which the dimension is $2\,(N-1) \times 2\,(N-1)$. It means that at least one complex-valued state variable have to be specified, i.e., is known.

As a further advantage provided by the Wirtinger calculus [2, 3], the Jacobian matrix which emerged in Cartesian coordinates needs lesser algebra task as well as minor implementation effort (encoding) than the former procedure in real domain [14]. Thereby, the Jacobian matrix in expanded form may be represented through four partitions matrix, yielding

$$\mathbf{J} = \begin{bmatrix} \frac{\partial \underline{M}_1}{\partial \underline{x}_1} & \frac{\partial \underline{M}_1}{\partial \underline{x}_2} & \cdots & \frac{\partial \underline{M}_1}{\partial \underline{x}_{N-1}} & \vdots & \frac{\partial \underline{M}_1}{\partial \underline{x}_1^*} & \frac{\partial \underline{M}_1}{\partial \underline{x}_2^*} & \cdots & \frac{\partial \underline{M}_1}{\partial \underline{x}_{N-1}^*} \\ \frac{\partial \underline{M}_2}{\partial \underline{x}_1} & \frac{\partial \underline{M}_2}{\partial \underline{x}_2} & \cdots & \frac{\partial \underline{M}_2}{\partial \underline{x}_{N-1}} & \vdots & \frac{\partial \underline{M}_2}{\partial \underline{x}_1^*} & \frac{\partial \underline{M}_2}{\partial \underline{x}_2^*} & \cdots & \frac{\partial \underline{M}_2}{\partial \underline{x}_{N-1}^*} \\ \frac{\partial \underline{M}_{N-1}}{\partial \underline{x}_1} & \frac{\partial \underline{M}_{N-1}}{\partial \underline{x}_2} & \cdots & \frac{\partial \underline{M}_{N-1}}{\partial \underline{x}_{N-1}} & \vdots & \frac{\partial \underline{M}_{N-1}}{\partial \underline{x}_1^*} & \frac{\partial \underline{M}_{N-1}}{\partial \underline{x}_2^*} & \cdots & \frac{\partial \underline{M}_{N-1}}{\partial \underline{x}_{N-1}^*} \\ \cdots & \cdots & \cdots\cdots & \cdots & \vdots & \cdots & \cdots & \cdots & \cdots \\ \frac{\partial \underline{M}_1^*}{\partial \underline{x}_1} & \frac{\partial \underline{M}_1^*}{\partial \underline{x}_2} & \cdots & \frac{\partial \underline{M}_1^*}{\partial \underline{x}_{N-1}} & \vdots & \frac{\partial \underline{M}_1^*}{\partial \underline{x}_1^*} & \frac{\partial \underline{M}_1^*}{\partial \underline{x}_2^*} & \cdots & \frac{\partial \underline{M}_1^*}{\partial \underline{x}_{N-1}^*} \\ \frac{\partial \underline{M}_2^*}{\partial \underline{x}_1} & \frac{\partial \underline{M}_2^*}{\partial \underline{x}_2} & \cdots & \frac{\partial \underline{M}_2^*}{\partial \underline{x}_{N-1}} & \vdots & \frac{\partial \underline{M}_2^*}{\partial \underline{x}_1^*} & \frac{\partial \underline{M}_2^*}{\partial \underline{x}_2^*} & \cdots & \frac{\partial \underline{M}_2^*}{\partial \underline{x}_{N-1}^*} \\ \frac{\partial \underline{M}_{N-1}^*}{\partial \underline{x}_1} & \frac{\partial \underline{M}_{N-1}^*}{\partial \underline{x}_2} & \cdots & \frac{\partial \underline{M}_{N-1}^*}{\partial \underline{x}_N} & \vdots & \frac{\partial \underline{M}_{N-1}^*}{\partial \underline{x}_1^*} & \frac{\partial \underline{M}_{N-1}^*}{\partial \underline{x}_2^*} & \cdots & \frac{\partial \underline{M}_{N-1}^*}{\partial \underline{x}_{N-1}^*} \end{bmatrix}. \tag{24}$$

For instance, **Figure 2** displays the pattern for the IEEE-57 bus system in $\mathbb{R}$-domain and complex plane. This latter is given by Eq. (24).

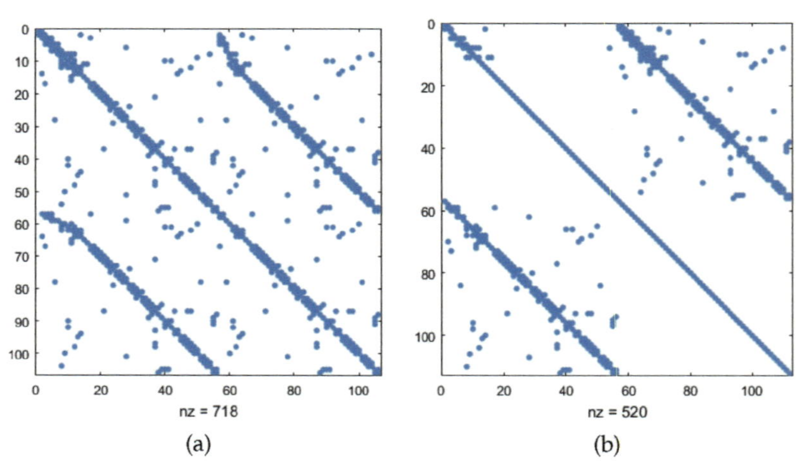

Figure 2.
Sparsity structure of (a) real-valued Jacobian matrix; (b) complex-valued Jacobian matrix of the IEEE 57-bus system.

4.1 Jacobian matrix factorization

In order to factorize the Jacobian matrix required in Eq. (23), the recommended procedure is to operate the factorization on the augmented Jacobian matrix, yielding

$$\mathbf{J}_a = \left[\mathbf{J}\ \underline{M}\left(\underline{x}_c^{(\nu-1)}\right)\right], \tag{25}$$

which the dimension is $2n \times (2n+1)$, resulting

$$\tilde{\mathbf{J}}_a = \left[\mathbf{T}_c\ \tilde{\underline{M}}\left(\underline{x}_c^{(\nu-1)}\right)\right], \tag{26}$$

where $\mathbf{T_c}$ is an upper triangular matrix of dimension $(2n \times 2n)$ and $\tilde{\underline{M}}\left(\underline{x}_c^{(\nu-1)}\right)$ comprises the corresponding rows in the updated *rhs* vector of dimension $(2n \times 1)$. Finally, Eq. (23) is solved by performing a back-substitution via

$$\Delta\underline{x}_c^{(\nu)} = \mathbf{T_c}\,\tilde{\underline{M}}\left(\underline{x}_c^{(\nu-1)}\right). \tag{27}$$

On the other hand, it is recommendable to perform the convergence checking over the infinity norm of two vectors. Firstly, as the former, it occurs over the corrections to be applied to the state variables and simultaneously over the mismatches vector. This latter is included, aiming to be aware against ill-conditioned systems [14], yielding

$$\left\|\Delta\underline{x}_c^{(\nu)}\right\|_\infty \textit{ and } \left\|M(\underline{x}_c)^{(\nu)}\right\|_\infty \le tol\ \left(e.g., 10^{-12}\right). \tag{28}$$

If Eq. (28) is satisfied, stop and print out the results. Otherwise, the state vector is updated as shown below:

$$\underline{x}_c^{(\nu)} = \underline{x}_c^{(\nu-1)} + \Delta\underline{x}_c^{(\nu)}, \tag{29}$$

and the iteration counter is increased followed by the updating of the mismatch vector and the Jacobian matrix factorization. This latter task can be mandatory or not once the Jacobian matrix may be kept constant throughout the iterative process (approximate, instead of full gain) which is a decision very often adopted after the second iteration aiming to lighten the computational burden. Further details can be found in [14], but in the sequence, a small example is presented forwarded of simulations carried out on large systems. However, as any other application in the industry, the power flow model lies in the solution of a system of linear algebraic equations which is summarized thereafter.

4.2 Nodal equation

This approach requires the nodal admittance matrix building, e.g.,

$$\underline{I} = \mathbf{Y_{bus}}\,\underline{V}, \tag{30}$$

thus the complex nodal power can be expressed as

$$\underline{S} = diag(\underline{V})\,\underline{I}^*, \tag{31}$$

or

$$\underline{S} = diag(\underline{V})\,\mathbf{Y}_{bus}^{*}\,\underline{V}^{*}. \tag{32}$$

Then, the nodal complex power at $bus - k$, i.e., S_k, is

$$S_k = V_k\, y_{kk}^{*}\, V_k^{*} + V_k \sum_{\substack{m=0\\ m\neq k}}^{N} y_{km}^{*}\, V_m^{*}, \tag{33}$$

where N is the number of network nodes. Therefore, the unknowns to be determined are the voltages at each node or bus into the system and the general power flow equations that model any type of branch in an electrical network, i.e., transmission lines and phase- and phase-shifting-transformers can be written, yielding

$$S_{km} = V_k \left(\frac{y_{km}^{*}}{t_{km} t_{km}^{*}} - j\, b_{km}^{sh}\right) V_k^{*} - V_k\, \frac{y_{km}^{*}}{t_{km}}\, V_m^{*}, \tag{34}$$

$$S_{mk} = V_m \left(y_{km}^{*} - j\, b_{km}^{sh}\right) V_m^{*} - V_m\, \frac{y_{km}^{*}}{t_{km}^{*}}\, V_k^{*}. \tag{35}$$

and their complex conjugate counterpart are

$$S_{km}^{*} = V_k^{*} \left(\frac{y_{km}}{t_{km}^{*} t_{km}} + j\, b_{km}^{sh}\right) V_k - V_k^{*}\, \frac{y_{km}}{t_{km}^{*}}\, V_m, \tag{36}$$

$$S_{mk}^{*} = V_m^{*} \left(y_{km} + j\, b_{km}^{sh}\right) V_m - V_m^{*}\, \frac{y_{km}}{t_{km}}\, V_k. \tag{37}$$

In Eqs. (34)–(37), $t_{km} = a_{km}\, e^{-j\varphi_{km}}$ is the general off-nominal tap transformer model which is composed by an ideal transformer with complex turns ratio $t_{km} : 1$ in series with its admittance or impedance. Thus, if the corresponding branch is referred to.

1. Off-nominal tap transformer: $b_{km}^{sh} = 0$ and $\varphi_{km} = 0$.
2. Pure-shifter: $b_{km}^{sh} = 0$ and $a_{km} = 1$.
3. Phase-shifter: $b_{km}^{sh} = 0$.
4. $\pi-$transmission line: $a_{km} = 1$ and $\varphi_{km} = 0$.

4.3 Small example

The power flow model in complex plane as detailed in [14] is applied to a small example system in which the diagram is shown in **Figure 3**, while the corresponding branch parameters and bus data, both in pu ($V_{base} = 230\, kV$; $S_{base} = 100\, MVA$), are presented in **Table 1**.

The nodal admittance matrix, $\mathbf{Y}_{bus}$, leads to

$$\mathbf{Y}_{bus} = \begin{bmatrix} +213.3474 - j\,380.8922 & -205.1282 + j\,358.9744 & -8.2192 + j\,21.9178 \\ -205.1282 + j\,358.9744 & +205.2414 - j\,359.3821 & -0.1132 + j\,0.6037 \\ -8.2192 + j\,21.9178 & -0.1132 + j\,0.6037 & +8.3324 - j\,22.3256 \end{bmatrix}. \tag{38}$$

The whole set of intermediary results throughout the iterative process is presented in the sequence.

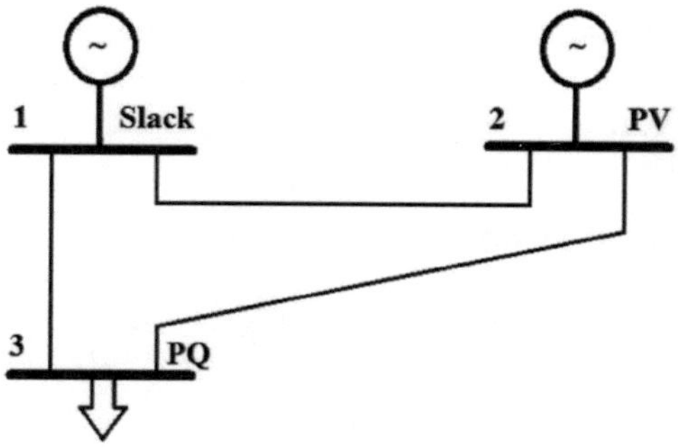

Figure 3.
Small 3-bus system.

Branch	Series		Shunt	
$i \to j$	R	X	Charging	Y/2
	pu	pu	MVAr	pu
1-2	0.0012	0.0021	39.2	0.196
1-3	0.0150	0.0400		
2-3	0.3000	1.6000		
Bus		**Specified quantities in pu**		
Type	P_g	V	P_{load}	Q_{load}
PV-2	1.0000	1.0000	0.2160	0.0918
PQ-3			2.700	1.620

Table 1.
Branch and bus data.

As in the real domain, the elements of the complex-valued Jacobian matrix remain practically unchanged after the second iteration, which suggest that we may keep them constant thereafter. Moreover, the computation of some entries can be avoided because they are complex conjugates of other entries; it turns out that these elements are PV-nodes.

$$\mathbf{J}^{(\nu=0)} = \left[\begin{array}{cc|cc} 413.6193\times e^{-j\,60.268} & 0.4232\times e^{-j\,74.484} & 413.6193\times e^{+j\,60.268} & 0.4232\times e^{+j\,74.484} \\ & 0.1960\times e^{+j\,90.000} & 0.6143\times e^{-j\,100.619} & 23.8298\times e^{+j\,69.533} \\ 1.0000\times e^{j\,0.000} & & 1.0000\times e^{j\,0.000} & \\ 0.6143\times e^{+j\,100.619} & 23.8298\times e^{-j\,69.533} & & 0.1960\times e^{+j\,90.000} \end{array}\right],$$

$$\mathbf{J}^{(\nu=1)} = \left[\begin{array}{cc|cc} 414.4312\times e^{-j\,60.323} & 0.4232\times e^{-j\,74.616} & 414.4312\times e^{+j\,60.323} & 0.3842\times e^{+j\,69.158} \\ & 3.1443\times e^{-j\,148.587} & 0.5577\times e^{-j\,105.946} & 21.6334\times e^{+j\,64.207} \\ 1.0000\times e^{-j\,0.132} & & 1.0000\times e^{+j\,0.132} & \\ 0.5577\times e^{+j\,105.946} & 23.8298\times e^{-j\,69.665} & & 3.1443\times e^{+j\,148.587} \end{array}\right],$$

$$\mathbf{J}^{(\nu=2)} = \left[\begin{array}{cc|cc} 414.3163\times e^{-j\,60.313} & 0.4232\times e^{-j\,74.599} & 414.3180\times e^{+j\,60.313} & 0.3765\times e^{+j\,68.935} \\ & 3.5321\times e^{-j\,143.603} & 0.5465\times e^{-j\,106.168} & 21.2006\times e^{+j\,63.984} \\ 1.0000\times e^{-j\,0.115} & & 1.0000\times e^{+j\,0.115} & \\ 0.5452\times e^{+j\,106.041} & 23.8298\times e^{-j\,69.648} & & 3.5232\times e^{+j\,144.712} \end{array}\right],$$

$$\mathbf{J}^{(\nu=3)} = \left[\begin{array}{cc|cc} 414.3115\times e^{-j\,60.313} & 0.4232\times e^{-j\,74.599} & 414.3133\times^{+j\,60.313} & 0.3763\times e^{+j\,68.932} \\ & 3.5408\times e^{-j\,143.485} & 0.5463\times e^{-j\,106.171} & 21.1905\times e^{+j\,63.982} \\ 1.0000\times e^{-j\,0.115} & & 1.0000\times e^{+j\,0.115} & \\ 0.5449\times e^{+j\,106.040} & 23.8298\times e^{-j\,69.648} & & 3.5316\times e^{+j\,144.620} \end{array}\right].$$

Interestingly, the numerical values of the state variables corrections, state variables, and mismatches vectors calculated in the complex plane are displayed in the **Tables 2–4**, respectively.

4.4 Performance in larger systems

The algorithm described earlier was encoded in MATLAB by using sparsity technique and column approximate minimum degree (*colamd*) ordering scheme. The numerical tests were executed by using an Intel® Core™ i5-4200 CPU at 1.60 Hz 2.30 GHz, 6GB of RAM, and 64-bit operating system. A flat start condition is assigned to the state variables in all simulations.

Thereby, **Table 5** presents the performance on larger systems of the Newton-Raphson method in complex plane which is highlighted in bold. The corresponding performance is compared with those of the former Newton-Raphson method developed in polar and rectangular coordinates, both in real domain. In all simulations the convergence criterion of 1×10^{-12} is assumed.

$\Delta\underline{x}$	$\Delta\underline{x}^{(\nu=0)}$	$\Delta\underline{x}^{(\nu=1)}$	$\Delta\underline{x}^{(\nu=2)}$	$\Delta\underline{x}^{(\nu=3)}$
Δx_2	$0.0023 \times e^{+j\ 90.00}$	$0.0003 \times e^{-j\ 90.39}$	$0.0127 \times e^{-j\ 90.08}$	$0.1708 \times e^{+j\ 89.92}$
Δx_3	$0.1278 \times e^{-j\ 138.75}$	$0.0185 \times e^{-j\ 174.56}$	$0.4267 \times e^{-j\ 179.44}$	$0.2326 \times e^{-j\ 179.18}$
Δx_2^*	$0.0023 \times e^{-j\ 90.00}$	$0.0003 \times e^{+j\ 90.37}$	$0.0127 \times e^{+j\ 90.07}$	$0.1708 \times e^{-j\ 89.91}$
Δx_3^*	$0.1278 \times e^{+j\ 138.75}$	$0.0203 \times e^{+j\ 178.81}$	$0.4795 \times e^{+j\ 173.22}$	$0.2615 \times e^{+j\ 173.47}$
$\Vert\Delta\underline{x}\Vert_\infty$ [a]	0.127809	0.020316	4.795255×10^{-4}	2.614490×10^{-7}

[a] *Convergence criteria:* $\Vert\Delta\underline{X}\Vert_\infty < tol. \approx 10^{-4}$.

Table 2.
Unknown correction vector.

$\underline{x}$	$\underline{x}^{(\nu=0)}$	$\underline{x}^{(\nu=1)}$	$\underline{x}^{(\nu=2)}$	$\underline{x}^{(\nu=3)}$
x_2	$1.000 \times e^{j\ 0.0}$	$1.000 \times e^{+j\ 0.132}$	$1.000 \times e^{+j\ 0.115}$	$1.000 \times e^{+j\ 0.115}$
x_3	$1.000 \times e^{j\ 0.0}$	$0.907 \times e^{-j\ 5.326}$	$0.889 \times e^{-j\ 5.548}$	$0.889 \times e^{-j\ 5.552}$
x_2^*	$1.000 \times e^{-j\ 180}$	$1.000 \times e^{-j\ 0.132}$	$1.000 \times e^{-j\ 0.115}$	$1.000 \times e^{-j\ 0.115}$
x_3^*	$1.000 \times e^{-j\ 180}$	$0.907 \times e^{+j\ 5.326}$	$0.887 \times e^{+j\ 5.421}$	$0.887 \times e^{+j\ 5.420}$

Table 3.
Unknown vector.

$\underline{M}$	$\underline{M}^{(\nu=0)}$	$\underline{M}^{(\nu=1)}$	$\underline{M}^{(\nu=2)}$	$\underline{M}^{(\nu=3)} \times 10^{-3}$
M_2	$-1.5680 + j\,0.0000$	$+0.2178 + j\,0.0000$	$+0.0093 + j\,0.0000$	$+0.1229 + j\,0.0000$
M_3	$+2.7000 + j\,1.4240$	$+0.1363 + j\,0.3648$	$+0.0021 + j\,0.0087$	$+0.0011 + j\,0.0047$
M_2^*	$+0.0000 + j\,0.0000$	$+0.0000 - j\,0.0000$	$+0.0000 - j\,0.0000$	$+0.0000 - j\,0.0000$
M_3^*	$+2.7000 - j\,1.4240$	$+0.1363 - j\,0.3648$	$0.0021 - j\,0.0087$	$0.0011 - j\,0.0047$

Convergence criteria: $\Vert\underline{M}\Vert_\infty < tol. \approx 10^{-4}$.

Table 4.
Mismatch vector.

	CV-Jacobian matrix dimension $2(N-1) \times 2(N-1)$	Algorithms	Number of iterations	Time/iteration (s)	Total time (s)
IEEE-14		$1.RV - NRM^{(p)}$	5	0.0184	0.1647
		$2.RV - NRM^{(r)}$	5	0.0150	0.0942
	26×26	$\mathbf{3.CV - NRM^{(r)}}$	**5**	**0.0098**	**0.0767**
IEEE-30		$1.RV - NRM^{(p)}$	5	0.0206	0.1791
		$2.RV - NRM^{(r)}$	6	0.0105	0.1121
	58×58	$\mathbf{3.CV - NRM^{(r)}}$	**6**	**0.0091**	**0.0645**
IEEE-57		$1.RV - NRM^{(p)}$	6	0.0132	0.1653
		$2.RV - NRM^{(r)}$	6	0.0137	0.1303
	112×112	$\mathbf{3.CV - NRM^{(r)}}$	**6**	**0.0110**	**0.0810**
IEEE-118		$1.RV - NRM^{(p)}$	5	0.0162	0.1575
		$2.RV - NRM^{(r)}$	6	0.0196	0.1840
	234×234	$\mathbf{3.CV - NRM^{(r)}}$	5	**0.0121**	**0.1056**
SIN-1916		$1.RV - NRM^{(p)}$	7	0.4642	3.4732
		$2.RV - NRM^{(r)}$	8	0.3095	2.6430
	3830×3830	$\mathbf{3.CV - NRM^{(r)}}$	7	**0.7699**	**4.5561**

(p)—polar coordinates; (r)—rectangular coordinates; tol., 1×10^{-12}.

Table 5.
Performance in larger systems—squared matrices.

The results presented in the aforementioned table allows us to infer that the Newton-Raphson method in complex plane has very good performance. Except for the SIN-1916 bus system, the time consuming required to achieve the solution is lower than the remainder approaches.

In the next section, the Gauss-Newton method is presented. The goal is to solve overdetermined systems of equations, i.e., the former nonlinear least-squares method in complex plane.

5. Complex-valued weighted-least-squares method (CV-WLS)

As shown in [3], the complex-valued WLS state estimator minimizes an objective function defined as

$$\underset{\underline{x}c}{\operatorname{argmin}} \ \mathcal{J}\left(\underline{x}_c\right) = \frac{1}{2}\left(\underline{z}_c - \underline{h}_c\left(\underline{x}_c\right)\right)^H \Omega_c^{-1}\left(\underline{z}_c - \underline{h}_c\left(\underline{x}_c\right)\right), \tag{39}$$

where $\underline{z}_c = (\underline{z}, \underline{z}^*)$ is a vector of specified complex values of dimension $(2m \times 1)$, $\underline{x}_c = (\underline{x}, \underline{x}^*)$ is a vector of complex-valued state variables of dimension $(2n \times 1)$, $\underline{h}_c(\underline{x}_c)$ is a vector of nonlinear functions of dimension $(2m \times 1)$ that maps $\underline{z}_c$ to $\underline{x}_c$, $\underline{\omega}_c$ is a vector of random errors in complex plane which dimension is $(2m \times 1)$, and

$\Omega_c = E\left(\underline{\omega}_c\, \underline{\omega}_c^H\right)$ is a Hermitian positive-definite covariance matrix of $\underline{\omega}_c$ which dimension is $(2m \times 2m)$. The superscript $(\cdot)^H$ stands for Hermitian operator, i.e., the transpose complex conjugate operation. Thus, the necessary condition of optimality is given by

$$\frac{\partial \mathcal{J}\,(\underline{x}_c)}{\partial \underline{x}_c} = -\mathbf{H}(\underline{x}_c)^H\, \Omega_c^{-1}\, (\underline{z}_c - \underline{h}_c(\underline{x}_c)) = 0. \tag{40}$$

By applying a first-order Taylor series expansion of $\underline{h}_c(\underline{x}_c)$ about $\underline{x}_c^{(\nu)}$, we get

$$\underline{h}_c(\underline{x}_c) = \underline{h}_c\left(\underline{x}_c^{(\nu)}\right) + \mathbf{H}\left(\underline{x}_c^{(\nu)}\right)\left(x_c - \underline{x}_c^{(\nu)}\right). \tag{41}$$

By replacing Eq. (41) into Eq. (40), we obtain

$$\mathbf{H}\left(\underline{x}_c^{(\nu)}\right)^H \Omega_c^{-1}\left[\underline{z}_c - \underline{h}_c\left(\underline{x}_c^{(\nu)}\right) - \mathbf{H}\left(\underline{x}_c^{(\nu)}\right)\left(x_c - \underline{x}_c^{(\nu)}\right)\right] = 0, \tag{42}$$

yielding the updated estimated state vector expressed as

$$\begin{aligned} \underline{x}_c^{(\nu+1)} &= \underline{x}_c^{(\nu)} + \mathbf{G}\left(\underline{\mathbf{x}}_\mathbf{c}^{(\nu)}\right)^{-1} \mathbf{H}\left(\underline{x}_c^{(\nu)}\right)^H \Omega_c^{-1}\, \Delta\underline{z}_c^{(\nu)}, \\ &= \underline{x}_c^{(\nu)} + \Delta\underline{x}_c^{(\nu)}, \end{aligned} \tag{43}$$

where

$$\Delta\underline{x}_c^{(\nu)} = \mathbf{G}\left(\underline{x}_c^{(\nu)}\right)^{-1} \mathbf{H}\left(\underline{\mathbf{x}}_c^{(\nu)}\right)^H \Omega_c^{-1}\, \Delta\underline{z}_c^{(\nu)}. \tag{44}$$

Notice $\mathbf{G}\left(\underline{x}_c^{(\nu)}\right) = \mathbf{H}\left(\underline{x}_c^{(\nu)}\right)^H \Omega_c^{-1}\, \mathbf{H}\left(\underline{x}_c^{(\nu)}\right)$ and $\Delta\underline{z}_c^{(\nu)} = \underline{z}_c - \underline{h}_c\left(\underline{x}_c^{(\nu)}\right)$. Thus, the iterations are stopped when

$$\left|\left|\Delta\underline{x}_c^{(\nu)}\right|\right|_\infty \le tol, e.g., 10^{-3}, \tag{45}$$

where $\|\cdot\|_\infty$ is the infinity norm and ν is the iteration counter.

Note that in Eq. (40), $\mathbf{H}(\underline{x}_c)$ is the Jacobian matrix of dimension $(2m \times 2n)$ defined in the complex domain, yielding

$$\mathbf{H}(\underline{x}_c) \triangleq \frac{\partial \underline{h}_c(\underline{x}_c)}{\partial \underline{x}_c} \triangleq \begin{pmatrix} \dfrac{\partial \underline{h}_c(\underline{x}_c)}{\partial \underline{x}} & \dfrac{\partial \underline{h}_c(\underline{x}_c)}{\partial \underline{x}^*} \\ \dfrac{\partial \underline{h}_c^*(\underline{x}_c)}{\partial \underline{x}} & \dfrac{\partial \underline{h}_c^*(\underline{x}_c)}{\partial \underline{x}^*} \end{pmatrix}. \tag{46}$$

Let $\mathbf{J_h} = \frac{\partial \underline{h}_c(\underline{x}_c)}{\partial \underline{x}}$ and $\mathbf{J_h^d} = \frac{\partial \underline{h}_c(\underline{x}_c)}{\partial \underline{x}^*}$ be Jacobian submatrices of dimension $(m \times n)$. They are obtained through the Wirtinger partial derivatives with respect to the complex and the complex conjugate state variables using the chain differentiation rule. Now, let us define the Jacobian matrix as

$$\mathbf{J}_c(\underline{x}_c) = \left(\mathbf{J_h}\ \mathbf{J_h^d}\right). \tag{47}$$

In the important special case given by Eq. (39) where $\mathcal{J}(\underline{x}_c)$ is a real-valued function of complex variables, the following property holds

$$\mathcal{J}(\underline{x}_c) \in \mathbb{R} \Rightarrow \frac{\partial h_c^*(\underline{x}_c)}{\partial \underline{x}} = \left(\frac{\partial h_c(\underline{x}_c)}{\partial \underline{x}^*} \right)^* = \left(\mathbf{J}_h^{\mathbf{d}} \right)^*. \tag{48}$$

Therefore, taking into account the chain rule differentiation mentioned earlier and the property stated in Eq. (48), Eq. (46) becomes

$$\mathbf{H}(\underline{x}_c) = \begin{pmatrix} \mathbf{J_h} & \mathbf{J_h^d} \\ \left(\mathbf{J_h^d}\right)^* & \left(\mathbf{J_h}\right)^* \end{pmatrix} = \begin{pmatrix} \mathbf{J}_c(\underline{x}_c) \\ \mathbf{J}_c^*(\underline{x}_c)\, \mathbf{S} \end{pmatrix}, \tag{49}$$

where $\mathbf{S}$ is a swap operator that permutes blocks of m rows or blocks of n columns depending upon whether $\mathbf{S}$ pre-multiples or post-multiples a matrix, respectively. Moreover, this operator is an isomorphism from $\mathbb{C}$ to the dual space $\mathbb{C}^*$, which obeys the properties $\mathbf{S}^{-1} = \mathbf{S}^T = \mathbf{S}$. It shows that $\mathbf{S}$ is symmetric and is equal to its own inverse, that is, $\mathbf{S}^2 = I$. For instance, as shown in [2], this matrix is defined as

$$\mathbf{S} \triangleq \begin{bmatrix} 0 & \mathbf{I}_n \\ \mathbf{I}_n & 0 \end{bmatrix}, \tag{50}$$

where $\mathbf{I}_n$ is the $(n \times n)$-identity matrix.

Now, the complex-valued gain matrix $\mathbf{G}(\hat{\underline{x}}_c)$ in expanded form can be expressed as

$$\mathbf{G}(\hat{\underline{x}}_c) = \begin{pmatrix} \mathbf{G}_{\underline{x}\,\underline{x}} & \mathbf{G}_{\underline{x}^*\,\underline{x}} \\ \mathbf{G}_{\underline{x}\,\underline{x}^*} & \mathbf{G}_{\underline{x}^*\,\underline{x}^*} \end{pmatrix}, \tag{51}$$

where $\mathbf{G}_{\underline{x}^*\,\underline{x}^*} = \left(\mathbf{G}_{\underline{x}\,\underline{x}}\right)^*$ and $\mathbf{G}_{\underline{x}^*\,\underline{x}} = \left(\mathbf{G}_{\underline{x}\,\underline{x}^*}\right)^*$, all of dimension $(n \times n)$. Then, it follows from Eq. (47) that

$$\begin{aligned} \mathbf{G}_{\underline{x}\,\underline{x}} &= \frac{1}{2}\left[\left(\frac{\partial \underline{h}}{\partial \hat{\underline{x}}}\right)^H \Omega_c^{-1} \left(\frac{\partial \underline{h}}{\partial \hat{\underline{x}}}\right) + \left(\left(\frac{\partial \underline{h}}{\partial \hat{\underline{x}}^*}\right)^H \Omega_c^{-1} \left(\frac{\partial \underline{h}}{\partial \hat{\underline{x}}^*}\right) \right)^* \right], \\ &= \frac{1}{2}\left[\mathbf{J_h}^H\, \Omega_c^{-1}\, \mathbf{J_h} + \left(\mathbf{J_h^d}^H\, \Omega_c^{-1}\, \mathbf{J_h^d} \right)^* \right], \end{aligned} \tag{52}$$

Similarly, we get

$$\begin{aligned} \mathbf{G}_{\underline{\mathbf{x}}^*\,\underline{\mathbf{x}}} &= \frac{1}{2}\left[\left(\frac{\partial \underline{\mathbf{h}}}{\partial \hat{\underline{\mathbf{x}}}}\right)^H \Omega_c^{-1} \left(\frac{\partial \underline{\mathbf{h}}}{\partial \hat{\underline{\mathbf{x}}}^*}\right) + \left(\left(\frac{\partial \underline{\mathbf{h}}}{\partial \hat{\underline{\mathbf{x}}}^*}\right)^H \Omega_c^{-1} \left(\frac{\partial \underline{\mathbf{h}}}{\partial \hat{\underline{\mathbf{x}}}}\right) \right)^* \right], \\ &= \frac{1}{2}\left[\mathbf{J_h}^H\, \Omega_c^{-1}\, \mathbf{J_h^d} + \left(\mathbf{J_h^d}^H\, \Omega_c^{-1}\, \mathbf{J_h} \right)^* \right]. \end{aligned} \tag{53}$$

The investigation of the sparsity structure of the Jacobian matrix in complex plane given by Eq. (49), e.g., **Figure 4**, reveals that the Jacobian matrices in the $\mathbb{C}$-domain are sparser than its counterpart in the $\mathbb{R}$-domain [15]. **Figure 4** is referred to the Brazilian equivalent 730-bus system which the Jacobian matrix in the $\mathbb{C}$-domain has 10,396 nonzero elements, while in the $\mathbb{R}$-domain, it has 18,403 nonzero elements; it is about 45% sparser.

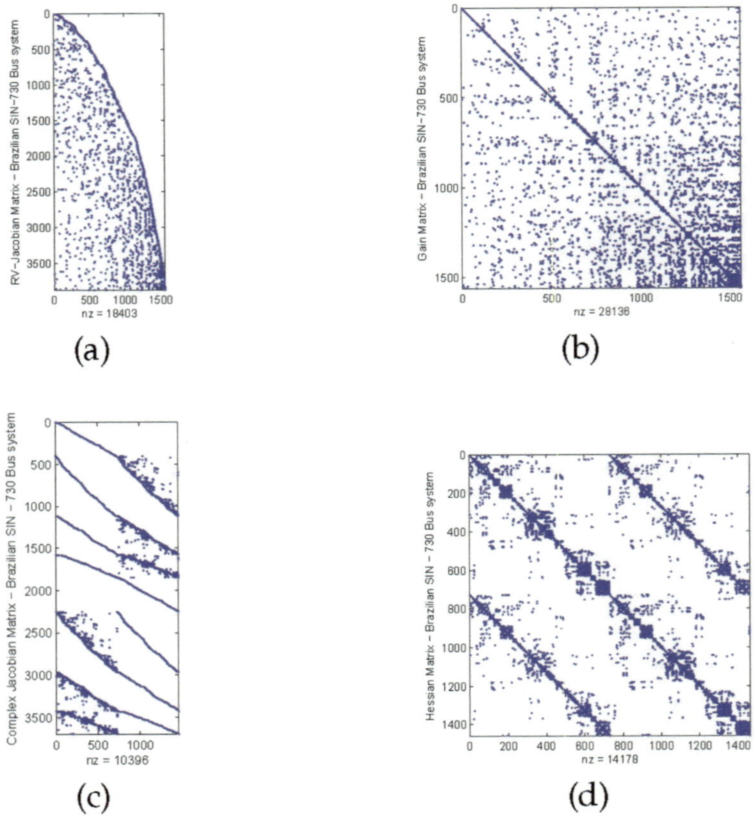

Figure 4.
Sparsity structure of (a) real-valued Jacobian matrix; (b) real-valued gain matrix; (c) complex-valued Jacobian matrix; and (d) complex-valued hessian matrix of the Brazilian equivalent 730-bus system.

Nonetheless, the recommended numerical procedure aiming to solve the complex-valued power system state estimation problem is addressed by solving the weighted form of the right-hand-side (*rhs*) of Eq. (40) instead of Eq. (44), yielding

$$\tilde{\mathbf{H}}(\underline{\hat{x}}_c)\;\Delta\underline{x}_c^{(\nu)} = \Delta\underline{\tilde{z}}_c, \tag{54}$$

where $\tilde{\mathbf{H}}(\underline{\hat{x}}_c) = \Omega_c^{-1/2}\,\mathbf{H}(\underline{\hat{x}}_c)$ is of dimension $(2m \times 2n)$ and $\Delta\underline{\tilde{z}}_c = \Omega_c^{-1/2}\,\Delta\underline{z}_c$ is of dimension $(2m \times 1)$. Thus, the incremental changes in the state vector are calculated via

$$\Delta\underline{x}_c^{(\nu)} = \tilde{\mathbf{H}}(\underline{\hat{x}}_c)^{\dagger}\;\Delta\underline{\tilde{z}}_c, \tag{55}$$

where the † operator is defined as the Moore-Penrose pseudoinverse [3].

Aiming to avoid explicitly store, the Q-matrix, we apply the QR-transformation to the augmented matrix, $\mathbf{H_a}(\underline{\hat{x}}_c)$, given by

$$\mathbf{H_a}(\underline{\hat{x}}_c) = \left[\tilde{\mathbf{H}}(\underline{\hat{x}}_c)\;\;\Delta\underline{\tilde{z}}_c\right]. \tag{56}$$

By storing the rotations in compact form, the complex-valued Jacobian matrix can be kept constant and only the right-hand-side vector is updated throughout the final iterations. The solution of the state vector increment given by Eq. (55) is found by executing a simple back-substitution of Eq. (56) after performing unitary transformations to the latter matrix, resulting in

$$\tilde{\mathbf{H}}_{\mathbf{a}}(\hat{\underline{x}}_c) = \left[\mathbf{T}_{\mathbf{c}} \;\; \Delta\tilde{\underline{\tilde{z}}}_c\right]. \tag{57}$$

Here, $\mathbf{T_c}$ is an upper triangular matrix of dimension $(2n \times 2n)$, and $\Delta\tilde{\underline{\tilde{z}}}_c$ comprises the corresponding rows in the updated *rhs* vector of dimension $(2n \times 1)$. Finally, Eq. (55) is solved by performing a back-substitution via

$$\Delta\underline{x}_c^{(\nu)} = \mathbf{T_c}\,\Delta\tilde{\underline{\tilde{z}}}_c. \tag{58}$$

5.1 Small example

The one-line diagram of a 2-bus system is depicted in **Figure 5**. The system is provided with two PMU measurements that meter the nodal voltage magnitudes and phase angles and two real and reactive power flow measurements, which are identified by means of black bullets and red triangles, respectively. In **Table 6**, the transmission line parameters are given in *pu*.

From **Figure 5**, the complex power injections at sending and receiving end, respectively, are written yielding

$$S_1 = V_1\left[\left(y_{12}^* - j\,b_{12}^{sh}\right)V_1^* - y_{12}^*\,V_2^*\right], \tag{59}$$

$$S_2 = V_2\left[\left(y_{12}^* - j\,b_{12}^{sh}\right)V_2^* - y_{12}^*\,V_1^*\right]. \tag{60}$$

Applying the Wirtinger calculus to Eqs. (59) and (60) leads to the Jacobian matrix given by Eq. (47) at each iteration as shown in the sequence. Here, the complex power injection measurement at each end, i.e., S_1 and S_2, is equal to the corresponding power flow measurement, i.e., S_{12} and S_{21}, respectively.

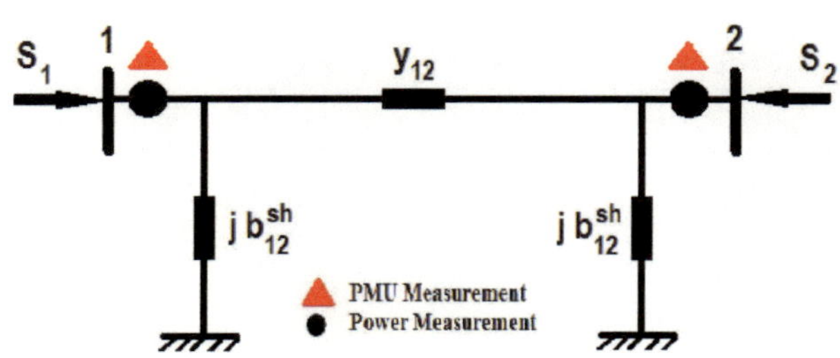

Figure 5.
2-Bus power system.

Branch	Series		Shunt	
$i \to j$	R	X	Charging	Y/2
	pu	pu	MVAr	pu
1-2	0.0203	0.1318	62.62	0.3131

Table 6.
Branch data.

$$\mathbf{J_c}^{(\nu=0)} = \left[\begin{array}{cc|cc} 1.0000 + j\,0.0000 & & & \\ & 1.0000 + j\,0.0000 & & \\ 0.0000 - j\,0.3131 & & +1.1415 + j\,7.0983 & -1.1415 - j\,7.4114 \\ & 0.0000 + j\,0.3131 & -1.1415 - j\,7.4141 & +1.1415 + j\,7.0983 \\ 0.0000 - j\,0.3131 & & +1.1415 + j\,7.0983 & -1.1415 - j\,7.4114 \\ & 0.0000 + j\,0.3131 & -1.1415 - j\,7.4141 & +1.1415 + j\,7.0983 \end{array}\right],$$

$$\mathbf{J_c}^{(\nu=1)} = \left[\begin{array}{cc|cc} +1.0000 + j\,0.0000 & & & \\ & +1.0000 + j\,0.0000 & & \\ +1.8414 + j\,0.2179 & & +0.9145 + j\,5.6849 & -0.9145 - j\,5.9356 \\ & -1.7683 - j\,0.6884 & -2.5295 - j\,4.9346 & +2.4565 + j\,4.7148 \\ +1.8414 + j\,0.2179 & & +0.9145 + j\,5.6849 & -0.9145 - j\,5.9356 \\ & -1.7683 - j\,0.6884 & -2.5295 - j\,4.9346 & +2.4565 + j\,4.7148 \end{array}\right],$$

$$\mathbf{J_c}^{(\nu=2)} = \left[\begin{array}{cc|cc} +1.0000 + j\,0.0000 & & & \\ & +1.0000 + j\,0.0000 & & \\ +1.8683 + j\,0.4802 & & +1.1653 + j\,7.1651 & -1.1658 - j\,7.4813 \\ & -1.7962 - j\,1.0677 & -2.7074 - j\,6.1598 & +2.6348 + j\,5.8884 \\ +1.8683 + j\,0.4802 & & +1.1653 + j\,7.1651 & -1.1658 - j\,7.4813 \\ & -1.7962 - j\,1.0677 & -2.7074 - j\,6.1598 & +2.6348 + j\,5.8884 \end{array}\right],$$

$$\mathbf{J_c}^{(\nu=3)} = \left[\begin{array}{cc|cc} +1.0000 + j\,0.0000 & & & \\ & +1.0000 + j\,0.0000 & & \\ +1.8828 + j\,0.4247 & & +1.1413 + j\,7.0982 & -1.1413 - j\,7.4113 \\ & -1.8098 - j\,1.0085 & -2.7148 - j\,6.1411 & +2.6417 + j\,5.8704 \\ +1.8828 + j\,0.4247 & & +1.1413 + j\,7.0982 & -1.1413 - j\,7.4113 \\ & -1.8098 - j\,1.0085 & -2.7148 - j\,6.1411 & +2.6417 + j\,5.8704 \end{array}\right].$$

As observed in the above expressions of $\mathbf{J_c}$, the sub-matrix $\mathbf{J_h}$ is more sparse than the sub-matrix $\mathbf{J_h^d}$, which affects the sparsity structure of the complex-valued Jacobian matrix as shown earlier in **Figure 4**. The state variables at each iteration are provided in **Table 7**, while the estimated measured quantities are given in **Table 8**.

$\underline{x}$	$\underline{x}^{(\nu=0)}$	$\underline{x}^{(\nu=1)}$	$\underline{x}^{(\nu=2)}$	$\underline{x}^{(\nu=3)}$
V_1	1.0000	1.0097	1.0000	1.0001
	$e^{+j\,0.0}$	$e^{-j\,0.1015}$	$e^{+j\,0.0018}$	$e^{+j\,0.0004}$
V_2	1.0000	0.8973	0.8954	0.8956
	$e^{+j\,0.0}$	$e^{-j\,14.9708}$	$e^{-j\,15.0924}$	$e^{-j\,15.0904}$
V_1^*	1.0000	1.0097	1.0000	1.0001
	$e^{+j\,0.0}$	$e^{+j\,0.1015}$	$e^{-j\,0.0018}$	$e^{-j\,0.0004}$
V_2^*	1.0000	0.8973	0.8954	0.8956
	$e^{+j\,0.0}$	$e^{+j\,14.9708}$	$e^{+j\,15.0924}$	$e^{+j\,15.0904}$

Table 7.
Estimated state variables.

$\hat{\underline{z}}_i$	$\hat{\underline{z}}^{(\nu=0)}$	$\hat{\underline{z}}^{(\nu=1)}$	$\hat{\underline{z}}^{(\nu=2)}$	$\hat{\underline{z}}^{(\nu=3)}$
S_{12}	0.0000 − j 0.3131	+1.4747 + j 0.1745	+1.8873 + j 0.4815	+1.8827 + j 0.4248
S_{21}	0.0000 − j 0.3131	−1.4014 − j 0.0707	−1.8036 − j 0.5094	−1.7997 − j 0.4500
S_1	0.0000 − j 0.3131	+1.4747 + j 0.1745	+1.8873 + j 0.4815	+1.8827 + j 0.4248
S_2	0.0000 − j 0.3131	−1.4014 − j 0.0707	−1.8036 − j 0.5094	−1.7997 − j 0.4500

Table 8.
CV-estimated quantities.

$\underline{r}^{(\nu=i)}$	$\underline{r}^{(\nu=0)}$	$\underline{r}^{(\nu=1)}$	$\underline{r}^{(\nu=2)}$	$\underline{r}^{(\nu=3)}$
r_{V_1}	$0.0000 + j\,0.0000$	$0.1991 + j\,0.0000$	$-0.0097 + j\,0.0018$	$0.0000 - j\,0.0000$
r_{V_2}	$-0.1349 - j\,0.2333$	$0.1634 - j\,0.0000$	$-0.0017 - j\,0.0015$	$0.0006 - j\,0.0001$
$r_{S_{12}}$	$1.8827 + j\,0.7375$	$0.4080 + j\,0.2499$	$-0.0046 - j\,0.0571$	$-0.0000 - j\,0.0004$
$r_{S_{21}}$	$-1.7998 - j\,0.1366$	$-0.3984 - j\,0.3790$	$0.0038 + j\,0.0597$	$-0.0001 + j\,0.0003$
r_{S_1}	$1.8827 + j\,0.7375$	$0.4080 + j\,0.2499$	$-0.0046 - j\,0.0571$	$-0.0000 - j\,0.0004$
r_{S_2}	$-1.7998 - j\,0.1366$	$-0.3984 - j\,0.3790$	$0.0038 + j\,0.0597$	$-0.0001 + j\,0.0003$
$\mathcal{J}(\hat{\underline{x}})^{(\nu=i)}$	14.7654	1.1288	0.013825	8.8×10^{-7}

Table 9.
CV-residual vector.

	CV-Jacobian matrix dimension $2m \times 2n$	Algorithms	Number of iterations	Time/ iteration (s)	Total time (s)
IEEE-14	60×28	**3.CV − NRM$^{(r)}$**	**3**	**0.045303**	**0.108547**
IEEE-30	124×60	**3.CV − NRM$^{(r)}$**	**3**	**0.067118**	**0.158415**
IEEE-118	368×236	**3.CV − NRM$^{(r)}$**	**8**	**0.150205**	**1.064942**
SIN-340	1704×680	**3.CV − NRM$^{(r)}$**	**7**	**0.992872**	**6.724038**
SIN-1916	9642×3832	**3.CV − NRM$^{(r)}$**	**8**	**29.856246**	**242.695989**

(r)—rectangular coordinates; tol.—1×10^{-3}.

Table 10.
Performance in larger systems—overdetermined matrices.

The residual vector and the chi-squared index throughout the iterations are presented in **Table 9**. Notice that the estimated values obtained in the $\mathbb{C}$-domain are exactly equal to those extracted from the power flow report in the $\mathbb{R}$-domain. Furthermore, the Gauss-Newton iterative algorithm converges in three iterations in both vector spaces, i.e., real and complex domain.

5.2 Performance in larger systems

In the sequel, **Table 10** presents the performance on larger systems of the Gauss-Newton method in complex plane which is highlighted in bold. In all simulations the convergence criterion of 1×10^{-3} is assumed.

The comparative analysis of the results presented in the aforementioned table allows us to infer that the Newton-Raphson method in complex plane has very good performance. Except for the SIN-1916 bus system, the time consuming required to achieve the solution is lower than the remainder approaches.

6. Conclusions and future developments

The chapter's prime goal is to present the advances aiming to solve nonlinear system of equations in complex plane, regardless if it is exactly or overdetermined. Firstly, it develops the former Newton-Raphson method addressed to solve exactly determined problem. Thereafter, the weighted-least-squares (WLS) is developed through the Gauss-Newton method. In both cases the applications are carried out on small examples and larger systems. All results demonstrate the advantages of the algorithms developed in complex plane over the former procedure, although the computational burden is still a bottleneck for larger systems. Highlight that there are many enhancements that can be addressed to mitigate this problem. To cite a few, they are shown as follows:

1. Ordering schemes based on rows overlapped by columns ordering schemes [12, 13].

2. Suppressing of complex conjugate calculation storing during the Jacobian matrices building.

Nomenclature

$\underline{x}_c$	Vector of the state variables in the conjugate coordinate system
x, x^*	Complex and complex conjugate state variables
t, t^*	Complex and complex conjugate tap position
$\Re\{\cdot\}$, $\{\cdot\}$	Real and imaginary part of a complex variable
$\mathbf{J}$	Complex-valued Jacobian matrix for the exactly determined system of equations
$\mathbf{H}$	Complex-valued Jacobian matrix for the overdetermined system of equations
$\underline{M}$	Complex-valued mismatch vector
$(\cdot)_c$	Quantity in the conjugate coordinate system
$\Vert\cdot\Vert^2$	Squared Euclidean norm
$\Vert\cdot\Vert_\infty$	Infinity norm
ν	Iteration counter

Author details

Robson Pires
Institute of Electric Systems and Energy—ISEE, Federal University of Itajubá—UNIFEI, Itajubá, Minas Geriais, Brazil

*Address all correspondence to: rpires@unifei.edu.br

References

[1] Steinmetz CP. Complex quantities and their use in electrical engineering. In: Proceedings of the International Electrical Congress. Chicago, IL: AIEE Proceedings; 1893. pp. 33-74

[2] Kreutz-Delgado K. The Complex Gradient Operator and the CR-Calculus. San Diego, USA: Electrical and Computer Engineering—Jacobs School of Engineering; University of California; 2009. pp. 1-74. ArXIV e-print, arXIV:0906.4835v1 [math.OC]

[3] Sorber L, Van Barel M, de Lathauwer L. Unconstrained optimization of real functions in complex variables. Society for Industrial and Applied Mathematics—SIAM. 2012; **22**(3):879-898

[4] Pires R. Complex-valued steady-state models as applied to power flow analysis and power system state estimation [PhD dissertation]. Itajuba, Brazil: Institute of Electrical Systems and Energy—ISEE; Federal University of Itajuba—UNIFEI, 2018. Available from: https://repositorio.unifei.edu.br/xmlui/handle/123456789/55

[5] David AHJ. A generalization of the conjugate-gradient method to solve complex systems. IMA Journal of Numerical Analysis. 1986;**6**(4): 447-452

[6] Maltsev A, Pestretsov V, Maslennikov R, Khoryaev A. Triangular systolic array with reduced latency for QR-decomposition of complex matrices. In: IEEE International Symposium on Circuits and Systems—ISCAS. 2006. pp. 385-388

[7] Awasthi A, Guttal R, Al-Dhahir N, Balsara PT. Complex QR decomposition using fast plane rotations for MIMO applications. IEEE Communications Letters. 2014;**18**(10): 1743-1746

[8] Gentleman WM. Least squares computations by givens transformations without square roots. Journal of Mathematical Analysis and Applications. 1974;**12**:329-336

[9] Simões-Costa AJA, Quintana VH. An orthogonal row processing algorithm for power sequential state estimation. IEEE Transactions on Power Apparatus and Systems. 1981;**100**(8):3791-3800

[10] Wang JW, Quintana VH. A decoupled orthogonal row processing algorithm for power system state estimation. IEEE Transactions on Power Apparatus and Systems. 1984;**PAS-103** (8):2337-2344

[11] Vempati N, Slutsker IW, Tinney WF. Enhancement to givens rotations for power system state estimation. IEEE Transactions on Power Systems. 1991;**6**(2):842-849

[12] Catalyurek UV, Aykanat CT, Kayaaslan E. Hypergraph partitioning-based fill-reducing ordering for symmetric matrices. SIAM Journal on Scientific Computing. 2011;**4**:1996-2023

[13] Kaya O, Kayaaslan E, Uçar B, and Duff I. Fill-in reduction in sparse matrix factorizations using hypergraphs [Research Report—8448]. 2014

[14] Pires R, Mili L, Chagas G. Robust complex-valued Levenberg-Marquardt algorithm as applied to power flow analysis. International Journal of Electrical Power & Energy Systems. 2019;**113**:383-392. DOI: 10.1016/j.ijepes.2019.05.032

[15] Pires RC, Mili L, Lemos FAB. Constrained robust estimation of power system state variables and transformer tap positions under erroneous zero-injections. IEEE Transactions on Power Systems. 2014;**29**(3):1144-1152. ISSN: 0885-8950

Section 3

Advanced Complex Analysis and Geometry Studies

Chapter 5

Variable Exponent Spaces of Analytic Functions

Gerardo A. Chacón and Gerardo R. Chacón

Abstract

Variable exponent spaces are a generalization of Lebesgue spaces in which the exponent is a measurable function. Most of the research done in this topic has been situated under the context of real functions. In this work, we present two examples of variable exponent spaces of analytic functions: variable exponent Hardy spaces and variable exponent Bergman spaces. We will introduce the spaces together with some basic properties and the main techniques used in the context. We will show that in both cases, the boundedness of the evaluation functionals plays a key role in the theory. We also present a section of possible directions of research in this topic.

Keywords: variable exponents, Hardy spaces, Bergman spaces, Carleson measures, analytic functions

1. Introduction

In recent years the interest for nonstandard function spaces has risen due to several considerations including their need in some fields of applied mathematics, differential equations, and simply the possibility to study extensions and generalizations of classical spaces.

One of such type of spaces is the variable exponent Lebesgue spaces. A first introduction to them was due to Orlicz in 1931. He considered measurable functions u such that

$$\int_0^1 |u(x)|^{p(x)}\,\mathrm{d}x < \infty,$$

the usual exponent p from the classical theory of Lebesgue spaces is replaced by a suitable function $p(\cdot)$. Orlicz was interested in the summability of Fourier series which led him to consider spaces of sequences (a_n) so that

$$\sum_{n=1}^{\infty} |\lambda a_n|^{p_n} < \infty,$$

for $\lambda > 0$ and $p_n \in [1, \infty)$.

Later generalizations consisted on considering real functions u on a domain Ω such that

$$\int_\Omega \varphi(x, |u(x)|)\,\mathrm{d}x < \infty,$$

where

$$\varphi : \Omega \times [0, \infty) \to [0, \infty)$$

is a suitable function. Such spaces are known nowadays as Musielak-Orlicz spaces. We are interested in the case

$$\varphi(x, y) = y^{p(x)},$$

which corresponds to variable exponent Lebesgue spaces, with some adequate restrictions for the *exponent* p.

The study of problems in spaces with nonstandard growth has been mainly related to Lebesgue spaces with variable order $p(x)$, to the corresponding Sobolev spaces, and to generalized Orlicz spaces (see surveys [1, 2]). The investigation of structural properties of variable exponent spaces and of operator theory in such spaces is of interest not only due to their intriguing mathematical structure—also worthy of investigation—but because such spaces appear in applications. One of these applications is the mathematical modeling of inhomogeneous materials, like electrorheological fluids. These are special viscous liquids that have the ability to change their mechanical properties significantly when they come in contact with an electric field. This can be explored in technological applications, like photonic crystals, smart inks, heterogeneous polymer composites, etc. [3–6].

Another known application is related to image restoration. Based on variable exponent spaces, the authors of [7] proposed a new model of image restoration combining the strength of the total variation approach and the isotropic diffusion approach. This model uses one value of p near the edge of images and another one near smooth regions, which leads to the variable exponent setting of the problem. Other references discussing image processing are [8–13]. This theory has also been applied to differential equations with nonstandard growth (see [14, 15]).

The theory of spaces of analytic functions on domains of the complex plane, or in general of $\mathbb{C}^n$, happens in parallel. Starting from the classical Hardy $H^p(\mathbb{D})$ and Bergman $A^p(\mathbb{D})$ spaces, the functional Banach spaces have had a preferential study.

A Banach space $\mathcal{X}$ of complex-valued functions on a domain Ω is said to be *a functional Banach space* (cf. [16]) if the following hold:

- Vectorial operations are precisely the pointwise operations on Ω.
- If $f(x) = g(x)$ for every $x \in \Omega$, then $f = g$.
- If $f(x) = f(y)$ for every $f \in \mathcal{X}$, then $x = y$.
- Evaluation functionals $x \mapsto f(x)$ are continuous on $\mathcal{X}$.

Classical Hardy and Bergman spaces are examples of functional Banach spaces. In the case of spaces of analytic functions, the evaluation functionals $K_x(f) = f(x)$ $(x \in \Omega)$ are an extension of the well-known *reproducing kernels* in Hilbert spaces of analytic functions. The analyticity property of the functions in the space interacts with the Banach space structure by means of the continuity of evaluation functionals raising a fruitful relation between function theory and operator theory.

The setting of nonstandard spaces of analytic functions is a young area of research; a lot is yet to be explored. In this chapter, an introduction to the subject of variable exponent spaces of analytic functions will be given, making emphasis in the special place that evaluation functionals have in the theory.

2. Variable exponents

Perhaps the most known function spaces in mathematical analysis are the *Lebesgue spaces* L^p. These are a fundamental basis of measure theory, functional analysis, harmonic analysis, and differential equations, among other areas. A recent generalization is the so-called *variable exponent Lebesgue spaces*. In this case, the defining parameter p is allowed to vary.

The basics on variable Lebesgue spaces may be found in the monographs [1, 17, 18]. For $\Omega \subset \mathbb{R}^d$ we put $p_\Omega^+ := \operatorname{ess\,sup}_{x\in\Omega}\, p(x)$ and $p_\Omega^- := \operatorname{ess\,inf}_{x\in\Omega}\, p(x)$; we use the abbreviations $p^+ = p_\Omega^+$ and $p^- = p_\Omega^-$. For a measurable function $p : \Omega \to [1,\infty)$, we call it a *variable exponent* and define the set of all variable exponents with $p^+ < \infty$ as $\mathcal{P}(\Omega)$.

For a complex-valued measurable function $\varphi : \Omega \to \mathbb{C}$, we define the *modular* $\rho_{p(\cdot),\mu}$ by

$$\rho_{p(\cdot),\mu}(\varphi) := \int_\Omega |\varphi(x)|^{p(x)}\, \mathrm{d}\mu(x)$$

and the *Luxemburg-Nakano norm* by

$$\|\varphi\|_{L^{p(\cdot)}(\Omega,\mu)} := \inf\left\{\lambda > 0 : \rho_{p(\cdot),\mu}\left(\frac{\varphi}{\lambda}\right) \leqslant 1\right\}. \tag{1}$$

Given $p(\cdot) \in \mathcal{P}(\Omega)$, the *variable Lebesgue space* $L^{p(\cdot)}(\Omega,\mu)$ is defined as the set of all complex-valued measurable functions $\varphi : \Omega \to \mathbb{C}$ for which the modular is finite, i.e., $\rho_{p(\cdot),\mu}(\varphi) < \infty$. Equipped with the Luxemburg-Nakano norm (1) is a Banach space.

Most of the research being done on variable exponent spaces makes use of a regularity condition in the variable exponent in order to have a "fruitful" theory.

Definition 1. A function $p : \Omega \to \mathbb{R}$ is said to be $\log$*-Hölder continuous*—or satisfy the *Dini-Lipschitz condition* on Ω if there exists a positive constant $C_{\log}$ such that

$$|p(x) - p(y)| \leqslant \frac{C_{\log}}{\log(1/|x-y|)},$$

for all $x, y \in \Omega$ such that $|x-y| < 1/2$, from which we obtain

$$|p(x) - p(y)| \leq \frac{2\ell C_{\log}}{\log\left(\frac{2\ell}{|x-y|}\right)}$$

for all $x, y \in \Omega$ such that $|x-y| < \ell$. We will write $p(\cdot) \in \mathcal{P}^{\log}(\Omega)$ when $p(\cdot)$ is $\log$-Hölder continuous.

This condition has proven to be very useful in the theory since, among other things, it implies the boundedness of the Hardy-Littlewood maximal operator in $L^{p(\cdot)}(\Omega)$. Such operator is defined as

$$Mf(x) := \sup_{r>0} \frac{1}{|B(x,r)|} \int_{B(x,r)} |f(y)|\mathrm{d}y$$

and represents an important tool in harmonic analysis. We used it in [19] to show that the Bergman projection is bounded on variable exponent Bergman spaces.

Another consequence of the $\log$-Hölder condition is the following inequality

$$|B|^{p_-(B)-p_+(B)} \leq C,$$

that hold for all balls $B \subset \mathbb{C}$. Here $|B|$ stands for the Lebesgue measure of B, $p^+(B) = \text{ess } \sup_{z \in B} p(z)$, and $p^-(B) = \text{ess } \inf_{z \in B} p(z)$. This will be a useful tool when studying complex function spaces since it allows to pass from an exponent that varies over a ball to a constant exponent at the center of such ball.

One interesting point of the theory of variable exponents is that, in general, the classical approach to Bergman spaces seems to fail in the variable framework. For example, in [19] it is shown that the Bergman projection is bounded from $A^{p(\cdot)}(\mathbb{D})$ to $A^{p(\cdot)}(\mathbb{D})$. This is done by using the theory of Békollé-Bonami weights and a theorem that extends Rubio de Francia's extrapolation theory to variable Lebesgue spaces. This method is quite different from the usual ways of showing that the Bergman projection is bounded, which use either Schur's test or Calderón-Zygmund theory.

3. Variable exponent Hardy spaces

In this section we will give an introduction to the variable exponent Hardy spaces and the results and techniques that are usually found. We will follow the presentation as in [20].

Definition 2. For each z in the unit disk $\mathbb{D}$, the Poisson kernel $P(z, \zeta)$ is defined as

$$P(z, \zeta) = \frac{1 - |z|^2}{|z - \zeta|^2},$$

and the Poisson transform of a function $f \in L^{p(\cdot)}(\mathbb{T})$ is defined as

$$Pf(z) = \int_{\mathbb{T}} P(z, \zeta) f(\zeta) m(\zeta),$$

where m denotes the normalized Lebesgue measure on $\mathbb{T}$.

We will use the following result from [21]:

Theorem 3. *Suppose that p is log-Hölder continuous. For each $0 \leq r < 1$, and $f \in L^{p(\cdot)}(\mathbb{T})$, the linear operator $P_r : L^{p(\cdot)}(\mathbb{T}) \to L^{p(\cdot)}(\mathbb{T})$ defined as*

$$P_r f(\zeta) = Pf(r\zeta)$$

is uniformly bounded on $L^{p(\cdot)}(\mathbb{T})$, $\|P_r(f)\|_{L^{p(\cdot)}(\mathbb{T})} \lesssim \|f\|_{L^{p(\cdot)}(\mathbb{T})}$, and for every $f \in L^{p(\cdot)}(\mathbb{T})$,

$$\|f - P_r f\|_{L^{p(\cdot)}(\mathbb{T})} \to 0, \quad \text{as } r \to 1^-.$$

We are now ready to define the harmonic Hardy spaces with variable exponents. Given $f : \mathbb{D} \to \mathbb{C}$ and $0 \leq r < 1$, the *dilations* $f_r : \mathbb{T} \to \mathbb{C}$ of f are defined as $f_r(\zeta) = f(r\zeta)$.

Definition 4. The *variable exponent harmonic Hardy space* $h^{p(\cdot)}(\mathbb{D})$ is defined as the space of harmonic functions $f : \mathbb{D} \to \mathbb{C}$ such that

$$\|f\|_{h^{p(\cdot)}(\mathbb{D})} = \sup_{0\le r<1} \|f_r\|_{L^{p(\cdot)}(\mathbb{T})} < \infty.$$

Notice that, since Pf is harmonic for $f \in L^{p(\cdot)}(\mathbb{T})$, then Theorem 3 shows that the Poisson transform $P : L^{p(\cdot)}(\mathbb{T}) \to h^{p(\cdot)}(\mathbb{D})$ is bounded. Moreover, we have the following theorem analogous to the constant exponent context.

Theorem 5. *Suppose that $p : [0, 2\pi] \to [1, \infty)$ is log-Hölder continuous. Then for every $U \in h^{p(\cdot)}(\mathbb{D})$, there exists $u \in L^{p(\cdot)}(\mathbb{T})$ such that $Pu = U$ and moreover, $\|U\|_{h^{p(\cdot)}(\mathbb{D})} \sim \|u\|_{L^{p(\cdot)}(\mathbb{T})}$.*

Theorem 6. *The following chain of inclusions holds*

$$h^{p^+}(\mathbb{D}) \subset h^{p(\cdot)}(\mathbb{D}) \subset h^{p^-}(\mathbb{D}),$$

and moreover, the inclusions are continuous.

Definition 7. The variable exponent Hardy space $H^{p(\cdot)}(\mathbb{D})$ is defined as the space of analytic functions $f : \mathbb{D} \to \mathbb{C}$ such that $f \in h^{p(\cdot)}(\mathbb{D})$.

In an analogous way to the classical setting $H^{p(\cdot)}(\mathbb{D})$ can be identified with the subspace of functions in $L^{p(\cdot)}(\mathbb{T})$ whose negative Fourier coefficients are zero, and as such, $H^{p(\cdot)}(\mathbb{D})$ is a Banach space.

Recall that for all functions $f \in H^1(\mathbb{D})$, we have the reproducing formula:

$$f(z) = \int_{\mathbb{T}} \frac{f(\zeta)}{1 - \overline{\zeta} z} \, dm(\zeta).$$

For each $z \in \mathbb{D}$, the functions $K_z : \mathbb{D} \to \mathbb{C}$ defined as

$$K_z(w) = \frac{1}{1 - \overline{z} w},$$

are called *reproducing kernels*. They are bounded on $\mathbb{D}$ and consequently belong to every space $H^{p(\cdot)}(\mathbb{D})$. Moreover, as a consequence of the reproducing formula and the Hahn-Banach theorem, the linear span of $\{K_z : z \in \mathbb{D}\}$ is dense in $H^{p(\cdot)}(\mathbb{D})$. Consequently, the set of polynomials is also dense in $H^{p(\cdot)}(\mathbb{D})$.

Theorem 8. *For each $z \in \mathbb{D}$ consider the linear functional $\gamma_z : H^{p(\cdot)}(\mathbb{D}) \to \mathbb{C}$ defined as $\gamma_z(f) = f(z)$. Then γ_z is a bounded operator for every $z = |z|e^{i\theta} \in \mathbb{D}$ and*

$$\|\gamma_z\| \lesssim \frac{1}{(1-|z|)^{1/p(\theta)}}.$$

Consequently, the convergence in the $H^{p(\cdot)}(\mathbb{D})$-norm implies the uniform convergence on compact subsets of $\mathbb{D}$.

The main tool for proving the previous theorem is following the version of a Forelli-Rudin inequality, adapted to the case of variable exponents. Here, the Log-Hölder continuity plays a key role.

Lemma 9. *Suppose $p : [0, 2\pi] \to [1, \infty)$ and $q : [0, 2\pi] \to [1, \infty)$ are such that $\frac{1}{p(\theta)} + \frac{1}{q(\theta)} = 1$ for every $\theta \in [0, 2\pi]$. Let $1/2 < r < 1$ and $z = |z|e^{i\theta}$. Define the function $\varphi : [0, 2\pi] \to \mathbb{R}^+$ as*

$$\varphi(t) = \frac{(1-|z|)^{1/q(\theta)}}{|1 - |z| r e^{i(t-\theta)}|}.$$

Then if $\varphi(t) > 1$, *it holds that*

$$\varphi(t)^{p(t)} \lesssim \varphi(t)^{p(\theta)}.$$

4. Variable exponent Bergman spaces

The theory of Bergman spaces was introduced by S. Bergman in [22] and since the 1990s has gained a great deal of attention mainly due to some major breakthroughs at the time. For details on the theory of Bergman spaces, we refer to the books [5, 23].

Definition 10. Given a measurable function $p \in \mathcal{P}(\mathbb{D})$, we define the *variable exponent Bergman space* $A^{p(\cdot)}(\mathbb{D})$ as the space of all analytic functions on $\mathbb{D}$ that belong to the variable exponent Lebesgue space $L^{p(\cdot)}(\mathbb{D})$ with respect to the area measure $\mathrm{d}A$ on the unit disk $\mathbb{D}$, i.e.,

$$A^{p(\cdot)}(\mathbb{D}) = \left\{ f \text{ is an analytic function and } \int_{\mathbb{D}} |f(z)|^{p(z)} \mathrm{d}A(z) < \infty \right\}.$$

One of the first results proven in [19] about this theory was the boundedness of the evaluation functionals that, as we saw before, will allow us to conclude that convergence in $A^{p(\cdot)}(\mathbb{D})$ implies uniform convergence on compact subsets of $\mathbb{D}$ and consequently $L^{p(\cdot)}$-limits of sequences in $A^{p(\cdot)}(\mathbb{D})$ are analytic. Hence $A^{p(\cdot)}(\mathbb{D})$ is a closed subspace of $L^{p(\cdot)}(\mathbb{D})$ (and hence a Banach space). The first approach to such result used the following interpolation result based on Forelli-Rudin estimates:

Lemma 11. *Let* $p \in \mathcal{P}(\mathbb{D})$, *then for every function* $f \in L^{p(\cdot)}(\mathbb{D})$ *we have*

$$\|f\|_{L^{p(\cdot)}(\mathbb{D})} \leqslant \|f\|_{L^1(\mathbb{D})}^{1/p^+} \|f\|_{L^\infty(\mathbb{D})}^{1-1/p^+}.$$

Using different techniques, the following sharp estimate was obtained in [24]:

Theorem 12. *Let* $p(\cdot) \in \mathcal{P}^{\log}(\mathbb{D})$. *Then for every* $z \in \mathbb{D}$ *we have that*

$$\|\gamma_z\|_{p(\cdot)} \asymp \frac{1}{\left(1 - |z|^2\right)^{2/p(z)}}. \tag{2}$$

The proof of this fact relies on the Log-Hölder condition and on the following version of a Jensen-type inequality for variable exponent spaces (see [17]).

Lemma 13. *Suppose that* $p(\cdot) \in \mathcal{P}^{\log}(\mathbb{D})$ *and let*

$$\frac{1}{q(z,y)} := \max\left\{\frac{1}{p(z)} - \frac{1}{p(y)}, 0\right\}.$$

Then for $0 < \gamma < 1$,

$$\left(⨍_{B(x,r)} |f(y)| \mathrm{d}A(y) \right)^{p(z)} \lesssim ⨍_{B(x,r)} |f(y)|^{p(y)} \mathrm{d}A(y) + ⨍_{B(x,r)} \gamma^{q(z,y)} \mathrm{d}A(y)$$

for all $z \in B(x,r)$ provided that $\|f\|_{L^{p(\cdot)}(\mathbb{D})} \leqslant 1$. The constant depends on γ and $p(\cdot)$.

The additional term that appears in the previous inequality makes the boundedness of the domain a necessary condition to use such technique. One question to address in future investigations is how the situation is for Bergman spaces defined on unbounded domains. In such case, the error term accumulates despite the regularity condition on $p(\cdot)$, and consequently a different technique is needed.

4.1 Mollified dilations

One technique developed to study variable exponent Bergman spaces is a combination of mollifiers and dilations. Such concept was developed for studying the density of the set of polynomials in Bergman spaces. In the classical case, this is a consequence of the fact that convergence in $A^p(\mathbb{D})$ implies convergence on compact subsets of $\mathbb{D}$ and that for any $f \in A^p(\mathbb{D})$, its *radial dilations*

$$f_r(z) = f(rz)$$

converge in norm to f for $r \to 1^-$. This is a simple fact that depends on the dilation-invariant nature of Bergman Spaces, something that does not hold in the case of variable exponent Bergman spaces. This is one of the main difficulties for generalizing the classical theory.

One way of overcoming this problem in the case of variable exponent Lebesgue spaces is the use of a *mollification operator*. But in the case of the unit disk, changes need to be made. That is, when we had the idea to introduce a *mollified dilation*, given a function $f \in A^{p(\cdot)}(\mathbb{D})$ and $r \in \left[\frac{1}{2}, 1\right)$, define the *mollified dilation* $f_r : \frac{1+r}{2r}\mathbb{D} \to \mathbb{C}$ of f as

$$f_r(z) := \int_{\mathbb{D}} f(rw)\eta_r(z-w)\mathrm{d}A(w).$$

where $\rho\mathbb{D}$ stands for the complex disk with radius ρ,

$$\eta_r(z) := \frac{4r^2}{(1-r)^2}\eta\left(\frac{2rz}{1-r}\right)$$

and

$$\eta(z) := \begin{cases} \exp\left(\dfrac{1}{|z|^2-1}\right), & \text{if } |z|<1, \\ 0, & \text{if } |z| \geqslant 1, \end{cases}$$

Mollified dilations allow us to approximate analytic functions in the variable exponent Bergman spaces by functions that are analytic on a neighborhood of the unit disk.

Theorem 14. *Let* $p \in \mathcal{P}^{\log}(\mathbb{D})$ *and let* $f \in A^{p(\cdot)}(\mathbb{D})$. *Then for* $1/2 \leqslant r < 1$, $f_r \in A^{p(\cdot)}(\mathbb{D})$, *and*

$$\sup_{1/2 \leqslant r < 1} \|f_r\|_{A^{p(\cdot)}(\mathbb{D})} \lesssim \|f\|_{A^{p(\cdot)}(\mathbb{D})}.$$

Moreover, $\|f_r - f\|_{A^{p(\cdot)}(\mathbb{D})} \to 0$ *as* $r \to 1^-$.

As a consequence of the previous theorem, we can approximate a function $f \in A^{p(\cdot)}(\mathbb{D})$ by a function f_r which is analytic in $\frac{1+r}{2r}\mathbb{D}$. Hence, the sequence of Taylor polynomials associated with f_r converges uniformly on $\mathbb{D}$ to f_r. Therefore, given $\varepsilon > 0$, there exists $1/2 \le r < 1$ such that $\|f - f_r\|_{A^{p(\cdot)}(\mathbb{D})} < \varepsilon/2$. And there exists a polynomial p such that $\|p - f_r\|_{A^{p(\cdot)}(\mathbb{D})} < \varepsilon/2$.

4.2 Carleson measures

Another classical problem that has a variable exponent equivalent consists on finding a geometrical characterization of Carleson measures in variable exponent Bergman spaces. Given a positive Borel measure μ defined on the unit disk $\mathbb{D}$, we say that μ is a *Carleson measure* for the variable exponent Bergman space $A^{p(\cdot)}(\mathbb{D})$ if there exists a constant $C > 0$ such that

$$\|f\|_{L^{p(\cdot)}(\mathbb{D},\mu)} \leqslant C\|f\|_{A^{p(\cdot)}(\mathbb{D})}.$$

In other words, μ is a Carleson measure on $A^{p(\cdot)}(\mathbb{D})$ if $A^{p(\cdot)}(\mathbb{D})$ is continuously embedded in $L^{p(\cdot)}(\mathbb{D},\mu)$.

Lennart Carleson gave a geometric characterization of Carleson measures on Hardy spaces H^p and used this result in his proof of the Corona theorem and some interpolation problems (cf. [25]). After that, Carleson measures have gained interest, and a geometric characterization is usually important in spaces of analytic functions.

In the case of the classical Bergman spaces $A^p(\mathbb{D})$, Carleson measures are characterized in terms of the measure on pseudo-hyperbolic disks (see [26]). An interesting fact is the independence of the characterization on the exponent p. In the case of variable exponent Bergman spaces, the independence of $p(\cdot)$ does not hold unless the $p(\cdot)$ satisfies the Log-Hölder condition. The counterexample for the general case and the theorem for the restricted case were found in [24].

Theorem 15. *Let μ be a finite, positive Borel measure on $\mathbb{D}$ and $p(\cdot) \in \mathcal{P}^{\log}(\mathbb{D})$. Then μ is a Carleson measure for $A^{p(\cdot)}(\mathbb{D})$ if and only if there exists a constant $C > 0$ such that for every $0 < r < 1$ and every $a \in \mathbb{D}$, $\mu(D_r(a)) \le C|D_r(a)|$, where $D_r(a)$ denotes pseudo-hyperbolic disk with center at $a \in \mathbb{D}$ and radius r:*

$$D_r(a) := \left\{ z \in \mathbb{D} : \left| \frac{a - z}{1 - \bar{a}z} \right| < r \right\}.$$

The main tool for the proof of the previous theorem is Eq. (2) that implies the following estimate for the reproducing kernels.

Theorem 16. *Let $p(\cdot) \in \mathcal{P}^{\log}(\mathbb{D})$. Then for every $z \in \mathbb{D}$ we have that*

$$\|k_z\|_{A^{p(\cdot)}(\mathbb{D})} \asymp \frac{1}{\left(1 - |z|^2\right)^{2(1-1/p(z))}}.$$

5. Open problems

5.1 Zero sets

An interesting area will be to study some analytic properties of functions belonging to variable exponent Bergman spaces. One starting point will be to study the structure of zero sets in the space.

A sequence of points $\{z_n\} \subset \mathbb{D}$ is a zero set for the Bergman space $A^p(\mathbb{D})$ if there exists $f \in A^p(\mathbb{D})$ such that $f(z_n) = 0$ for all n and $f(z) \neq 0$ if $z \notin \{z_n\}$.

Although the problem of completely describing the zero sets in $A^p(\mathbb{D})$ is still open, some information is available. For example, if $n(r)$ denotes the number of zeroes of a function $f \in A^p(\mathbb{D})$ having modulus smaller than $r > 0$, then it is known that

$$n(r) = O\left(\frac{1}{1-r}\log\left(\frac{1}{1-r}\right)\right), \qquad r \to 1^-.$$

This result depends on studying the radial growth of functions in the Bergman space and on Jensen's formula for the sequence $\{z_k\}$ of zeroes of f such that $|z_k) < r$.

$$\log|f(0)| = \sum_{k=1}^{n(r)} \log\left(\frac{|z_k|}{r}\right) + \frac{1}{2\pi}\int_0^{2\pi} \log|f\left(re^{i\theta}\right)|\,d\theta.$$

This equation holds for every analytic function on $\mathbb{D}$. Consequently, if we want to find out whether a similar result about the growth of the zeroes holds in the variable exponent case, then it is necessary to study the radial growth of functions in $A^{p(\cdot)}(\mathbb{D})$. Such results, in the case of a constant exponent again, depend on the subharmonicity of $|f|^p$.

Another result involving zero sets is that if $f(0) \neq 0$, then

$$\prod_{k=1}^{n(r)} \frac{1}{|z_k|} = O\left(n(r)^{1/p}\right), \qquad r \to 1^-.$$

Finding an extension of such result to variable exponents would include making sense of the right-hand side term that is not even clear in this context.

5.2 Sampling sequences

A related concept that we would like to address in variable exponent Bergman spaces is that of sampling sequences. A sequence of points $\{z_k\} \subset \mathbb{D}$ is sampling in $A^p(\mathbb{D})$ if there exists constants $c > 0$ and $C > 0$ such that for all $f \in A^p(\mathbb{D})$

$$c\|f\|_p^p \leq \sum_{k=1}^{\infty} \left(1 - |z_k|^2\right)^2 |f(z_k)|^p \leq C\|f\|_p^p.$$

One difference that is expected to occur in the case of variable exponents is that sampling sequences will probably not be invariant under automorphism of the unit disk. This is true for a constant exponent, and it will be interesting to find counter-examples if the exponent varies. Sampling sequences are related to the concept of "frames" in Hilbert spaces and can be thought as sequences that contain great information of the space. It is expected that a sampling sequence is a somehow "big" and "spread out" subset of the unit disk. The notion is clearly related in A^p to the concept of Carleson measures.

If we define a discrete measure μ as

$$\mu = \sum_{k=1}^{\infty} \left(1 - |z_k|^2\right)^2 \delta_{z_k}$$

where δ_{z_k} is the Dirac measure with a point mass at z_k, then the sequence $\{z_k\}$ is sampling if μ is a Carleson measure and satisfies a "reverse" Carleson condition. Then it becomes relevant to find a geometric characterization of the measures that satisfy a reverse Carleson condition (see [27–29]). The characterization depends on the concept of dominant sets and it is independent of p. The methods used by Luecking for Bergman spaces rely on a calculation of the norm of evaluation functionals and a submean value property. Different techniques must be developed for the variable exponent counterpart.

5.3 Operators in variable exponent Bergman spaces

The characterization of Carleson measures obtained in [24] opens the possibility of studying the boundedness and compactness of certain operators acting on variable exponent Bergman spaces.

Among those operators worth studying are multiplication operators. Those are formally defined on a functions space $\mathcal{F}$ as

$$M_f(g) = fg$$

where $g \in \mathcal{F}$. One natural question is to find the set of symbols f that make the operator M_f map the space $A^{p(\cdot)}(\mathbb{D})$ to itself.

Such question has been addressed in the case of weighted Bergman spaces in [23]. The proof relies on a geometric characterization of Carleson measures, a composition with a disk isomorphism, and a theorem of change of variables. Such tool is difficult to use in the setting of variable exponents since any change of variables will also affect the exponent and consequently the spaces are not necessarily invariant under composition with isomorphisms. This makes the situation different from the case of a constant exponent.

Other operators related to multiplication are Toeplitz operators. Those have already being studied in [30] for the case of weighted Bergman spaces with non-radial weights. Given a function $\varphi \in L^1(\mathbb{D})$, the Toeplitz operator T_φ is defined on the set of polynomials as

$$T_\varphi p(z) = \int_{\mathbb{D}} p(w) k_w(z) \varphi(w) \mathrm{d}A(w).$$

One natural question is to ask whether this operator can be extended boundedly to the space $A^{p(\cdot)}(\mathbb{D})$. This question is addressed in [31] were a characterization of the boundedness and compactness of T_φ is found in terms of Carleson measures and the Berezin transform associated with T_φ. This type of results are sometimes referred to as Axler-Zheng theorems, and similar questions looking to establish the relation between the Berezin transform of a finite product of Toeplitz operators with its compactness have been addressed by several authors; a survey of this type of results is given in [32]. It is then reasonable to ask weather an Axler-Zheng type result for products of Toeplitz operators holds in the context of variable exponents.

The composition operators are another type of operators to be studied. Given an analytic self-map φ of the unit disk, the composition operator C_φ can be formally defined as

$$C_\varphi(f) = f \circ \varphi.$$

A natural question is to find function-theoretic conditions on φ that guarantee the boundedness and/or compactness of its associated composition operator acting on $A^{p(\cdot)}(\mathbb{D})$. One approach to follow is to address the boundedness problems of linear operators acting on $A^{p(\cdot)}(\mathbb{D})$ through the use Rubio de Francia extrapolation. Given an open set $\Omega \subset \mathbb{C}$, we denote by $\mathcal{F}$ a family of pairs of non-negative, measurable functions defined on Ω, and by A_1 we denote the class of Muckenhoupt weights w. That is, the non-negative functions w such that

$$\text{ess sup}_{z\in\Omega} \frac{Mw(z)}{w(z)} < \infty$$

where M denotes the Hardy-Littlewood maximal operator. Rubio de Francia extrapolation in the setting of variable exponent spaces can be stated as follows.

Proposition 17 (Thm. 5.24 in [1]). *Suppose that for some $p_0 \geq 1$ the family of pairs of functions $\mathcal{F}$ is such that for all $w \in A_1$,*

$$\int_\Omega F(x)^{p_0} w(x) \mathrm{d}x \leq C_0 \int_\Omega G(x)^{p_0} w(x) \mathrm{d}x, \quad (F, G) \in \mathcal{F}.$$

Given $p \in \mathcal{P}(\Omega)$, if $p_0 \leq p_- \leq p_+ < \infty$ and the maximal operator is bounded on $L^{(p(\cdot)/p_0)'}(\Omega)$, then

$$\|F\|_{L^{p(\cdot)}(\Omega)} \leq C_{p(\cdot)} \|G\|_{L^{p(\cdot)}(\Omega)}.$$

This result allows, under certain conditions, to pass from the of studying operators defined on variable exponent spaces, to study operators defined on weighted constant exponent spaces, and therefore it is possible to use known results from the Muckenhoupt weights theory.

5.4 Analytic Besov spaces

Another type of spaces we are interested is the class of analytic Besov spaces B_p. These are the spaces of all analytic functions in the unit disk such that

$$\int_\mathbb{D} |f'(z)|^p \left(1 - |z|^2\right)^{p-2} \mathrm{d}A(z) < \infty.$$

For each p this is a normed space with norm

$$\|f\|_{B_p} = |f(0)| + \left(\int_\mathbb{D} |f'(z)|^p \left(1 - |z|^2\right)^{p-2} \mathrm{d}A(z)\right)^{1/p}.$$

One particular property of this space is that they are Möbius invariant in the sense that $\|f \circ \varphi\|_{B_p} = \|f\|_{B_p}$ for every automorphism of the unit disk φ. This is probably not true in general for a variable exponent version due to the problems with the change of variables formula. A first question to address is to characterize the exponents that leave the space invariant under disk automorphisms.

One useful technique to study such spaces is a derivative-free characterization of functions in B_p. It can be seen (see, e.g., [33]) that $f \in B_p$ if and only if

$$\int_\mathbb{D}\int_\mathbb{D} \frac{|f(z) - f(w)|^p}{|1 - z\overline{w}|^4} \mathrm{d}A(z)\mathrm{d}A(w) < \infty.$$

A similar result in the case of variable exponents could serve as a starting point for investigating other properties of the space.

Author details

Gerardo A. Chacón[1*] and Gerardo R. Chacón[2]

1 Universidad Antonio Nariño, Bogotá, Colombia

2 Gallaudet University, Washington, D.C., USA

*Address all correspondence to: gerardo.chacon@gallaudet.edu

References

[1] Cruz-Uribe D, Fiorenza A. Variable Lebesgue Spaces: Foundations and Harmonic Analysis. Basel: Birkhäuser; 2013

[2] Samko S. On a progress in the theory of Lebesgue spaces with variable exponent: Maximal and singular operators. Integral Transforms and Special Functions. 2005;**16**(5–6): 461-482

[3] Acerbi E, Mingione G. Regularity results for electrorheological fluids, the stationary case. Comptes rendus de l'Académie des Sciences. 2002;**334**(9): 817-822

[4] Acerbi E, Mingione G. Regularity results for stationary electrorheological fluids. Archive for Rational Mechanics and Analysis. 2002;**164**(3):213-259

[5] Růžička M. Electrorheological Fluids, Modeling and Mathematical Theory. Lecture Notes in Mathematics. Berlin: Springer-Verlag; 2000

[6] Růžička M. Modeling, mathematical and numerical analysis of electrorheological fluids. Applications of Mathematics. 2004;**49**(6):565-609

[7] Chen Y, Levine S, Rao M. Variable exponent, linear growth functionals in image restoration. SIAM Journal on Applied Mathematics. 2006;**66**(4): 1383-1406 (electronic)

[8] Aboulaich R, Boujena S, El Guarmah E. Sur un modèle non-linéaire pour le débruitage de l'image. Comptes Rendus de l'Académie des Sciences. 2007;**345**(8):425-429

[9] Aboulaich R, Meskine D, Souissi A. New diffusion models in image processing. Computers & Mathematics with Applications. 2008;**56**(4):874-882

[10] Blomgren P, Chan T, Mulet P, Wong CK. Total variation image restoration, numerical methods and extensions. In: Proceedings of the 1997 IEEE International Conference on Image Processing, Volume III; 1997. pp. 384-387

[11] Bollt EM, Chartrand R, Esedoglu S, Schultz P, Vixie KR. Graduated adaptive image denoising, local compromise between total variation and isotropic diffusion. Advances in Computational Mathematics. 2009;**31** (1-3):61-85

[12] Chen Y, Guo W, Zeng Q, Liu Y. A nonstandard smoothing in reconstruction of apparent diffusion coefficient profiles from diffusion weighted images. Inverse Problems and Imaging. 2008;**2**(2):205-224

[13] Wunderli T. On time flows of minimizers of general convex functionals of linear growth with variable exponent in BV space and stability of pseudo-solutions. Journal of Mathematical Analysis and Applications. 2010;**364**(2):5915-5998

[14] Harjulehto P, Hästoö P, Lê ÚV, Nuortio M. Overview of differential equations with non-standard growth. Nonlinear Analysis: Theory Methods & Applications. 2010;**72**(12):4551-4574

[15] Mingione G. Regularity of minima, an invitation to the dark side of the calculus of variations. Applications of Mathematics. 2006;**51**(4):355-426

[16] Cowen CC Jr, MacCluer BI. Composition Operators on Spaces of Analytic Functions (Studies in Advanced Mathematics). Boca Ratón, FL: CRC Press; 1995

[17] Diening L, Harjulehto P, Hästö P, Růžička M. Lebesgue and Sobolev Spaces with Variable Exponents, Lecture Notes in Mathematics. Berlin: Springer-Verlag; 2011

[18] Rafeiro H, Rojas E. Espacios de Lebesgue con exponente variable: Un espacio de Banach de funciones medibles (Spanish). Vol. 2014. Caracas: IVIC—Instituto Venezolano de Investigaciones Científicas. p. XI+136

[19] Chacón GR, Rafeiro H. Variable exponent Bergman spaces. Nonlinear Analysis: Theory Methods & Applications. 2014;**105**:41-49

[20] Chacón GA, Chacón GR. Analytic variable exponent Hardy spaces. Advances in Operator Theory. 2019;**4**: 738-749

[21] Sharapudinov II. Uniform boundedness in L^p $(p = p(x))$ of some families of convolution operators. Mathematical Notes. 1996;**59**:205-212

[22] Bergman S. The Kernel Function and Conformal Mapping. 2nd ed. Providence, R. I.: American Mathematical Society; 1970

[23] Zhao R. Pointwise multipliers from weighted Bergman spaces and Hardy spaces to weighted Bergman spaces. Annales Academiæ Scientiarum Fennicæ. 2004;**29**:139-150

[24] Chacón GR, Rafeiro H, Vallejo JC. Carleson measures for variable exponent Bergman spaces. Complex Analysis and Operator Theory. 2017;**11**: 1623-1638. DOI: 10.1007/s11785-016-0573-0

[25] Garnett JW. Bounded Analytic Functions. Berlin: Springer-Verlag; 2007

[26] Duren P, Schuster A. Mathematical surveys and monographs, 100. In: Bergman Spaces. Providence, RI: American Mathematical Society; 2004

[27] Luecking D. Closed-range restriction operators on weighted Bergman spaces. Pacific Journal of Mathematics. 1984;**110**:145-160

[28] Luecking D. Forward and reverse Carleson inequalities for functions in Bergman spaces and their derivatives. American Journal of Mathematics. 1985; **107**:85-111

[29] Mengestie T. Carleson type measures for Fock-Sobolev spaces. Complex Analysis and Operator Theory. 2014;**8**:1225-1256. DOI: 10.1007/s11785-013-0321-7

[30] Chacón GR. Toeplitz operators on weighted Bergman spaces. Journal of Function Spaces and Applications. 2013; **2013**:5. Article ID: 753153. DOI: 10.1155/2013/753153

[31] Chacón GR, Rafeiro H. Toeplitz operators on variable exponent Bergman spaces. Mediterranean Journal of Mathematics. 2016;**13**:3525-3536. DOI: 10.1007/s00009-016-0701-0

[32] Cucković Z, Şahutoğlu S, Zheng A. Type theorem on a class of domains in $\mathbb{C}^n$. Integral Equations and Operator Theory. 2013;**77**:397

[33] Zhu K. Operator Theory in Function Spaces, Mathematical Surveys and Monographs. Providence, RI: American Mathematical Society; 2007

Chapter 6

Integral Geometry and Cohomology in Field Theory on the Space-Time as Complex Riemannian Manifold

Francisco Bulnes

Abstract

The study of the relationships between the integration invariants and the different classes of operators, as well as of functions inside the context of the integral geometry, establishes diverse homologies in the dual space of the functions. This is given in the class of cohomology of the integral operators that give solution to certain class of differential equations in field theory inside a holomorphic context. By this way, using a cohomological theory of appropriate operators that establish equivalences among cycles and cocycles of closed submanifolds, line bundles and contours can be obtained by a cohomology of general integrals, useful in the evaluation and measurement of fields, particles, and physical interactions of diverse nature that occurs in the space-time geometry and phenomena. Some of the results applied through this study are the obtaining of solutions through orbital integrals for the tensor of curvature $R^{\mu\nu}$, of Einstein's equations, and using the imbedding of cycles in a complex Riemannian manifold through the duality: line bundles with cohomological contours and closed submanifolds with cohomological functional. Concrete results also are obtained in the determination of Cauchy type integral for the reinterpretation of vector fields.

Keywords: complex Riemannian manifold, cocycles, cohomology, cohomology of cycles, geometrical integration, integral curvature, integration invariants, integral operators

AMS Classification: 32A19 32C26 32C30 23C15 58 K70 14 J17

1. Introduction

Obtaining an integral cohomology of general integral operators that determine complex analytic solutions through classes of cohomology born of the $\bar{\partial}$-cohomology is necessary to use a holomorphic language with the purpose of obtaining the holomorphic forms that involve exact forms. In fact, this methodology is a way of so many perspectives that suggest the use of complex hyperholomorphic functions in approaching functions in complex analysis, although using fibrations on some quaternionic algebra. The holomorphic forms required in this language, are good to express the integral of complex vector fields as integral of line, which have more than enough lines and hyperplanes, respectively, in $\mathbb{CP}^n$ and $\mathbb{C}^n$, visualizing these fields like holomorphic sections of complex holomorphic bundles of fibrations $X \to M$.

But the $\bar{\partial}$-cohomology exists naturally in coverings of Stein $X \to M$, like holomorphic forms. Then, the integral can be expressed on spaces M_δ, and Δ_Z, [1, 2], that are given as lines and hyperplanes of $\mathbb{CP}^n$ and $\mathbb{C}^n$, and that as such they are integral orbital of the complex manifolds $M = G/L$ and $\Delta = \Gamma/\Sigma$, belonging to a $\bar{\partial}$-cohomology in holomorphic language.

The cohomologies of functionals and functions, respectively, that they can built through the complex cohomology of hyperspaces are generalizable for vector fields in the same sense of the coverings of Stein and therefore of the $\bar{\partial}$-cohomology.

The following question arises, how to establish isomorphisms of cohomological classes for functions, functional, and vector fields inside the holomorphic context possible? How to determine a cohomological theory of integral operators that establish equivalences among these objects and the geometric objects of closed submanifolds, bundles of lines, and Feynman diagrams? How everything can decrease to a single cohomology of general integrals on contours or a cohomology of generalized functionals?

Before giving an answer to the previous questions, we give some preliminary definitions that we will use to fix concepts and outlines of the wanted general theory.

Let M, be a complex Riemannian manifold and be a sheaf of germs of holomorphic sections of a vector holomorphic sheaf.

Definition 1.1. We say that a space$H^\bullet(M, \mathfrak{J})$, is an integral cohomology (not in the sense of the set $\mathbb{Z}$, but yes in the sense of the integrals of partial differential equations) of those $\bar{\partial}$-equations, if this is a class of solutions or general integrals of these equations in M [1, 3].

Definition 1.2. An integral as generalized solution of a $\bar{\partial}$-equation is a realization of an irreducible representation of a $\bar{\partial}$-cohomology of complex closed submanifolds [2–4].

If the irreducible representations are unitary, then we have a complex L^2-cohomology or $\bar{\partial}$-cohomology with coefficients in L^2. The corresponding integral operators to their integral cohomology are those of the complex Fourier analysis, which in the complex geometrical context (geometrical analysis) could be integrals constructed through integral transforms as the Hilbert transforms and other [3].

In the case of a real reductive Lie group, the generalized integrals come to be determined by their orbital integrals. Let G, be a real form of $G^{\mathbb{C}}$, and P, their parabolic subgroup. The generalized integrals in G, are the integrals on open orbits of the generalized flag manifold $G^{\mathbb{C}}/P$. For this way, if $G = U(n, 1)$, and the generalized flag manifold is then $\mathbb{P}^n$, the open orbit is the group of positive lines $\mathbb{P}^+$, which is an $U(n, 1)-$orbit in $\mathbb{P}^n(\mathbb{C})$. The integrals are of John type [3, 5, 6]:

$$\varphi(P) = \int_{L^+ \subset \mathbb{P}^n(\mathbb{C})} f, \tag{1}$$

The general integral in this case is given by the twistor transform [7] on the corresponding homogeneous bundle of lines, that is to say:

$$\mathcal{T} : H^1(\mathbb{P}^+, O(-n-2)) \to H^1(\mathbb{P}^{+*}, O(n-2)), \tag{2}$$

Using the twistor transform like intertwining operator of induced tempered representations on a $\bar{\partial}$-cohomology, we have representations of $SU(2, 2)$ that are orbits of a fundamental unitary $(g, K)-$module of the electrodynamics [8]

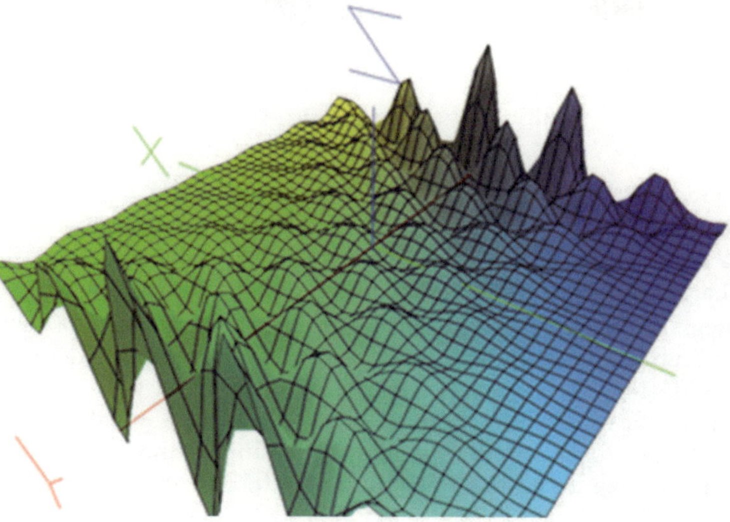

Figure 1.
Electromagnetic waves in conformal actions of the group SU(2, 2) *on a two-dimensional flat model of the space-time [9–11].*

(see **Figure 1**). Then, it is possible to assign a vector bundle of lines with a unitary representation, where it can be classified.

The concepts of general integral and generalized integral are different because one refers to the whole class of cohomology of solutions of those $\bar{\partial}$-equations about a complex analytic manifold, and the other refers to the classes of cohomology of solutions on cycles or cocycles of the complex Riemannian manifold [1, 2].

Another example in the recovery of a space of functions mainly the space M, is the recovery of real functions in the space $\mathbb{R}^n$, through values of certain integral operators. Such is the case of the formula tof(x), recovered on $\mathbb{R}^n$,

$$f(x) = c\int_{\Gamma}\left\{\int_{-\infty}^{\infty} f^{\wedge}(\xi, p)[p - (\xi, x)]^{-n}dp\right\}\omega(\xi) \tag{3}$$

where the integral on p, is understood in terms of its regularization (role that carries out the Hilbert transform). The constant c depends on the dimension parity of the space $\mathbb{R}^n$, where it was carrying the tomography [6].

To answer the first question, we need a structure of complexes that induce isomorphisms in integral cohomology.

Definition 1.3. A covering of Stein is a set of manifolds of Stein[1] M_δ and Δ_z, of the corresponding fibers $X \rightarrow M$ and $X \rightarrow \Delta$, of the double fibration [1].

Let us consider the complexes given in Ref. [1], and let us consider the structure defined by a covering of Stein given by the set of open $\{M_\delta\}$, and $\{\Delta_z\}$, in the topology

$$\tau_X = \{(z, \xi) \in M \times \Xi | X \subset M \times \Xi(\Leftrightarrow M_\delta \cap \Xi_z)\}, \tag{4}$$

1 A Stein manifold is an open orbit of a semi-simple Lie group G, in a generalized flag manifold whose nilpotent radical is opposite to the parabolic subgroup P, of G [12]. A definition of the Stein manifold that uses the Hermitian structure of a complex holomorphic manifold is:
Let be $G = G_0$, a real form of $G_{\mathbb{C}}$, and $F_D = G/H$, an open orbit in the flag manifold $F = G_{\mathbb{C}}/P = G_0/U$. F_D is Stein if H is compact (or equivalently, if F_D is Hermitian symmetric). Likewise, a Stein manifold is a Hermitian symmetric flag domain.

Then, a complex in X is the space such that Ω^r_h, for any complex Ω^r, in a corresponding long succession is given as follows:

$$\{\Omega^r_h\} \subsetneq \{\Omega^r\} \tag{5}$$

(i.e., to say, all the subcomplexes Ω^r_h, of the complex Ω^r). Then, the integral operator cohomology $H^\bullet(M, \mathfrak{J})$, in a complex manifold M, is that whose complexes conform a holomorphic structure that induces (in the corresponding integral manifold) a generalized according structure of integral submanifolds.

The integral submanifolds represent solutions of those $\bar{\partial}$-equations in cycles of M. The integral submanifolds are the corresponding cocycles of M, under the integral operators of $H^\bullet(M, \mathfrak{J})$.

For example, if we take the complex manifold M, like a manifold of rational curves E_z, of a twistor manifold $\mathcal{I}$ [where should understand each manifold $\mathcal{I}$, as the manifold of integral submanifolds (locally)], then its structure comes from a structure projective of their line on E_z, guided according to the vectors in T_zM.

These correspond to sections of a normal bundle $\mathcal{N}E_z$, to the curve E_z (infinitesimal deformations to the curve), that is to say, these conform the holomorphic structure that will induce the corresponding structure (that is to say in the corresponding integral manifold). In this case, the generalized structure of integral submanifolds is the $V^{(k)}$-conformal integrable structure given by $\mathcal{I}$. The integral cohomology in this case is given by the family of rational curves.

The twistor content in this case helps and is necessary to establish the deformation of the integral curves of the vector sheaf of lines O(k). In such case, the integral cohomology is $H^\bullet(M, \mathfrak{J}) = H^0(\mathcal{I}, O(k))$.

This example is interesting not only for the fact of the definition of the integral cohomology, which defines, for this way, a class of integrals for M, but also for the fact of satisfaction of the integrability condition for the equation of the tensor of Weyl $W_{ij} = 0$, where $H^0(\mathcal{I}^+, O(k))$ (respectively, $H^0(\mathcal{I}, O(k))$) are the solutions or integral of $W^+ = 0$ (respectively, $W^- = 0$ [13, 14].

2. Duality: line bundles with cohomological contours and closed submanifolds with cohomological functional

We consider the following result on integral cohomology for integral geometry.

Proposition 2.1. In the integral cohomology $H^\bullet(M, \mathfrak{J})$, on complex manifolds, the following statements are equivalent:

a. The open M_δ, and Δ_z, are G−orbits opened up in X, and their integrals are generalized integral for M,

b. Exists an integral operator T, such that $H^\bullet(M, \mathfrak{J}) \cong_T \ker\{D\text{-equations}\}$,

c. $M_\delta = \cup_M \underline{\pi}/\underline{z}$, and $\Delta_z = \cup_\Delta \underline{z}/\underline{\pi}$, where $H^\bullet(M, \mathfrak{J}) = H^{n-1}(U, \rho^{-1}O(V))$.

Proof. The integrals on the open G− orbits satisfy the G−invariant integration:

$$\int_{G/H} f d\Phi(\phi^r) = \int_{G/H} (f \circ \Phi^{-1})\phi^r, \tag{6}$$

For the theorem of Buchdall Eastwood [12], we have that the orbits generalized in X, give us a new cohomological class that is related to the previous for an integral operator T, defined for

$$H^{\bullet}(M, \mathfrak{J}(\nu)) \to H^{\bullet}(\Xi, \tau^{-1}\mathfrak{J}(\nu)), \tag{7}$$

and such that $H^{\bullet}(\Xi, \tau^{-1}\mathfrak{J}(\nu)) \cong_T \ker\{D\text{-equations } G/H\}$, has more than enough. By the theorem II.1 [1][2], the G−orbits are K−orbits in X. Then (i) == > (ii). Now for the theorem II.2 [1],[3] we have that each canonical fibration of a flag manifold will give a G−orbit in Z, for some internal symmetrical G−space M.

In particular, ker{D-equations}, takes place the correspondence with the cycles of $H^{\bullet}(M, \mathfrak{J})$. In fact, ker{$D$-equations}, is similar to a compact number of components on which G, acts transitively, and these belong together to the cocycles of $H^{\bullet}(\Xi, \tau^{-1}\mathfrak{J}(\nu))$.

But ker{D-equations} only exists as integral of those $\overline{\partial}$-equations in M (with M, integrable) if $|R_{\mathcal{I}}^{M}(j) = 0$. This $g_{\mathbb{C}}$ establishes a generalized structure of M, which underlies in its composition (in fact$[m^{+,}, m^{+}] \subset m$, for integrability). Then, $\forall z \in M$ and $\sigma \in \Sigma(\cong \sum_i V_z)$ exist $z \in F$, such that $T_zF = \sigma T_wF \in \sum_i(V_w), \forall w \in F$. Then, $M = \cup_{\sigma \in \Sigma} V_\sigma$, and $\Xi = \cup_{\gamma \in \Sigma} V_\gamma$, then for n-dimensional planes of a Grassmann manifold, $G_{1,n}$ had that $M_\delta = \cup_{M} \underline{\pi}/\underline{z}$, and $\Delta_z = \cup_{\Delta} \underline{z}/\underline{\pi}$, which defines cycles in $H^{n-1}(U, \rho^{-1} O(V))$, with $U \subset M$. Then (ii) implies (iii).

However, fixed G exists alone a finite number of flag manifolds of certain biholomorphism of this type. These are in bijective correspondence with the conjugated classes of parabolic subalgebras of $g_{\mathbb{C}}$, and each flag manifold admits a finite number of canonical fibrations.

Then, ker{D-equations}, is made of a finite number of G−orbits, all which are closed and (iii) == > (ii). Then since each one of these G−orbits exists like an K−orbit of the space of classes G/K, with Nijenhuis null curvature tensor, then each flag submanifold is an K−orbit of the vector holomorphic G−bundle of the 2n− dimensional irreducible symmetrical Riemannian manifold J(M).

Its integrals are orbital, and their extensions to M_δ, and Δ_z, are generalized integrals (since they are integral of line along the fibers of M_δ, and Δ_z, respectively) for which it is continued. Then, (ii) implies (i).◆.

---

[2] **Theorem.** The K− invariance given for the G−structure $S_G(M)$, of complex holomorphic M, is induced to each closed submanifold given for the flag manifolds of the corresponding vector holomorphic G−bundle. Furthermore, the given integral cohomology on such complex submanifolds is equivalent to the integral cohomology on submanifolds of a maximum complex torus.

[3] **Theorem.** Let be $M = G/K$, an internal symmetric simply connected Riemannian manifold and of compact type. Then

$$Z = \{R_{\mathcal{I}}^{M}(j) \in End(\wedge^2 T*(M) \otimes_{\mathbb{R}} E) | R_{\mathcal{I}}^{M}(j) = 0\},$$

It consists of a finite number of connected components on each a G, that acts transitively. Further, any flag G−manifold is realized as a such orbit for some M.

The requirement of the transitive action of G, on the orbits is, for example, indispensable to the spatial isotropy hypothesis in the constructions of an integral cohomology to the space–time curvature, since the curvature integrals must be determined on G−invariant orbits and will be calculated for reduction of the corresponding holonomy group on K− invariant orbits.

Proposition 2.2. The $(n-1)-\overline{\partial}-$ complex cohomology with coefficients in a complex holomorphic bundle of M, is a cohomology of hyperlines and hyperplanes[4].

---

[4] We can have a little digression with certain details on the complex Radon transform using submanifolds in the space $\mathbb{CP}^1$, to the $\overline{\partial}-$ cohomology. Let be M, a complex holomorphic manifold (or complex Riemannian manifold [15]). We consider its corresponding reductive homogeneous space determined for the flag manifold $F = G_{\mathbb{C}}/P$, with P, a parabolic subgroup of $G_{\mathbb{C}}$. We consider the open orbit given for the Stein manifold $F_D = G/H$ (as was defined in the footnote 1) with H, a compact subgroup of the real form G_0, of $G_{\mathbb{C}}$.
Let be $M \cong \mathbb{C}^n$, and we consider concave linearly domains D, in $\mathbb{C}^n$ (or so better in $\mathbb{PC}^n$ [16]). D, has structure of complex vector space. Let be $D_1 = \xi^n/\overline{D}$, a holomorphic convex linear domain conformed for holomorphic hyperplanes $\pi_i(D)$, $i = 1, 2, 3, \ldots$, in D_1. Let be $H^1(D)$, the complex holomorphic functions space defined on D_1. Let $D \to M$, be a fiber vector bundle seated in the complex holomorphic manifold M. Let $A^{p,q}(D)$, be the (p, q)-forms space on M, with values in D (that is to say, the global sections space of the fiber tangent bundle $\wedge^{p,q}T*(M) \otimes D$).
Of this way, the bi-graded algebra is the space

$$\mathcal{A}(D) = \oplus_{n+m=p} A^{n,m}(D),$$

Let $\overline{\partial}$-be the scalar operator on the complex manifold M, with values on the vector bundle of global sections $\mathcal{E}(\wedge^{p,q}T*(M) \otimes D)$, that is to say, the differential operator

$$\overline{\partial} : \mathcal{E}(\wedge^{p,q}T*(M) \otimes D) \to \mathcal{E}(\wedge^{p,q+1}T*(M) \otimes D),$$

The operator $\overline{\partial}$, complies certain anticommutative properties [1]. Now, we consider the Radon transform on the complex holomorphic functions H(D), and its analogous for the complex holomorphic functionals $H(D*)$, through the corresponding diagram:

$$\begin{array}{l} D \xrightarrow{f} H(D) \xrightarrow{R_{\overline{\partial}}} L(D) \\ \downarrow \text{Functional} \downarrow \text{Functional} \downarrow \text{Functional} \quad , \\ D* \xrightarrow{\varphi} H(D*) \xrightarrow{R_{\overline{\partial}}*} L(D*) \end{array}$$

and we consider an $\overline{\partial}$-operator in D. The before diagram represents a first cohomological advance on the relation between functionals of the $(n-1)-$dimensional $\overline{\partial}$- cohomology with coefficients in a complex vector bundle Ω^n (holomorphic complex bundle) and the integration of the cohomology on hyperplanes in D, which an integral geometry is equivalent to consider an adequate Radon transform in D. Likewise, and using the satellites $\overline{\partial}R$, and $\overline{\partial}R^{-1}$, of the before diagram and composing the diagram with the correspondences to R, on D, and $D*$, we can have:

$$\overline{\partial} R(f) = R\overline{\partial}(f),$$

The details of the demonstration of this identity can be seen in Ref. [1].
Due to that R, is injective, this is equivalent to have the exact succession of Radon transform images:

$$0 \to R_0 A^{0,0}(L(D)'') \to RA^{0,1}(H(D)'') \to R*A^{0,1}(L(D)') \to 0,$$

or in equivalent way, for the exact succession:

$$0 \to R_0^{-1} B^{0,0}(L(D)'') \to R^{-1}B^{0,1}(H(D)'') \to R*^{-1}B^{0,1}(L(D)') \to 0,$$

Here the $''$ and $'$ denote the projectivizing of spaces for R. Then the Radon transform can be generalized to the $\overline{\partial}$-cohomology classes on the complex spaces D, respectively D_1, in $\mathbb{C}^n$, as the mapping:
$R_{\overline{\partial}}$: $\overline{\partial}$-cohomology of dimension n $\to$ $\overline{\partial}$-cohomology of dimension (n-1),
whose restriction to a domain D, is the mapping:

$$R_{\overline{\partial}}|_D : H(D) \to L(D),$$

which satisfies the diagram of correspondences for functionals of a (n-1)-dimensional cohomology with coefficients in a holomorphic vector bundle $\mathcal{E} \to M$.
The natural question arises, what relation there is between the two different corresponding objects to functionals, that is to say, cohomology and functions?
The relation is an integral relation of certain $\overline{\partial}$-cohomology, which comes defined for the Radon transform of the Dolbeault cohomology $R_{\overline{\partial}}$.
The Radon transform can be viewed as the mapping of cohomological spaces:

$$R_{\overline{\partial}} : H^{p,n}(D, V) \to H^{p,n-1}(D, V),$$

Therefore, it is enough to demonstrate that $R_{\overline{\partial}}(H^{p,n}(D, V))$, is the qth-projection (n-1)-dimensional of $H^{p,n}(D, V)$, in $H^{0,q}(D, V) = H^{0,n}(D, V)$. Remember that the Radon transform in the complex context D, is the continuous and analytic mapping [17]:

Their demonstration is a simple consequence of the digression in part II of Ref. [1], on some basic integral $\bar{\partial}$–cohomologies on n–dimensional complex spaces (see **Figure 2**), of this same philosophical dissertation of integral operators published in 2007.

Proposition 2.3. The integrals of contour are generalized function in a cohomology of contours (cohomological functional).

We define the following concept.

Definition 2.1. Cohomological function of a cohomology $H^{\bullet}(M - \text{Sing}M, \Omega^r)$, [5] is an integral cohomology of the form $H^{\bullet}(\mathcal{M} - \text{Sing}\, M, \mathbb{C})$, where $\mathcal{M}$, can be understood as a twistor space corresponding to M. (see **Figure 3**).

For example, this class belongs to the Feynman integrals.

We consider p and differential q forms of the cohomologies on the complex manifolds X, and Y, respectively, $\alpha \in H^p(X, S)$, and $\beta \in H^q(Y, S)$.

We consider their cup product given for $\alpha \cup \beta \in H^{p+q}(X \cap Y, S \otimes T)$, and the connecting map in the succession of Mayer-Vietoris:

$$\partial * : H^{p+q}(X \cap Y, S \otimes T) \to H^{p+q+1}(X \cup Y, S \otimes T), \tag{8}$$

$$R : H(D) \to L(D),$$

with rule of correspondence for a complex coordinates system $z_1, z_2, \ldots, z_n$,

$$f^{\wedge}(\zeta_1, \zeta_2, \ldots, \zeta_n) = \left(\frac{i}{2}\right)^{n-1} \int_D f(z_1, z_2, \ldots, z_n)\delta(s\text{-}[(\zeta_1, \zeta_2, \ldots, \zeta_n), (z_1, z_2, \ldots, z_n)]) \bullet$$
$$< dz_1, dz_2, \ldots, dz_n, d\bar{z}_1, d\bar{z}_2, \ldots, d\bar{z}_n),$$

$\forall f \in H(D)$.

We consider $\bar{\partial}$, complex scalar mapping defined to Dolbeault cohomology. Let $D* = \mathcal{L}(H(D), \mathbb{C})$, be the set of hyperplanes corresponding to D. Let

$$ev_f : \mathcal{L}(H(D), \mathbb{C}) \to \mathbb{C},$$

the evaluation of $f \in H(D)$, in the complex hyperplane $\pi(z)$, of D, with rule of correspondence:

$$\pi(z)(f) = <\pi(z), f>,$$

Due to that $\bar{\partial} R(f) = R\bar{\partial}(f), \forall f^{\wedge} \in L(D)$, we have that:

$$\bar{\partial}\,(f^{\wedge}(z)) = \bar{\partial}(f^{\wedge}) \otimes z + f^{\wedge}\bar{\partial}(z) = \bar{\partial}(z) \otimes R(f) \in A^{p,q-1}(V),$$

where in particular the exterior algebra $\wedge^{0,q}(T*(M) \otimes V_C)$, is generated for elements $\pi(z) \wedge \bar{\partial} R(f)(z))$. Then

$$R_{\bar{\partial}}(f) \otimes ev_f = <\pi(z)f, \bar{\partial}(RF)>,$$

Therefore $p = 0$. Then $R_{\bar{\partial}}(f) \otimes ev_f \in A^{0,q}(V)$. Then $H^{0,q}(\mathbb{C}^n/D, V) = H^{0,q}(D_1, V)$, which is a Dolbeault cohomology. Of this form, it can be established that through the hyperspaces geometry can be determined a certain class of holomorphic complex functions using an appropriate $\bar{\partial}$- cohomology. Also Gindikin generalizes this idea using the (n-1-q)-$\bar{\partial}$-cohomology determining the Radon transform on hyperplanes defined as linearly concave domains of dimension q, first to the real case and after to the complex case [16]. For example, a good modern research to the respect is the followed residual $\bar{\partial}$-cohomology and the complex Radon transform on subvarieties of $\mathbb{CP}^1$ [16].

[5] Here, $\mathcal{M}$, is the product of all the twistor spaces and Sing M, is the union of all the subspaces on which the $(Z^{\alpha}W_{\alpha})^{-1}$, and $(Z^{\alpha}A_{\alpha})^{-1}$, are singular factors. Its differential form is integrated over a contour, which can be traditional contour, for example with cohomology space $H_{3\upsilon}(\mathcal{M} - \text{Sing}\, M, \mathbb{C})$.

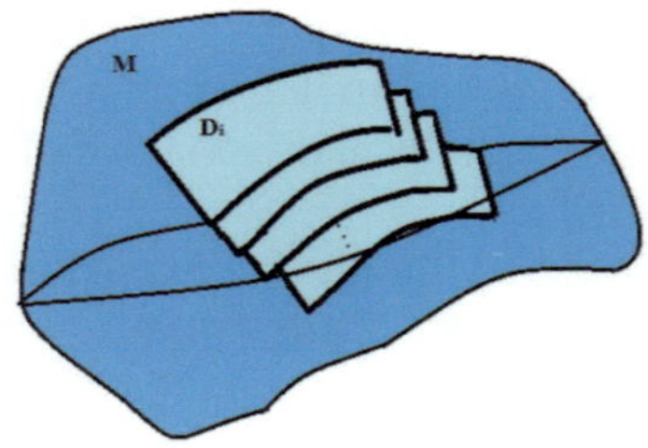

Figure 2.
Convex domains conformed for holomorphic hyperplanes $\pi_i(D)$.

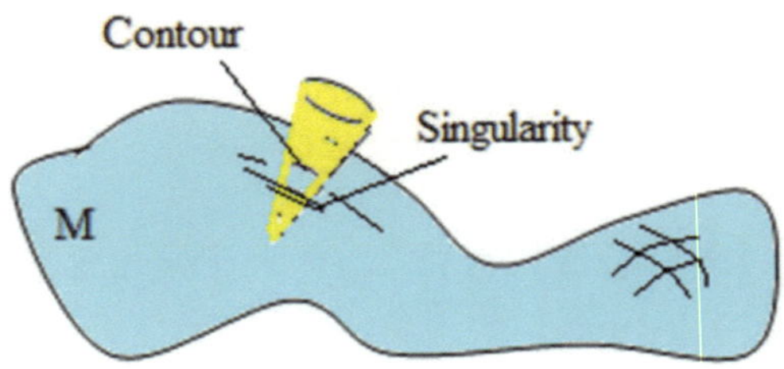

Figure 3.
Cohomology of contours isomorphic to $H^{\bullet}(M - \text{Sing}\, M, \Omega^r)$.

We consider for the inner product of α, and β, the relation is

$$\alpha \bullet \beta = \partial * (\alpha \cup \beta), \tag{9}$$

This description of the inner product has been used in a new development of the cohomology for twistor diagrams foreseen in Refs. [14, 18]. This new method is almost opposed to the procedure that we want to use in the unification of contour integrals on diagrams, in respect of the Feynman integral, although also proper to the Conway integrals, Cauchy integrals,[6] and some integral transforms as the Hilbert transforms.

We want to assemble a Feynman diagram for applications of the product "cup." The interior edges of a Feynman diagram are taken again as elements of groups H^0 (such extra elements have to be abandoned in a cohomology, for example, $H^{\bullet}(M, \tau^{-1}\, \mathfrak{J}(\nu))$, and the interior edges form the fields (assuming that they are elementary states) in several cohomology groups H^1.

Let denote $\mathcal{M}$, for Π, and sing $M = \ell$. Likewise, if f, is one of these elements of H^1, this new procedure determines an element of the cohomology $H^f(\Pi\text{-}\ell', \Omega^d)$, where ℓ', is the union of all the subspaces defined by internal edges, always with the subspaces $\mathbb{CP}^1$, on whose elementary states f, are singular.

Then for Proposition 2.1 (b), the following mapping exists

$$H^f(\Pi\text{-}\ell', \Omega^d) \to H^{f+d}(\Pi\text{-}\ell', \mathbb{C}), \tag{10}$$

[6] For example, to this case for holomorphic functions, we have the generalized Cauchy formula:

$$f^{(n)}(a) = \frac{n!}{2\pi i} \oint_{\gamma} \frac{f(z)}{(z\text{-}a)^{n+1}} dz.$$

using the description of Dolbeault of the first group, forgetting the bi-graduation (d, f), (d, f) and reminding only the total grade $d + f$. A description of Cěch of this mapping is used for the evaluation of twistor cohomology. In our case, we will only use the duality of Poincaré to know in what moment of the evaluation of an element of $H^{f+d}(\Pi\text{-}\ell', \mathbb{C})$, one can need a contour in $H_{f+d}(\Pi\text{-}\ell', \Omega^d)$. This can define in a more general sense the cohomological functional. Likewise, the mapping Eq. (10) is an example of the cohomological functional.

This contour "cohomologic" is easy to relate it with a traditional in $H_d(\Pi\text{-}\ell, \mathbb{C})$, due to that the following mapping exists

$$H_{f+d}(\Pi\text{-}\ell', \Omega^d) \to H_d(\Pi\text{-}\ell', \mathbb{C}), \tag{11}$$

given for iteration of the constant mapping of Mayer-Vietoris (in homology) f-times; one for each field.

For example, for diagram, product can be demonstrated that $H_8(\Pi\text{-}\ell, \mathbb{C})$, and that the image of the generator of this group low two mappings of Mayer-Vietoris as is the usual in the physical contour for the product of diagrams given. This affirms that only exists a cohomological contour for the product climb (as is expected) and suggests a method for contours that verifies and observes which belong to cohomologics.

Definition 2.2. (Hyperfunction). A hyperfunction on $\mathbb{R}^n$, is an element of the $(n-1)$-$\overline{\partial}-$ cohomology $H^{(n-1)}(M, \mathfrak{J})$, with $M = \mathbb{C}^n/\mathbb{R}^n$.

Proposition 2.4. The general integrals of line are functional on arches γ, in geometry of conformal generalized structure.

Proof: Consider a vector holomorphic G-invariant sheaf and their corresponding bundle of lines associated with those (r, 0)-forms on the corresponding topological vector space. Then, the integrals on the fibers of the vector holomorphic sheaf are the integrals of line on the cycles of the sections X, of the vector sheaf, given by $\int_\gamma X \bullet \delta, \forall\ \delta \in \Omega^r$ [where Ω^r is a complex defined in Eq. (5)]. Then the holomorphic structure that constitutes these complexes induces (in the corresponding integral manifold) a conformal generalized structure of integral submanifolds where the arches γ, are local parts of integral curves of the fibers of the vector sheaf of lines. In other words, $\forall\ \gamma \in \sum_i(V_z)$ exists locally an integral submanifold S, with $z \in S$, such that $T_z S = \gamma$, and $T_w S \in \sum_i(V_w)$, $\forall w \in S$. Then the integral of line can be re-written in this conformal generalized structure as

$$\int_\gamma X \bullet \delta = \int_{T_z S} f \bullet \delta, \quad \forall \quad \delta \in \Omega^r, f \in \mathcal{T}, \tag{12}$$

where $\mathcal{T}$, is the tube domain (in the local structure where the integral submanifold S, exists) $\mathcal{T} = \mathbb{R}^n + iV$, where V, is a cone, not necessarily convex (that has applicability on the fibers of the sheaf of lines). The idea is to define the expressionf $\bullet\ \delta$, inside the context of the integral of line in such case that the values of f, on the arch γ, are values off, a hyperfunction represented this like a variation of holomorphic functions $f(z|\delta)$, in a submanifold of Stein M_δ, such that $M_\delta \supset \mathcal{T}$.

Then, the sesquilinear coupling of the hyperfunction corresponding to f, and the function f itself, is an integral of contour, and for Proposition 2.3, a generalized functional in the cohomology $H^1(\Pi\text{-}\ell, \mathbb{C})$. Indeed, let be $\mathcal{T} = \mathbb{R}^n + iV$, the tube domain where the cone V, is not necessarily convex. This cone $V = \cup_{\gamma \in \Sigma} V_\gamma$, in the conformal generalized structure where the V_γ, are the convex maximal sub-cones in V. Considers our manifold, complex Riemannian manifold. The idea is that a holomorphic form required in this language is a good expression to write the integral of complex vector fields as an integral of line through more than enough bundles of hyperlines and hyperplanes. As for example, we have more than enough hyperlines and hyperplanes, respectively, in $\mathbb{RP}^n$, and $\mathbb{C}^n$, visualizing these fields like holomorphic sections of complex holomorphic bundles of fibers $X \to M$. In Δ, exists q-dimensional cycles such that $V = \cup_{\delta\in\gamma} V_\delta$. Let be $\mathcal{T}_\delta = \mathbb{R}^n + iV_\delta$, with covering of Stein $\mathcal{T} = \cup_{\delta\in\gamma}\mathcal{T}_\delta$. Let us consider the vector cohomology $H^{(q)}(\mathcal{T}, \mathfrak{J})$, using this covering. Then for proposition 2. 1, incise b), a canonical operator exists (of values frontier for f) defined for

$$H^{(q)}(\mathcal{T}, \mathfrak{J}) \to H^{(q)}(\mathbb{C}^n/\mathbb{R}^n, \mathfrak{J}), \tag{13}$$

Then, the integral can be expressed on spaces M_δ and Δ_z, which are affined to lines and hyperplanes $\mathbb{CP}^n$ and $\mathbb{C}^n$ and that such are orbital integrals of the complex manifolds $M = G/L$ and $\Delta = \Gamma/\Sigma$, belonging to a $\bar{\partial}$-cohomology in holomorphic language.

In particular, if $f(z|\delta, d|\delta) \in \Omega^q_{\mathcal{T}}$ has regular values $\forall z \in \mathbb{R}^n$, then

$$\varphi(x) = \int_\gamma \varphi(x|\delta, d|\delta), \quad \forall \quad x \in \mathbb{R}^n. \tag{14}$$

Then, in the integral submanifold M_δ, said integrals take the form

$$\int_\gamma X \bullet G = \int_\gamma \varphi(z|\delta, d|\delta) f(z) = \int_\gamma f(z|\delta). \tag{15}$$

However, these integrals are integral of contour belonging to a cohomology $H^1(\Pi\text{-}\ell, \mathbb{C})$ of cohomological functional. Then, the integral $\int_\gamma f(z|\delta)$ is a functional inside the integral cohomology $H^{(n-1)}(\mathbb{C}^n/\mathbb{R}^n, \mathfrak{J})$ (**Figure 4**).

The previous Propositions 2.3 and 2.4 establish that the structure of complexes for the integral operator cohomology does suitable to induce isomorfisms in other object classes of the manifold M, doing arise the question to some procedure that exists inside the relative cohomology on $\mathfrak{J}$: can we induce isomorfisms of integral cohomologies?

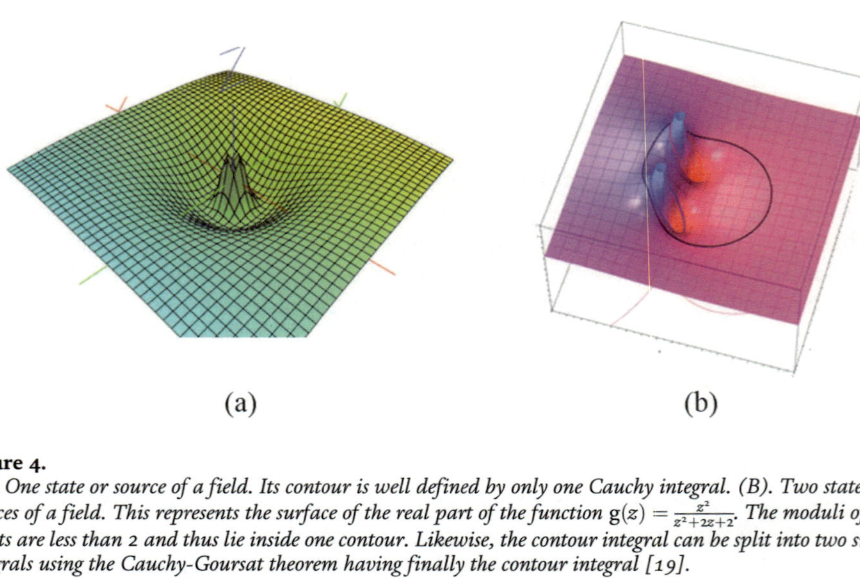

(a) (b)

Figure 4.
(A). One state or source of a field. Its contour is well defined by only one Cauchy integral. (B). Two states or sources of a field. This represents the surface of the real part of the function $g(z) = \frac{z^2}{z^2+2z+2}$. *The moduli of these points are less than 2 and thus lie inside one contour. Likewise, the contour integral can be split into two smaller integrals using the Cauchy-Goursat theorem having finally the contour integral [19].*

Now, we consider a closed subset (or relatively closed) F, of a space X, and a sheaf $\mathfrak{J}$, on X. In a way more than enough, we choose an open covering Y, of X, with a subcovering Y′, of X/F.

A relative co-chain of Cěch is a co-chain of Cěch with regard to the covering Y, subject to the condition of annulling when we restrict to the subcovering Y′. Then, it had the exact succession of relative co-chains groups:

$$0 \rightarrow C_F^p(X, \mathfrak{J}) \rightarrow C^p(X, \mathfrak{J}) \rightarrow C_F^p(X/F, \mathfrak{J}) \rightarrow 0, \tag{16}$$

where $C_F^p(X, \mathfrak{J})$ is the group of relative co-chains. The inherent relative co-chain to a co-opposite operator of the ordinary co-chains and the limit on fine coverings of the homology of $C_F^*(X, \mathfrak{J})$ give the groups of relative cohomology $H_F^p(X, \mathfrak{J})$.

$$\oint_C g(z)dz = \oint_C \left(1 - \frac{1}{z-z_1} - \frac{1}{z-z_2}\right)dz = 0 - 2\pi i - 2\pi i = -4\pi i.$$

This is a good example of traditional cohomological functional element of $H^f(\Pi\text{-}\ell', \Omega^r) = \mathbb{C}$.

In this case is not necessary to take the limit since ahead of time one has the relative theorem of Leray, which establish that if $H^p(U, \mathfrak{J}) = 0, p \geq 1$, for each set U, in the covering Y, then this covers enough to calculate the relative cohomology. The exact long succession cohomology of the exact short succession defined in Eq. (16) determines the exact succession of relative cohomology

$$0 \rightarrow H_F^0(X, \mathfrak{J}) \rightarrow H^0(X, \mathfrak{J}) \rightarrow C^0(X/F, \mathfrak{J}) \rightarrow H^1(X, \mathfrak{J}) \rightarrow \ldots, \tag{17}$$

where the mappings of the cohomology on X, to the given on X/F, are restrictions.

Other important result on the relative cohomology is the split theorem, which establishes in shallow terms that the relative cohomology depends only on the immediate neighborhoods of the embedding of F, in X. With more precision, giving an open subset X, such that$(X/X') \cap F = \emptyset$, a canonical isomorfism exists if$H_F^n(X, \mathfrak{J}) = H_F^n(X', \mathfrak{J})$.

This is the form to induce isomorfisms. In our case, the covering Y, is a covering of Stein where the integral operator cohomology $H^\bullet(M, \mathfrak{J})$, should exist such as we wish. Why? Because the natural place, where a $\overline{\partial}-$cohomology exists, is in a covering of Stein and is because we want to obtain the solutions of $\overline{\partial}-$partial differential equations.

We apply the relative cohomology to cohomologies of contours because we want generalized function as solutions of the differential equations [5, 18].

We consider the following general procedure due to Baston [8] for the exhibition of all the cohomological functional on a collection of fields given. This procedure is required for the evaluation of boxes diagram, that is to say, the obtaining of the elementary states $\varphi^i(i = 1, 2, 3, 4, \ldots)$ of the field through a local cohomology.

We consider a complex manifold given for $X \cup Y$, the closed subsets $F \subset X$, and $G \subset Y$, and elements $\alpha \in H^p(X\text{-}F, S)$, and $\beta \in H^q(Y\text{-}G, T)$. Then we can use the connecting mappings in the exact successions of relative cohomology

$$H^p(X, S) \rightarrow H^p(X\text{-}F, S) \xrightarrow{r} H_F^{p+1}(X, S) \rightarrow H^{p+1}(X, S), \tag{18}$$

and

$$H^q(Y, T) \rightarrow H^q(Y\text{-}G, T) \xrightarrow{r} H_G^{q+1}(Y, T) \rightarrow H^{q+1}(Y, T), \tag{19}$$

to obtain elements $r\alpha$, and $r\beta$. Then, the cup product on relative cohomology is defined as:

$$\begin{aligned}\cup : H^{p+q+1}(X \cup Y, S \otimes T) &\xrightarrow{r} H^{p+q+1}(X \cup Y\text{-}F \cap G, S \otimes T) \\ &\rightarrow H^{p+q+2}_{F \cap G}(X \cup Y, S \otimes T) \rightarrow H^{p+q+2}(X \cup Y, S \otimes T),\end{aligned} \tag{20}$$

and this demonstrates that

$$\alpha \bullet \beta = r^{-1}(r\alpha \cup r\beta), \tag{21}$$

Due to that in the diagram boxes, the interactive vector fields φ, are given as elements of groups H^1, defined on different spaces, we need the vector product in relative cohomology:

$$\times : H^{p+1}_F(X, S) \otimes H^{q+1}_G(Y, T) \rightarrow H^{p+q+2}_{F \times G}(X \times Y, S \otimes T), \tag{22}$$

Likewise, for diagram box of four states, we have the cohomology of the left side of Eq. (22) that can be illustrated (**Figure 5**).

Strictly speaking $S \otimes T$, could be $\pi *_X S \otimes \pi *_Y T$. As before $r\alpha \times r\beta$, is in the image of the connecting mapping r, in:

$$H^{p+q+1}(X \cup Y\text{-}F \cap G, S \otimes T) \xrightarrow{r} H^{p+q+2}_{F \times G}(X \times Y, S \otimes T) \rightarrow H^{p+q+2}(X \times Y, S \otimes T), \tag{23}$$

with

$$\alpha \bullet \beta = r^{-1}(r\alpha \times r\beta)\left(\in \nu^{-1}O(p, q, \mathbf{r})\right), \tag{24}$$

The following technical question arises: how to relate contour cohomology as $H^{f+d}(\Pi\text{-}\ell', \mathbb{C})$, with an integral cohomology of vector fields?

Part of the replay to this question is found when are considered the complex components $F_i = P_i - U_i$, with $i = 1, 2, 3, 4, \ldots, f$; being P_i, P, $P*$, and U_i, open subsets of $\mathbb{P}_i$, belonging to the correct cohomology to the Penrose transform on $H^1(U, O(-\mathbf{r}))$.

The idea is to obtain an image of the vector field as element of a cohomology on homogeneous bundles of lines in each component of the field (that is to say, determine a cohomology for each line integral of each field component). Beforehand this is foreseen that will happen with the Penrose transform, which is an integral transform on the homogeneous bundles of lines.

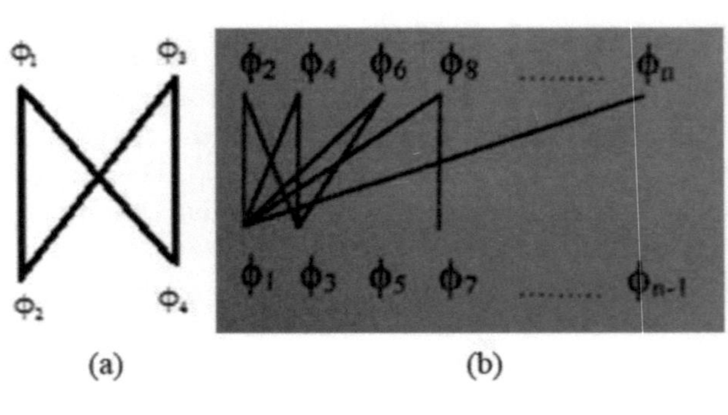

Figure 5.
Feynman boxes diagrams [1].

Let $F = F_1 \times \ldots \times F_f$. We denote for L_i, a projective line included in F_i, and let $L = L_1 \times \ldots \times L_f$. For f vector fields, we have an element in the cohomological group $H^1(U_1, O(-r_1)) \otimes \cdots \otimes H^1(U_f, O(-r_f))$. For relative cohomology and projective twistor diagram results [18], the inner product for the line integrals for all these fields is not lost. Then for the Künneth formula to relative cohomology, we have:

$$H^1(U_1, O(-r_1)) \otimes \cdots \otimes H^1(U_f, O(-r_f)) \cong H_F^{2f}(\Pi, O(\mathbf{r})), \tag{25}$$

where $\mathbf{r} = r_1 \times \ldots \times r_f$. Each linear continuous functional on these fields is thus an element of the compact relative cohomology group $H_F^{2f}(\Pi, \Pi\text{-}F, O(\mathbf{r}))$. We must establish that Eq. (25) and the group $H_F^{2f}(\Pi, \Pi\text{-}F, O(\mathbf{r}))$, are not in general dual.

Now well, considering this cohomology of vector fields, is necessary to decide how the interior of a diagram choose some of these functionals. We remember the interior of a diagram as the holomorphic nucleus $h \in H^{3f,q}(\Pi\text{-}\ell, O(\mathbf{r}))$. For example, in the scalar product (spin zero) $h = \frac{DW \wedge DZ}{(W_\alpha Z^\alpha)^2} \in H^{6,q}(\Pi\text{-}\ell, O(\text{-}2\text{-}2))$. While in the box $h = \frac{DW \wedge DZ \wedge DX \wedge DY}{(W_\alpha Z^\alpha W_\beta Y^\beta Z_\gamma X^\gamma Y_\delta Z^\delta)^2} \in H^{6,q}(\Pi\text{-}\ell_0, O(\text{-}2\text{-}2\text{-}2\text{-}2))$. Usually $q = 0$. In these cases h, can be determined for integration without the interior vertices of the twistor diagram, although it is not always easy. If $q \neq 0$, the determination of h in none time is clear. How to do about it?

We consider the complex cohomology, and also we consider an element $\alpha \in H_{\mathbb{C}}^{0,f\text{-}q}(\Pi - \ell, \Pi\text{-}\ell \cup F)$. Then $\alpha \cup h \in H_{\mathbb{C}}^{3f,f}(\Pi - \ell, \Pi\text{-}\ell \cup F; O(\text{-}\mathbf{r}))$. This is an induced mapping for the inclusion

$$i : H_{\mathbb{C}}^{3f,f}(\Pi - \ell, \Pi\text{-}\ell \cup F; O(\text{-}\mathbf{r})) \to H_{\mathbb{C}}^{3f,f}(\Pi, \Pi - F; O(\text{-}\mathbf{r})), \tag{26}$$

where such $i(\alpha \cup h)$, is a chosen functional for the interior of the diagram (that is to say h) as required. However, as this was done through α, the results are hard to view α as a contour. For it, we first note that the embedding of the constant sheaf $\mathbb{C}$, in $O(\text{-}\mathbf{r})$, induces a mapping:

$$H_{\mathbb{C}}^{f\text{-}q}(\Pi - \ell, \Pi\text{-}\ell \cup F; \mathbb{R}) \to H_{\mathbb{C}}^{f\text{-}q}(\Pi - \ell, \Pi - \ell \cup F; O(\text{-}\mathbf{r})), \tag{27}$$

and second, the cohomology groups $\alpha \in H_{5f+q}(\Pi - \ell, \Pi\text{-}\ell \cup F)$ and $H_{\mathbb{C}}^{f\text{-}q}(\Pi - \ell, \Pi\text{-}\ell \cup F; \mathbb{R})$ are isomorphic. Now, it is necessary to insist in that α is in the image of the mapping Eq. (27), which will produce a viewing as contour. Being α a contour, we call to $i(\alpha \cup h)$, the functional "associated with" the kernel h, and we remark strongly that this not exists if $F \subset \ell$, then $H_{5f+q}(\Pi - \ell, \Pi\text{-}\ell \cup F) = 0$, which is hoped. We can refer to this problem as impossible, since necessarily $\ell \neq F$, for the chosen fields in this cohomology, which are the most general possible. The idea is to wobtain an image of the vector field as an element of a cohomology on homogeneous bundles of lines in each component of the field. We note that our defined fields are generally perfect. In fact, if the vector fields are elemental states, then $F_i = L_i$, and F, is equal to a closed submanifold Λ (of real codimension 4f, with normal orientable bundle). Using the Thom isomorphism, we have:

$$H_{f+q}(\Lambda - \ell) \xrightarrow{\cong} H_{5f+q}(\Pi - \ell, \Pi\text{-}\ell \cup \Lambda) = 0, \tag{28}$$

which is deduced that the viewed contours are given in $H_{f+q}(\Lambda - \ell)$. If the vector fields are not elemental states along $(\Pi - \ell, \Pi\text{-}\ell \cup F)$, then $(\Pi - \ell, \Pi\text{-}\ell \cup F)$, is homotopic to $(\Pi - \ell, \Pi\text{-}\ell \cup \Lambda)$, which establishes its generality in homology.

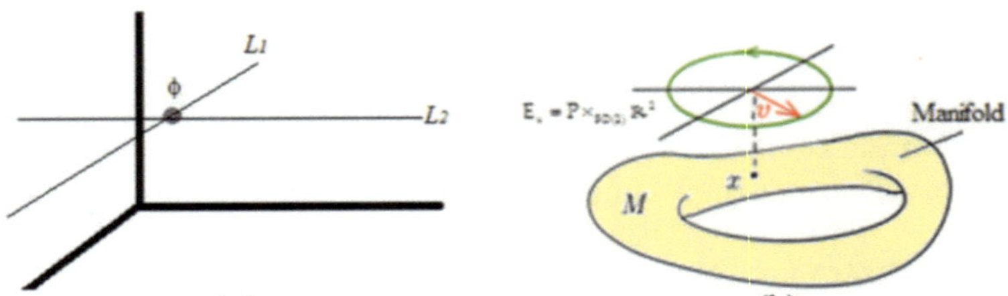

(a) (b)

Figure 6.
(a). Field state in a cohomology $H^{3,0}(\mathbb{R}^3, \mathcal{L})$*, to the line bundle* $\mathcal{L}$*.. (b).* P, *is a principal* $SO(2)-$*bundle. The fiber of the fiber bundle is the points* $E_x = P\times_{SO(2)}\mathbb{R}^2$.

Likewise we have demonstrated that if$(\Pi - \ell, \Pi\text{-}\ell \cup F)$, is homotopic to $(\Pi - \ell, \Pi\text{-}\ell \cup \Lambda)$, then the functionals on $H^1(U_1, O(-r_1)) \otimes \cdots \otimes H^1(U_f, O(-r_f))$, associated with the kernel $h \in H^{3f,q}(\Pi\text{-}\ell, O(\text{-}\mathbf{r}))$, are given for elements of the homology group $H_{f+q}(\Lambda - \ell)$. Now, which of these contours are cohomological? A classes of contours are the classic or traditional contours. However, realizing extensions of these contour classes through twistor geometry, we can consider cohomological contours to all image elements of the generator of $H_d(\Pi\text{-}\ell'{\prime}, \mathbb{C})$, under two mappings of Mayer-Vietoris. Likewise, the box nonprojective diagram also engages three cohomological contours. Can this particular theory of contours to the spin context be understood?

The response is yes, for example, of the foreseen construction given in **Figure 6b**).

If $f \in C^1(\Omega) \cap C(\overline{\Omega}) \cap \ker D_{\pm a}(\Omega)$, with $f = K_{\pm a}\overline{f} \in H^0(\Pi - \wp, \mathbb{C})$, being $\wp = \{\pm a\}$, then $h = \frac{1}{(z\pm a)} \in H^1(\Pi - \wp, O(-2))$. Then an integral formula in hypercomplex analysis of a vector field is an element of the integral cohomology $H^1(\Pi - \wp, \mathbb{H})$. We can realize more work in this sense until we can arrive to the Penrose transform on hypercomplex numbers.

3. The main conjecture and some notes of integral cohomology in low dimension of a complex Riemannian manifold

Using definitions and results exposed with before can be enunciated and demonstrated the following conjectures:

Conjecture 3.1. The cohomology of closed submanifolds of co-dimensions k-1, n-k, and n(k-1), can be represented and evaluated by a function cohomology. The cohomology of contours is represented and evaluated by a complex functional cohomology. The cohomology of line bundles is represented and evaluated by a vector field cohomologies under the $\overline{\partial}$-cohomology corresponding.

There are indicium of that the differential operator class that accepts a scheme of integral cohomology (integral cohomology) like due for the Penrose transform, twistor transform, and so on is the class conformally invariant differential operators, of fact the Penrose transform generates these conformally invariant operators. Some examples of these differential operators are for the massless field equations (for flat versions and some curved versions [20]) and the conformally invariant wave operator due to the mapping:

$$\square + -R/6 : O[-1] \rightarrow O[-3], \tag{29}$$

or also the Einstein's operator

$$\nabla^{(A}{}_{(A'}\nabla^{B)}{}_{B')} + \Phi^{(AB))}_{(A'B')} : O[-1] \rightarrow O^{(AB))}_{(A'B')}[-1], \tag{30}$$

or the conformally invariant modification of the square of the wave operator O[-1] → O[-4], that is to say, the wave operator that involves in its term Ricci tensors:

$$\square^2 : \phi \rightarrow \nabla_b \left[\nabla^b \nabla^a - 2R^{ab} + (2/3)\left(Rg^{ab}\right)\nabla_a\right], \tag{31}$$

Then, the integration of the partial differential equations corresponding to these linear invariant differential operators is realized due to integral transforms of the Penrose type since the irreducible unitary representation scheme to these operators is unitary representations of components of the group $SL(4, \mathbb{C})$, such as $SO(2n)$.

In fact, in the flat case, the invariant differential operator classifications were described to determine a problem of representation theory of Lie groups applied to the Lie group $SL(4, \mathbb{C})$ and its compact subgroups. Then, own vision to these operators through $SL(4, \mathbb{C})$ will be as equivariant operators between homogeneous vector bundles on M, considering to $SL(4, \mathbb{C})$ as homogeneous space or class space. The integrals in this case are realizations of these representations and are orbital integrals of the integral transform of the resolutions to these differential equations, which, in this concrete case, are the Penrose transform.

Then, the resolution problem of the partial differential equations is reduce to the use of representation theory, but for this case, no always can construct the curved analogues of conformally invariant differential operators of the flat space. This demonstrates that cannot be generated a curved analogous under an integral transform on homogeneous bundles of lines that are direct images of the operators D^n, of $\mathcal{G}$, of G/L. However, yes is possible to obtain a complete list under this procedure as a mapping of unitary modules.

Also, the scheme of the $\mathbb{H}$-modules in the quaternion analysis serves to compute and determine the properties of manifold through the scheme of fibers that can be in closed complex submanifolds. In fact, this is an alternative for the determination of vector fields through line bundles, which defined these as spin bundles.

Now well, cohomologically: How similar are these two methodologies for the study in field theory? Can the direct product of Lie groups $SU(2)T$, subjacent in the structure of a complex Riemannian manifold that models the space-time to its vector field study and its integration through the isometries of the space $\mathcal{L}(H)$ be carried? Which are the integration limitations for the integral transforms on homogenous bundles in global descriptions of the vector fields?

The first question is related to the double fibration that can be realized on some complex projective spaces and their quaternion equivalent. Since it always exists this bijection due to this double fibration with some corresponding homotopy group that is frequently given for spheres, some real and complex projective spaces that are necessarily identified with some n-dimensional sphere exist. Such is the case, for example, of the projective spaces $\mathbb{RP}^1 \cong S^1$, $\mathbb{HP}^1 \cong S^4$, or $\mathbb{CP}^7 \cong Spin(2, 6)$. Then can be determined isomorphic cohomological spaces via some integral transform of the mentioned for the double fibrations. Some of these integrals result be of Feynman type due to the complex projective bundles are spin bundles in some sphere that determines some state space in quantum mechanics. For example, for the complex case, is had in an infinite succession of non-trivial bundles, the infinite set of bundles $S^1 \rightarrow \mathbb{P}_k^{2\ell-1} \rightarrow \mathbb{CP},^{\ell\text{-}1}$ with $k \in \mathbb{Z}$, and $k \neq \ell$, which represents the infinite set of corresponding monopoles bundles to the case $\ell = 2$.

These with proper connections represent Dirac magnetic monopoles of charge k.

The constitutive integrals of these monopoles are Cauchy integrals that for diagrams of a cohomology $H^1(\Pi\text{-}\ell, \mathbb{C})$, these are reduced to integrals of Feynman type on the diagrams-boxes corresponding to the state monopoles vertices. These are identified for the factors $1/Z_\alpha W^\alpha$. Likewise, an integral of Cauchy type given for an integral for a ϕ^4-vertex representing the projective space $\mathbb{P}$, or its dual $\mathbb{P}^*$, comes given for

$$\mathcal{IF}(\phi^4) = \oint D^1(Z)f(Z_\alpha)g(W^\alpha)h(X_\alpha)j(Y^\alpha)/Z_\alpha W^\alpha X_\alpha W^\alpha X_\alpha Y^\alpha Z_\alpha Y^\alpha, \tag{32}$$

which is not different to the Cauchy integral for a monopole in $z = z_0$, and representing the space $\mathbb{P}^1(\mathbb{R})$.

The response to the second question also is positive since it is possible to determine a cohomology of the space–time based on light geodesics as orbits of a complex torus T, when we consider our Universe as a complex hyperbolic manifold. The corresponding integral operators on the corresponding orbits result to be n- dimensional Fourier transforms $\mathcal{F}_n$, that can be calculated for the relation

$$f, = \mathcal{F}_n^{-1}\mathcal{F}_1\mathcal{R}f, \tag{33}$$

in a n-dimensional manifold. The operator $\mathcal{R}$, is the Radon transform calculated on the corresponding cycles. It is well known that $\mathcal{F} \in \mathcal{L}(H)$, and that the integral cohomology given for$\mathcal{F}_n$, is the $\bar{\partial}$- cohomology of one codimensional submanifolds in M.

A response to the last question could be the limitations that are observed when it is wanted to extend the integration on the orbits of M, to a global integration of vector fields, since it is required the global integration of a vector field without the necessity of calculating previously the integrals on orbits of sections of a homogeneous bundle.

However, certain feasibility exists to obtain a methodology in this respect, generalizing, in some sense, the concept of conformal generalized structure on the manifold M.

The existing equivalences between twistor spaces, quaternion spaces, and Riemannian manifolds establish isomorphisms between different cohomology classes whose geometrical invariants are with similar invariant properties in such different cohomology classes. Likewise, we have, for example, a John integral on a complex bundle of lines F, which includes the same integration invariants with respect to the line bundle of the linear concave domains in the space $\mathbb{C}^n$ (respectively, $\mathbb{CP}^n$) for the integral of the Radon transform. The cohomology of the singularities in the description of the massless fields can be done through a twistor description of the fields using a relative cohomology of sheaves on the massless fields distributed on a real Minkowski space. Likewise, we can have other examples of equivalences for different cohomology classes.

Much results in complex analysis in $\mathbb{C}$, or $\mathbb{C}^2$, can be generalized on a context of analytic functions more extensive, using a holomorphic language of a $\bar{\partial}$- cohomology. Example of it is the use of hyperfunctions for generalizing some contour integrals. If $F \subset \mathbb{R}$, where F, is a closed interval and the hyperfunctions of F, are given for the quotient space $O(\mathbb{C}\text{-}F)/O(\mathbb{C})$, and iff, is an analytic complex function (analytic in a real sense), the sesquilinear coupling with a hyperfunction represented by the holomorphic function φ (which can be a hypercomplex function) on ($\mathbb{C}$-F), is given for the contour integral:

$$(\phi, f) = \oint \varphi(z)f(z)dz, \tag{34}$$

where the function f, must be extended holomorphically to a little portion of F, and the contour in ($\mathbb{C}$-F), transits around of F, sufficiently near of the definition domain off. This integral is not more different than the Cauchy integral, in fact, in certain sense, this is a generalization. Further, this is not more different than the John integrals, Conway integrals, and Penrose integrals on $\mathbb{R}$. The first two are used on the circle S^1, the third, for obtaining the harmonic functions of three and four variables determining the solution of the wave equation in $\mathbb{R}^4$.

The Penrose line integral in integral geometry has the interpretation as was mentioned in the Radon transform on lines of a flag manifold $F = \{L | L \subset \mathbb{R}^4\}$. All these integrals belong to a same cohomological class, which can be determined calculating the cohomology of $\mu^{-1}O(p, q, r)$, using the spectral sequence:

$$E^{p,q} = \Gamma(U, \nu_*^q(\mathbb{R}^p)), \tag{35}$$

Then it is possible to calculate the cohomology groups $H^{p,q}(U', \mu^{-1}O(p, q, r))$, in terms of $H^{p,q}(U', \nu_*^q(\mathbb{R}^p))$, taking the meaning of Eq. (35). These cohomology groups are sections of the sheaf with coefficients on the fibered bundle $O(p, q, r)$. The space $\mu^{-1}O(p, q, r)$, represents the inverse image of said sheaf. $U \subset M$, and $U' = \nu^{-1}(U) \subset F$, and $\mu^{-1}(U') \subset \mathbb{P}$, with μ, and ν, are the corresponding homomorphisms of the double fibration in integral geometry to relate objects in M, and $\mathbb{P}$, can be a projective twistor space and F, the flag manifold.

Finally, we can say that the descriptions in Section 3 are only few examples of our theory of integrals that we want to construct, and that are examples to enforce our conjecture on the integral geometry bases obtained from the geometry and analysis.

4. Conclusions

The idea to obtain an integral operator cohomology is develop a theory through integral invariants, that is to say, explore the complex Riemannian manifolds though the value of its integrals along the cycles and the corresponding cocycles (submanifolds, contours, vertices, edges, complexes, and so on) of the manifold. The duality between these cycles obeys to the spectral transformation that follows much of these integrals as solution of the corresponding differential equations. For example, in some case, it is used the tomography of Riemannian manifold whose cocycles are submanifolds. However, this idea can be generalized and induced beyond the tomography, for example, the integral transforms that generate differential operators with certain property of invariance inside the manifold and establish solution classes through these properties as the case to the conformally invariant differential operators. Then, the representation of objects, such as differential operators, functions, hyperfunctions, and fields, through integrals also appears in a natural way using the cohomology groups of its cocycles as first, second, ..., nth integrals for a problem of the differential or functional equations.

Likewise, much of these solutions are given through the integral transforms that search solution classes as equivalence classes in the dual problem. The inverse problems are developed in the geometrical analysis corresponding. The cohomological problem consists in developing a cohomology $H^{\bullet}(M, \mathfrak{J})$, the sufficiently general that means the solution to enlarge number of differential equations and that can be applied in the solution of the field equations in exploring the Universe.

The reinterpretation for physics phenomena in the case when said complex Riemannian manifold models the space-time, results interestingly, and let open the possibility of constructing an Universe theory that includes macroscopic and microscopic phenomena through a good integral theory.

Author details

Francisco Bulnes
IINAMEI, Research Department in Mathematics and Engineering, TESCHA, Chalco, Mexico

*Address all correspondence to: francisco.bulnes@tesch.edu.mx

References

[1] Bulnes F, Shapiro M. On general theory of integral operators to analysis and geometry. In: Cladwell JP, editor. Monograph in Mathematics. 1st ed. México: IM/UNAM and IPN/SEPI; 2007

[2] Bulnes F. Integral Geometry Methods in the Geometrical Langlands Program. USA: SCIRP; 2016

[3] Bulnes F. On the last progress of cohomological induction in the problem of classification of lie groups representations. In: International Conference of Infinite Dimensional Analysis and Topology, Book of Plenary Conferences. Ukraine: Precarpatinan National University; 2009

[4] F. Bulnes, "Conferences of lie groups (representation theory of reductive lie groups)", Monograph in Pure Mathematics, SEPI-ESIME/IPN, 2nd Edition by Paul Cladwell, Mexico, 2005.

[5] Bateman H. The solution of partial differential equations by means of definite integrals. Proceedings of the London Mathematical Society. 1904; **1**(2):451-458

[6] Bulnes F. Radon transform, generalizations and penrose transform. In: Proceedings of 4th International Congress in Applied Mathematics, Special Section in Functional Analysis and Differential Equations. Mexico: IMUNAM and IPN/SEPI; 2008. pp. 63-76

[7] Dunne EG, Eastwood MG. The Twistor Transform. London Mathematical Society Lecture Note Series, 156. Cambridge, United Kingdom: Cambridge University Press; 1990

[8] Bulnes F. Doctoral course of mathematical electrodynamics. Journal of Conferences and Advanced Courses of Applied Math II. SEPI-ESIME/IPN, editor. Vol. 4(30) 1 of Advanced Course in Applied Mathematics, National Polytechnique Institute. 2006;**8**(1): 398-447

[9] Bulnes F. Mathematical electrodynamics: Groups, cohomology classes, unitary representations, orbits and integral transforms in electrophysics. American Journal of Electromagnetics and Applications. 2015;**3**(6):43-52. DOI: 1011648/j. ajea.20150306.12

[10] Bulnes F, Fominko S. Dx-schemes and jets in conformal gravity using integral transforms. International Journal of Mathematical Research. 2016; **5**(2):154-165

[11] Bulnes F. lectromagnetic waves in conformal actions of the group SU(2, 2) on a dimensional flat model of the space-time. In: VI International Conference on Geometry, Dynamics, Integrable Systems-(GDIS 2016), 2–5 June; Izhevsk, Russia; 2016

[12] Dunne EG, Zierau R. Twistor theory for indefinite Kahler symmetric spaces. In: Contemporary Mathematics. Vol. 154. USA: AMS; 1993

[13] Eastwood M, Penrose R, Wells RO Jr. Cohomology and massless fields. Communications in Mathematical Physics. 1981;**78**:26-30

[14] Baston RJ. Local Cohomology, Elementary States and Evaluation. Vol. 22. Twistor, Newsletter (Oxford Preprint). United Kingdom: Oxford; 1986. pp. 8-13

[15] Kobayashi K, Nomizu K. Foundations of Differential Geometry. (Vol. II). New York: Wiley and Sons; 1969

[16] Gindikin SG, Henkin GM. Integral geometry for ∂-cohomology in q-linear

concave domains in CPn. Funktsional. Anal. i Prilozhen. 1978;**12**(4):6-23

[17] Gel'fand IM, Graev MI, Shapiro IIP. Generalized Functions. New York, USA: Academic Press; 1952

[18] S. Huggett and Singer, "Cohomology of contours and residues", Transactions of the American Mathematical Society. 1982. pp. 308-316

[19] Derbyshire S. An illustration to Cauchy's integral formula in complex analysis. Available from: http://en.wikipedia.org/wiki/File:ComplexResiduesExample.png

[20] Bulnes F. Cohomology of moduli spaces in differential operators classification to the field theory (II). In: Proceedings of FSDONA-11 (Function Spaces, Differential Operators and Non-linear Analysis, 2011); Tabarz Thur. Vol. 1, No. 12; 2011. pp. 1-22

Section 4

Complex Functional Transforms and Their Applications

Chapter 7

Extracting Coherent Structures in Near-Wall Turbulence Based on Wavelet Analysis

Peng Du, Haibao Hu and Xiao Huang

Abstract

To analyze the properties of the coherent structures in near-wall turbulence, an extraction method based on wavelet transform (WT) and a verification procedure based on correlation analysis are proposed in this work. The flow field of the turbulent boundary layer is measured using the hot-film anemometer in a gravitational low-speed water tunnel. The obtained velocity profile and turbulence intensity are validated with traditional boundary layer theory. The fluctuating velocities at three testing positions are analyzed. Using the power spectrum density (PSD) and WT, coherent and incoherent parts of the near-wall turbulence are extracted and analyzed. The probability density functions (PDFs) of the extracted signals indicate that the incoherent structures of turbulence obey the Gaussian distribution, while the coherent structures deviate from it. The PDFs of coherent structures and original turbulence signals are similar, which means that coherent structures make the most contributions to the turbulence entrainment. A correlation parameter is defined at last to prove the validity of our extraction procedure.

Keywords: coherent structure, wavelet transform, correlation analysis, turbulence

1. Introduction

Turbulence is a commonly seen but very complicated phenomenon in nature. Numerous tests have proven that turbulence is not a pure random process but contains different scales of fluctuations called coherent structures [1–3]. These structures significantly contribute to fluid entrainment and mass, momentum, and heat transfer [4, 5]. Therefore, investigating the coherent structures is of great significance to undercover the physics and to realize flow control.

Among the techniques of turbulence analysis, wavelet transform has been proven feasible and power to detect and extract the coherent structures in turbulence [6–9]. Early works are based on continuous wavelet transform (CWT). Liandrant [10] and Jiang [11, 12] proposed the maximum energy principle, which considered the signal at the maximum energy scale as the burst events in turbulence. Kim [13] identified the coherent structure around a vibrating cantilever based on CWT. However, a drawback of CWT is that it is unable to reconstruct the signal if the mother wavelet is not orthogonal [14–16]. To solve this problem, Longo [17] used the multiresolution analysis technique based on the discrete wavelet transform (DWT) and extracted the structures in turbulence. DWT has evident

IntechOpen

advantages compared with CWT since it is invertible and multi-scaled scales can be analyzed. Kadoch [18] combined DWT and direct numerical simulation (DNS), whose results proved that coherent structures preserve the vortical structures with only about 4% of the wavelet coefficients but retain 99.9% of the turbulence energy.

In this work, measurement of the turbulent boundary layer is carried out using hot-film anemometer in a gravitational low-speed water tunnel. A procedure based on the WT and correlation analysis is proposed to extract and verify the coherent and incoherent structure in turbulence.

2. Experimental tests and analysis

2.1 Experimental apparatus

A gravitational low-speed water tunnel was constructed for the experiment. The gravity generated by the water level difference drives the water flow in the tunnel, and the flow can be tested in the experimental section (**Figure 1**). A maximum water speed of 2.0 m/s can be reached, and the turbulence intensity is less than 2%. The IFA300 hot-wire anemometer was used to measure the turbulence boundary layer flow at a series of positions in the vertical direction (**Figure 2**). Detailed setups in the experimental section can be observed in **Figure 2**. A probe penetrates into the

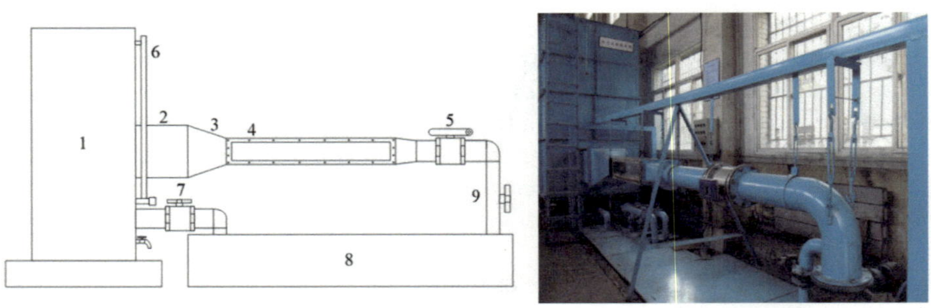

Figure 1.
Sketch (left) and photo (right) of the gravitational low-speed water tunnel. (1) Water tank; (2) stabilization section; (3) contraction section; (4) experimental section; (5) electromagnetism flowmeter; (6) water level observation section; (7) water pump; (8) water storage basin; (9) switch valve.

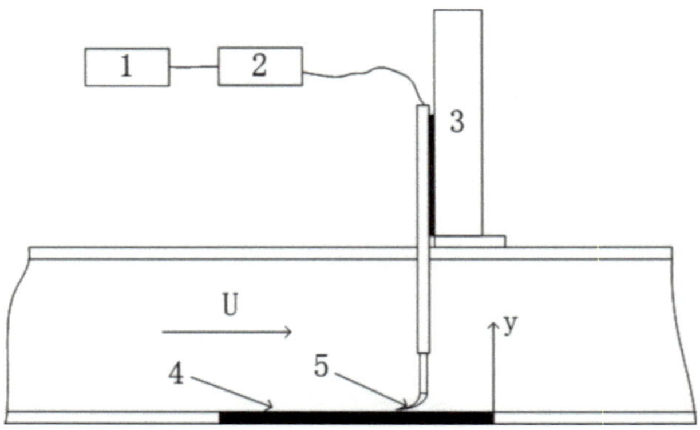

Figure 2.
Sketch of experimental setups. (1) PC; (2) hot-film anemometer; (3) coordinate frame; (4) experimental plate; (5) hot-film probe.

flow to measure the flow field. A coordinate frame was used to move the probe in the vertical direction, with a precision of 0.01 mm. During the experiment, the sampling frequency and sampling time were set to 50 kHz and 10.24 s.

2.2 Verification of turbulent boundary layer flow

By using the experimental setups in **Figure 2**, the flow velocity of the turbulence boundary layer was measured at a series of positions in the vertical direction. The mean velocity profile and the turbulence intensity distribution at the water speed 0.4 m/s can are analyzed in **Figures 3** and **4**, which agree with the turbulence boundary

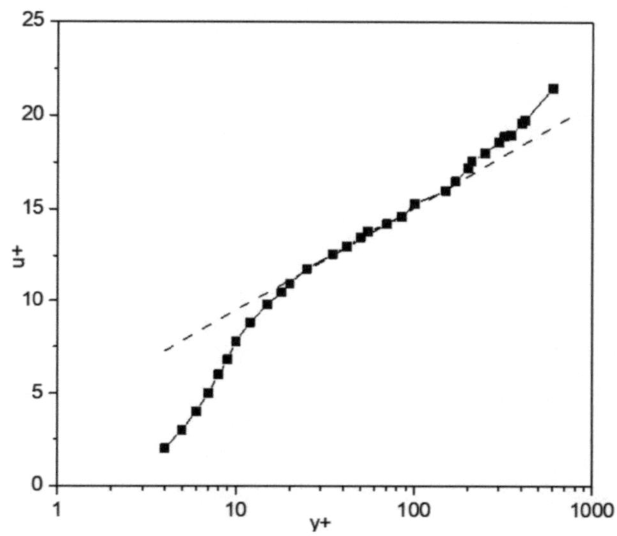

Figure 3.
The profile of mean velocity at the water speed 0.4 m/s.

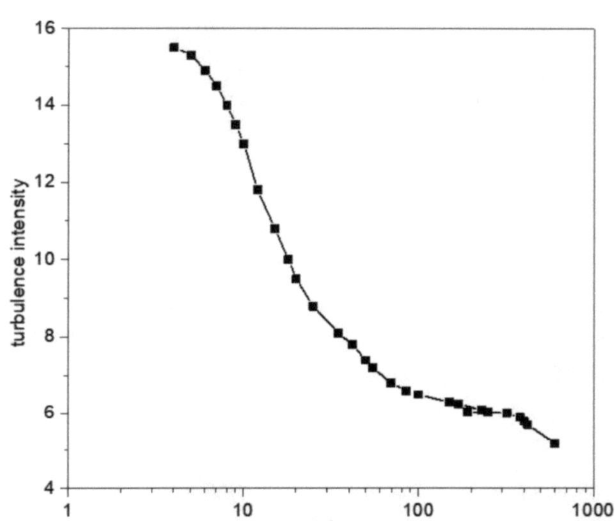

Figure 4.
Turbulence intensity at the water speed 0.4 m/s.

layer theory. This means that the flow field in the experimental section is fully developed. Our setups and techniques are ready for turbulent boundary layer tests.

3. Theoretical background of wavelet transform

WT is a mapping of a time function, in a one-dimensional case, to the two dimensional time-scale joint representation. The temporal aspect of the signal can be preserved. The wavelet transform provides multiresolution analysis with dilated windows. The high-frequency part of the signal is analyzed using narrow windows, and the low-frequency part is done using wide windows. WT decomposes the signal into different frequency components and then studies each component with a resolution matched to its scale. It has advantages over traditional Fourier methods in analyzing physics where the signal contains discontinuities and sharp spikes.

WT of a signal $s(t)$ is defined as the integral transform of $\psi_{a,b} = \frac{1}{\sqrt{a}}\psi\left(\frac{t-b}{a}\right)$, which can be expressed as:

$$\begin{aligned} W_f(a,b) &= \int_{-\infty}^{\infty} s(t)\psi_{a,b} dt \\ &= \int_{-\infty}^{\infty} s(t)\frac{1}{\sqrt{a}}\psi\left(\frac{t-b}{a}\right)dt \end{aligned} \tag{1}$$

where $\varphi_{m,n}(t)$ is the scaling function, which is defined as $\varphi_{m,n}(t) = 2^{-m/2}\varphi(2^{-m}t - n)$, and where a and b are the scale and position [19].

Scale a and position b should be discretized for applications. Usually we choose $a = 2^m(m \in Z, a_0 > 1)$, $b = n \cdot 2^m(b_0 > 0, n \in Z)$. When $\psi(t)$ obeys the orthogonal condition $\int \psi_{m,n}(t)\psi_{m',n'}(t)dt = \delta_{m,m'}\delta_{n,n'}$, the functions of the orthogonal basis can be written as:

$$\begin{aligned} \psi_{m,n}(t) &= \frac{1}{\sqrt{2^m}}\psi\left(\frac{t - n \cdot 2^m}{2^m}\right) \\ &= 2^{-m/2}\psi(2^{-m}t - n) \end{aligned} \tag{2}$$

The corresponding DWT can be expressed as:

$$\begin{aligned} <s, \psi_{m,n}> &= 2^{-m/2}\int_{-\infty}^{\infty} s(t)\psi_{m,n}(t)dt \\ &= 2^{-m/2}\int_{-\infty}^{\infty} s(t)\psi(2^{-m}t - n)dt \end{aligned} \tag{3}$$

The orthogonality of $\psi_{m,n}(t)$ eliminates the relevance between the points in wavelet space because of redundancy. The analyzing result of WT can thus reflect the characteristics of the original signal. Based on OWT, the signal $s(t)$ can be written as:

$$s(t) = \sum_{-\infty}^{\infty}\sum_{-\infty}^{\infty} <s, \psi_{m,n}> \psi_{m,n}(t) \tag{4}$$

By choosing the scale m_0 as the critical value, the signal $s(t)$ can be divided into the approximate and detailed parts:

$$
\begin{aligned}
s(t) &= \sum_{m=m_0+1}^{\infty}\sum_{n=-\infty}^{\infty} <s, \psi_{m,n}> \psi_{m,n}(t) + \sum_{m=-\infty}^{m_0}\sum_{n=-\infty}^{\infty} <s, \psi_{m,n}> \psi_{m,n}(t) \\
&= \sum_{n=-\infty}^{\infty} <s, \varphi_{m,n}> \varphi_{m_0,n}(t) + \sum_{m=-\infty}^{m_0}\sum_{n=-\infty}^{\infty} <s, \psi_{m,n}> \psi_{m,n}(t) \\
&= \sum_{n=-\infty}^{\infty} a_{m_0}[n]\varphi_{m_0,n}(t) + \sum_{m=-\infty}^{m_0}\sum_{n=-\infty}^{\infty} d_m[n]\psi_{m,n}(t) \\
&= A_{m_0} + \sum_{m=1}^{m} D_m
\end{aligned}
\tag{5}
$$

where $\psi_{m,n}(t)$ is the wavelet function. $\varphi_{m,n}(t)$ can be viewed as a low-pass filter, while $\psi_{m,n}(t)$ as a band-pass filter. The first part of the above equation is the low-frequency approximation of the signal $s(t)$ at the scale 2^{-m0}; the high-frequency part is the details of the signal $s(t)$ [15, 20].

For turbulence, the fluctuating velocity of turbulence can be normally divided into two subparts:

$$s = \tilde{s} + s' \tag{6}$$

where $\tilde{s}$ is the coherent part and s' is the incoherent part. The signals $\tilde{s}$ and s' are statistically independent.

By adopting the multiresolution analysis (**Figure 5**), the turbulence signal $s(t)$ can be divided into different frequencies. Coherent structures can thus be reconstructed in a selected frequency domain. Other redundant signals can then be eliminated. Therefore, the frequency range determination and localization of the coherent structures are critical in this process. The frequency can be determined as:

$$f = \frac{f_c f_i}{a} \tag{7}$$

where f_s and f_c are the sampling frequency and the central frequency of a particular wavelet basis. a is the scale, denoted as 2^m (m is a particular level of decomposition) in OWT. It represents the original frequency range of the turbulence signal when $m = 0$ (i.e., $a = 1$), $f = f_0$.

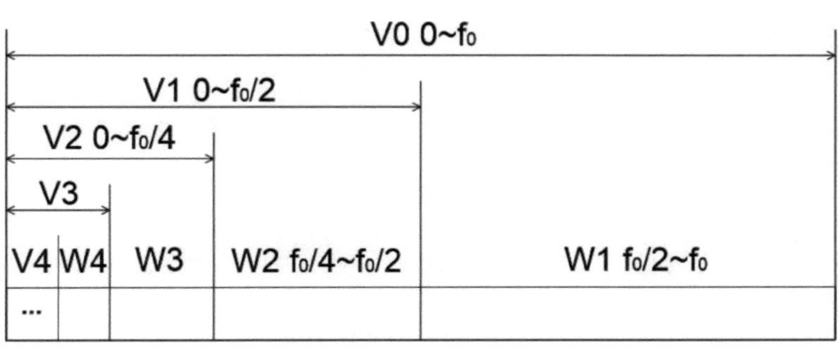

Figure 5.
Sketch of the multiresolution analysis.

4. Extraction and verification of turbulent structures

To extract the coherent structures in turbulence, the signals at the central area of turbulence should be selected. According to previous studies [20–22], the formation of the coherent structures in turbulence is formed in the area of $0 < y^+ < 30$, and the self-sustaining of the coherent structures is in the area of $20 < y^+ < 60$. As a result, three testing positions with the y^+ 20.8, 33.5, and 42.6 were selected, whose fluctuating velocity signals are shown in **Figure 6**.

4.1 Preliminary evaluation of coherent structures

For preliminary evaluations of the coherent structures, CWT is first utilized for the analysis. CWT is a mathematical mapping similar to the Fourier transform [23, 24]. It is linear, invertible, and orthogonal. However, the Fourier transform uses basis functions, including the sines and cosines, which extend to infinity in time, while wavelet basis functions drop towards zero outside a finite domain (compact support). This allows for an effective localization in both time and frequency. CWT uses inner products to measure the similarity between the turbulence signal and the wavelet function, which defines a mapping between the two. CWT compares the turbulence signal to shifted and compressed/stretched versions of the wavelet function. Compressing/stretching is also referred to as dilation or scaling and corresponds to the physical notion of scale. By continuously varying the values of the scale parameter, a, and the position parameter, b, one can obtain the CWT coefficients at last.

In the work, the 5th order of Daubechies wavelet was selected as the basis function, whose central frequency fc is 0.6667 Hz. The calculated CWT coefficients of the three signals are shown in **Figure 7**, where the quasi-periodic structures (coherent structures) of turbulence can be clearly observed. The modulus of the wavelet coefficients shows that during the vortex breakdown, which is caused by the strong nonlinear flow instability, energy is spread over a wide range of scales. Large-scale structures exhibit anisotropic properties in the flow. Their peaks and troughs appear at the scale about 300, corresponding with a frequency of 0.6667/300 = 0.0022 Hz. These dominant scales will have the highest level of energy in turbulence. At the smaller scales, the vortices break up into intermittent small-scale features. Some organizations are evident here, with periodical and intermittent turbulent bursts. The low-frequency structures will decay to isotropic structures and dissipate in turbulence at last.

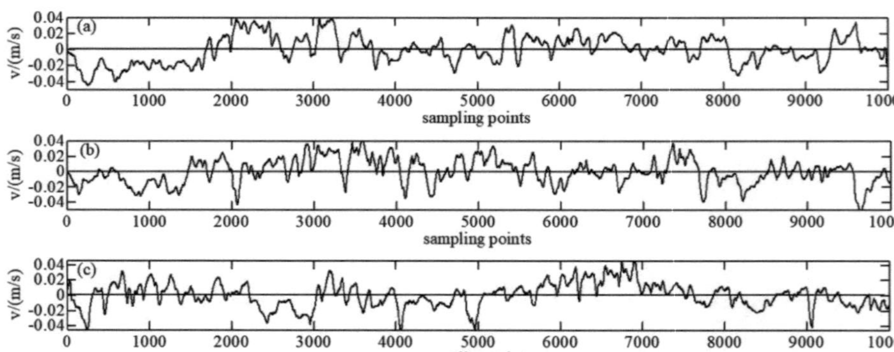

Figure 6.
Fluctuating velocity signals at three positions (a) $y^+ = 20.8$, (b) $y^+ = 33.5$, (c) $y^+ = 42.6$.

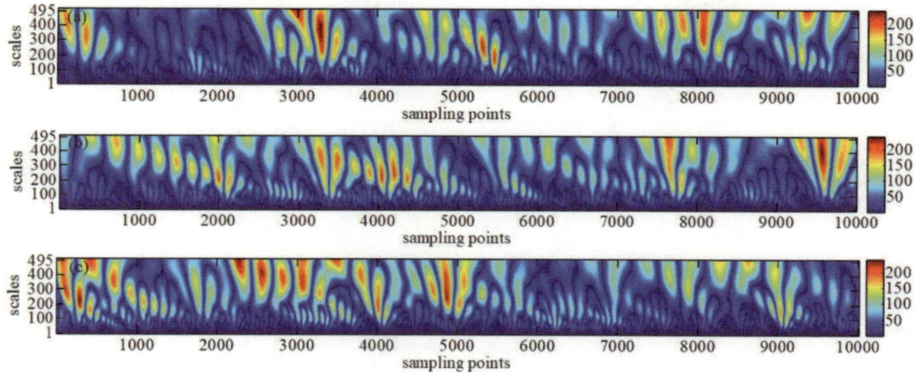

Figure 7.
Continuous wavelet transform coefficients at (a) $y^+ = 20.8$, (b) $y^+ = 33.5$, (c) $y^+ = 42.6$.

4.2 Extraction of coherent structures

To obtain the frequency range of coherent structures in turbulence, power spectrum densities of the three selected signals were calculated in **Figure 8**. The centralized frequencies of the coherent structures are found in the range $0 \sim 230\ Hz$, $0 \sim 240\ Hz$, $0 \sim 230\ Hz$. The rapid attenuation of PSD demonstrates the low noise of our experimental system. Multiresolution analysis of OWT was used to extract the coherent structures in turbulence [9, 25, 26].

WT of a signal is equivalent to local cross-correlation analysis between the signal and wavelet function. OWT carries out the multi-resolution analysis for both decomposition and reconstruction of the original turbulence signal. It is thought of the wavelet coefficients as digital filters as which the original signal is passed through low-pass filters to decompose into low-frequency components and passed through high-pass filters to analyze into high-frequency components.

Using the multiresolution analysis of OWT, the turbulence signal was split into seven scales as in **Table 1**, which eliminates most of the redundant signals. The frequency range of the approximate signal is mainly in the range $0 \sim 260\ Hz$, which covers most of the coherent structures. In **Table 1**, the coherent structures are found to take almost 75 % of the whole energy in turbulence.

The extracted signals of each level are shown in **Figure 9**, where "A7" is the approximate signal, i.e., the coherent structures; where "sD7" is the incoherent structures, which is calculated by:

$$\text{sD7} = \text{s} - \text{A7} = \text{D1} + \text{D2} + \cdots + \text{D7}, \tag{8}$$

and where "s" is the original signal. "D1 ~ D7" are the detailed signals of each level.

4.3 Verification of extracted signals

To characterize the properties of the extracted signals, the probability density functions (PDFs) were analyzed in **Figure 10**. It can be observed that the incoherent structures are approximately Gaussian, demonstrating isotropic characteristics. The PDFs of coherent structures deviate from the Gaussian distribution, presenting strong anisotropic characteristics. And the PDFs of the coherent structures resemble that of the original turbulence signals. This means that coherent structures contribute the most to turbulence entrainment.

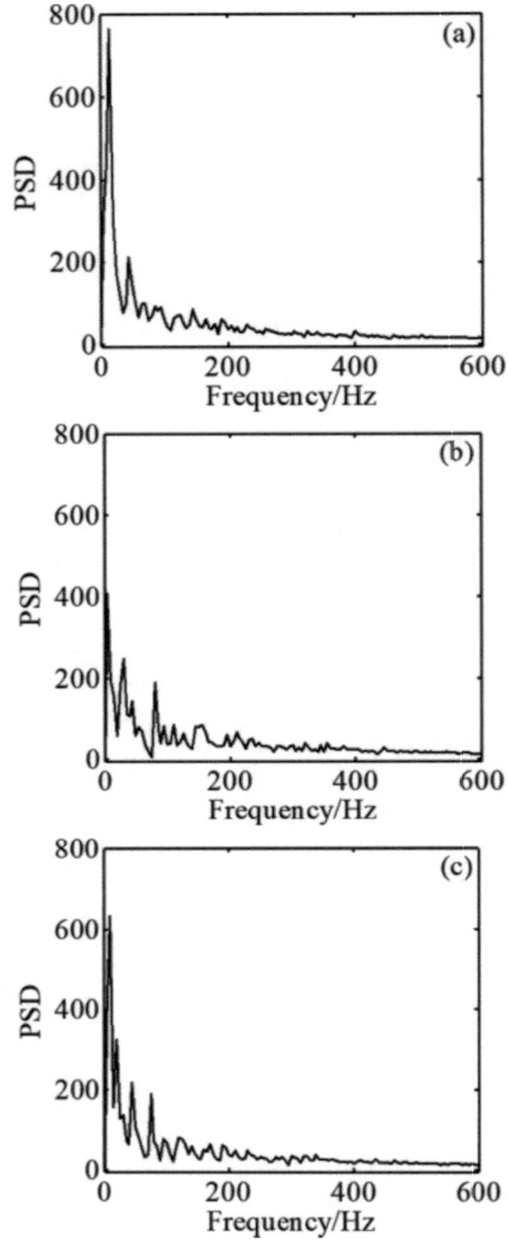

Figure 8.
Power spectrum densities at the three positions (a) $y^+ = 20.8$, *(b)* $y^+ = 33.5$, *(c)* $y^+ = 42.6$.

For further validation of the extracted coherent and incoherent structures, correlation analysis was carried out here. A correlation parameter β between these structures was defined [27]:

$$\beta = \frac{\overline{v_a v_d}}{\overline{v^2}} = \frac{\frac{1}{N}\sum v_{ai} v_{di}}{\frac{1}{N}\sum v_i^2} \tag{9}$$

where v is the fluctuating velocity signal. The subscripts "a" and "d" represent the coherent and incoherent structures. N is the number of the sampling points. $\overline{v_a v_d}$ can be regarded as the stress between the coherent and incoherent structures.

Signal	Frequency/*Hz*		Energy/%	
		$y^+ = 20.8$	$y^+ = 33.5$	$y^+ = 42.6$
s	$0 \sim 33{,}335$	100	100	100
A7	$0 \sim 260$	85.6498	77.0677	81.3847
D7	$260 \sim 520$	0.0147	0.0200	0.0259
D6	$520 \sim 1042$	0.0062	0.0086	0.0129
D5	$1042 \sim 2083$	0.0019	0.0036	0.0042
D4	$2083 \sim 4167$	0.0464	0.0703	0.0868
D3	$4167 \sim 83{,}334$	0.3957	0.8099	0.8505
D2	$83{,}334 \sim 16{,}668$	3.5993	5.5974	5.2322
D1	$16{,}668 \sim 33{,}335$	10.2411	16.4225	12.4028

Table 1.
Frequency and energy distribution of seven level decompositions.

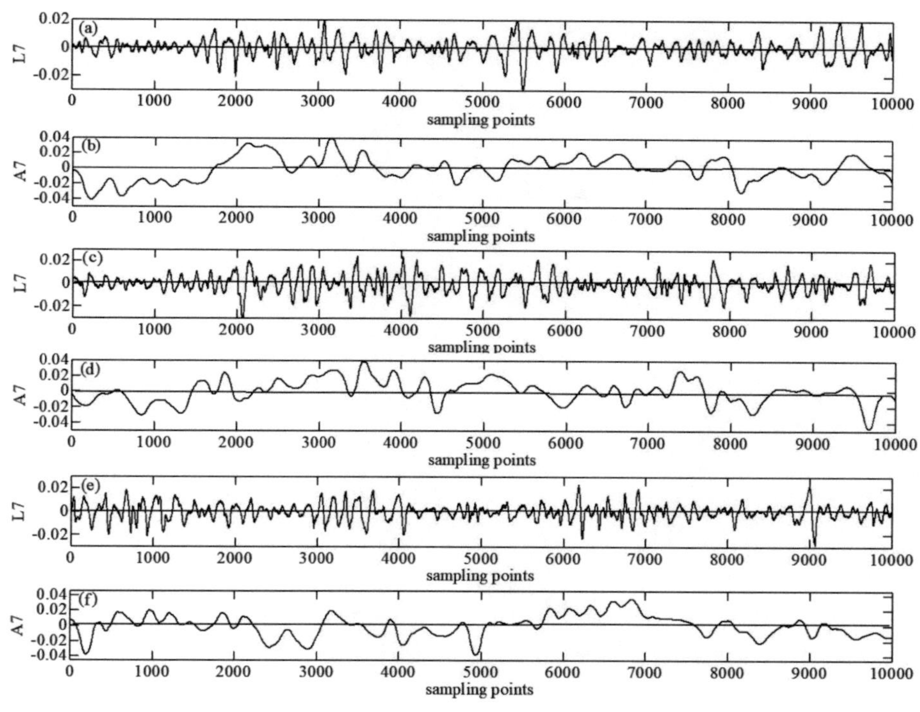

Figure 9.
Extracted signals in turbulence. (a) Incoherent structure ($y^+ = 20.8$); (b) coherent structure ($y^+ = 20.8$); (c) incoherent structure ($y^+ = 33.5$); (d) coherent structure ($y^+ = 33.5$); (e) incoherent structure ($y^+ = 42.6$); (f) coherent structure ($y^+ = 42.6$).

Value of β represents the correlation between coherent and incoherent structures. A large value of β means that the coherent structures are divided into detailed signals as incoherent structures, denoting an inappropriate selection of the decomposition level. If the coherent structures are correctly extracted, the correlation parameter β should be 0. According to Eq. (9), β of our three selected signals at the level 7 are -3.8444×10^{-4}, 7.2638×10^{-4}, and 3.2677×10^{-4}, respectively, demonstrating the low correlation between the extracted coherent and incoherent structures. This proves the validity of the proposed extraction process.

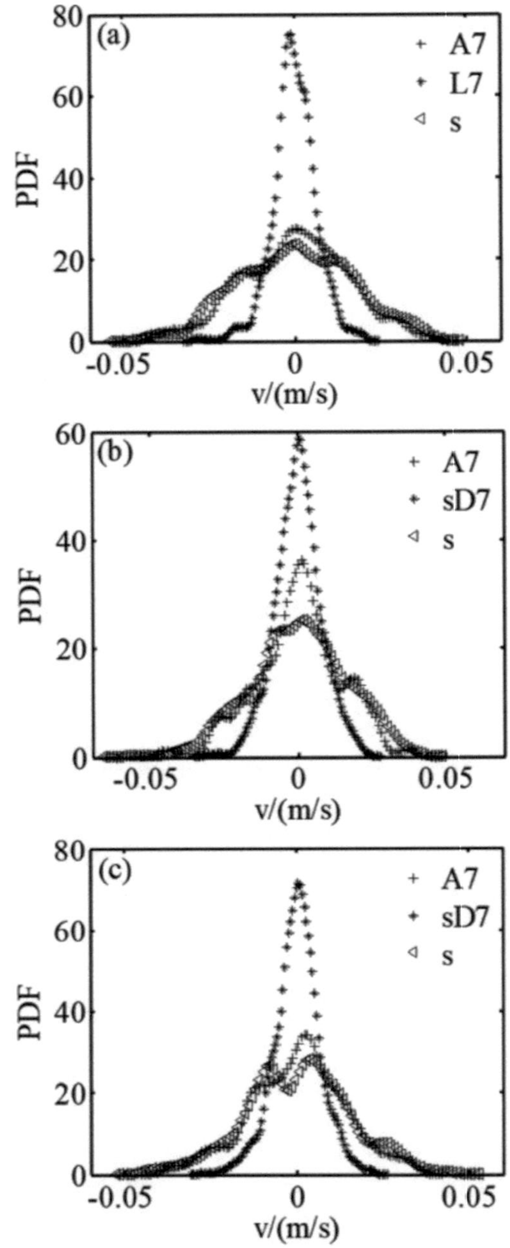

Figure 10.
Probability density functions at three testing positions (a) $y^+ = 20.8$, *(b)* $y^+ = 33.5$, *(c)* $y^+ = 42.6$.

5. Conclusion

The flow field of the turbulence boundary layer was measured using hot-film anemometer in a gravitational low-speed water tunnel. The coherent and incoherent structures in turbulence were separated successfully with an extraction method based on WT. With CWT, the turbulent structures can be observed in various scales. With DWT, multiresolution analysis can be carried out for the decomposition and reconstruction of vortical structures in different scales. The PDF of the incoherent structures was found to obey the Gaussian distribution, while that of the coherent structures deviate from it. The similarity of the PDFs of the coherent structures and the original turbulence signal demonstrate that the coherent structures make most contributions to turbulence. A correlation parameter between coherent and incoherent structures was defined, which proves the successful separation of coherent structure from turbulence.

Acknowledgements

The authors acknowledge the support from the National Natural Science Foundation of China (Grant No. 51879218, 51679203) and Fundamental Research Funds for the Central Universities (Grant No. 3102018gxc007, 3102020H HZY030004).

Conflict of interest

The authors declare no conflict of interest.

Notes

Reprinted (adapted) with permission from Chinese Physics B, 2013, 22(7): 074703.

Abbreviations

WT	wavelet transform
PSD	power spectrum density
OWT	orthogonal wavelet transform
PDF	probability density function
CWT	continuous wavelet transform
DWT	discrete wavelet transform
DNS	direct numerical simulation

Nomenclature

$s(t)$	original turbulence signal
$\varphi_{m,n}(t)$	scaling function
a	scale parameter
b	position parameter
m_0	critical scale
$\psi_{m,n}(t)$	wavelet function
$\tilde{s}$	coherent part of the signal
s'	incoherent part of the signal
f	frequency
f_s	sampling frequency
f_c	central frequency of particular wavelet basis
y^+	dimensionless wall distance
$A7, \ D1 \sim D7$	detailed signal of each level
v	fluctuating velocity signal
β	correlation parameter

Appendix I: complex wavelet transform

The continuous wavelet transform (CWT) has the drawback of redundancy. As the dilation parameter a and the shift parameter b take continuous values, the resulting CWT is a very redundant representation. Therefore, the discrete wavelet transform was proposed to overcome this problem by setting the scale and shift parameters on a discrete set of basis functions. Their discretization is performed by:

$$a = a_0^j \cdots b = ka_0^j b_0 \cdots \text{for} \cdot j, k \in Z \tag{10}$$

where $a_0 > 1$ is the dilation and $b_0 \neq 0$ is the translation. The family of wavelets can be expressed as:

$$\psi_{j,k}(t) = a_0^{-j/2} \psi\left(a_0^{-j} t - kb_0\right) \tag{11}$$

and the discrete wavelet decomposition of a signal $f(t)$ is:

$$f(t) = \sum_j \sum_k D_f(j,k) \psi_{j,k}(t) \tag{12}$$

where $D_f(j,k)$ is the DWT of the signal $f(t)$. The most widely used dilation and shift parameters are $a = 2$ and $b = 1$.

The basis function set $\left\{\psi_{j,k}\right\}$ should be orthonormal such that:

$$D_f(j,k) = \int_{-\infty}^{\infty} \psi_{j,k}^*(t) f(t) dt = \left\langle \psi_{j,k}(t) f(t) \right\rangle \tag{13}$$

The advantage of the DWT is the multi-resolution analysis ability. Although the standard DWT is powerful, it has three major disadvantages that undermine its applications: shift sensitivity, poor directionality, and absence of phase information.

Complex wavelet transform can be used to overcome these drawbacks. It uses complex-valued filtering and decomposes the signal into real and imaginary parts, which can be used to calculate the amplitude and phase information.

For turbulence analysis, the complex wavelet transform should be used since the modulus of the wavelet coefficients allows characterizing the evolution of the turbulent energy in both the time and frequency domains. The real-valued wavelets will make it difficult to sort out the features of the signal or the wavelet. On the contrary, the complex-valued wavelets can eliminate these spurious oscillations. The complex extension of a real signal $f(t)$ can be expressed as:

$$x(t) = f(t) + jg(t) \tag{14}$$

where $g(t)$ is the Hilbert transform of $f(t)$ and is denoted as $H\{f(t)\}$ and $j = (-1)^{1/2}$. The instantaneous frequency and amplitude of the signal $x(t)$ can then be calculated as:

$$\begin{aligned} \text{Magnitude of } x(t) &= \sqrt{\left(f(t)^2 + g(t)^2\right)} \\ \text{Angle of } x(t) &= \tan^{-1}[g(t)/f(t)] \end{aligned} \tag{15}$$

The complex wavelet transform is able to remove the redundancy for turbulence analysis where the directionality and phase information play important roles.

Author details

Peng Du†, Haibao Hu*† and Xiao Huang
School of Marine Science and Technology, Northwestern Polytechnical University, Xi'an, P.R. China

*Address all correspondence to: huhaibao@nwpu.edu.cn

† These authors are contributed equally.

References

[1] Kowal G, Lazarian A. Velocity field of compressible magnetohydrodynamic turbulence: Wavelet decomposition and mode scalings. The Astrophysical Journal. 2010;**720**(1):742

[2] Xiao-Bing L, Zheng-Qing C, Chao-Qun L. Late-stage vertical structures and eddy motions in a transitional boundary layer. Chinese Physics Letters. 2010;**27**(2):024706

[3] Rinoshika A, Omori H. Orthogonal wavelet analysis of turbulent wakes behind various bluff bodies. Experimental Thermal and Fluid Science. 2011;**35**(7):1231-1238

[4] Rinoshika A, Watanabe S. Orthogonal wavelet decomposition of turbulent structures behind a vehicle external mirror. Experimental Thermal and Fluid Science. 2010;**34**(8): 1389-1397

[5] Okamoto N, Yoshimatsu K, Schneider K, et al. Coherent vortices in high resolution direct numerical simulation of homogeneous isotropic turbulence: A wavelet viewpoint. Physics of Fluids. 2007;**19**(11):115109

[6] De Stefano G, Vasilyev OV. A fully adaptive wavelet-based approach to homogeneous turbulence simulation. Journal of Fluid Mechanics. 2012;**695**: 149-172

[7] Futatani S, Bos WJT, del-Castillo-Negrete D, et al. Coherent vorticity extraction in resistive drift-wave turbulence: Comparison of orthogonal wavelets versus proper orthogonal decomposition. Comptes Rendus Physique. 2011;**12**(2):123-131

[8] de la Llave PM, Cant S, Prosser R. On the use of biorthogonal interpolating wavelets for large-eddy simulation of turbulence. Journal of Computational Physics. 2012;**231**(20):6754-6769

[9] Khujadze G, Schneider K, Oberlack M, et al. Coherent vorticity extraction in turbulent boundary layers using orthogonal wavelets. Journal of Physics: Conference Series. 2011;**318**(2): 022011

[10] Liandrat J, Moret-Bailly F. The wavelet transform-some applications to fluid dynamics and turbulence. European Journal of Mechanics - B/Fluids. 1990;**9**:1-19

[11] Nan J, Jin Z. Detecting multi-scale coherent eddy structures and intermittency in turbulent boundary layer by wavelet analysis. Chinese Physics Letters. 2005;**22**(8):1968

[12] Jian-hua L, Nan J, Zhen-dong W, et al. Multi-scale coherent structures in turbulent boundary layer detected by locally averaged velocity structure functions. Applied Mathematics and Mechanics. 2005;**26**(4):495-504

[13] Kim YH, Cierpka C, Wereley ST. Flow field around a vibrating cantilever: Coherent structure education by continuous wavelet transform and proper orthogonal decomposition. Journal of Fluid Mechanics. 2011;**669**:584-606

[14] Yoshimatsu K, Schneider K, Okamoto N, et al. Intermittency and geometrical statistics of three-dimensional homogeneous magneto-hydrodynamic turbulence: A wavelet viewpoint. Physics of Plasmas. 2011; **18**(9):092304

[15] Baars WJ, Talluru KM, Hutchins N, et al. Wavelet analysis of wall turbulence to study large-scale modulation of small scales. Experiments in Fluids. 2015;**56**(10):188

[16] Camussi R. Coherent structure identification from wavelet analysis of particle image velocimetry data. Experiments in Fluids. 2002;**32**(1):76-86

[17] Longo S. Turbulence under spilling breakers using discrete wavelets. Experiments in Fluids. 2003;**34**(2): 181-191

[18] Arimitsu T, Arimitsu N. Analysis of PDFs for energy transfer rates from 40963 DNS-verification of the scaling relation within MPDFT. Journal of Turbulence. 2011;**12**:N1

[19] Gang D, Shi-Sheng Z, Yang L. Time series prediction using wavelet process neural network. Chinese Physics B. 2008;**17**(6):1998

[20] Asai M, Minagawa M, Nishioka M. The instability and breakdown of a near-wall low-speed streak. Journal of Fluid Mechanics. 2002;**455**:289-314

[21] Chen L, Tang DB. Study on turbulent spots in plane Couette flow. Transactions of Nanjing University of Aeronautics & Astronautics. 2007; **24**(3):211-217

[22] Hu HB, Du P, Huang SH, Wang Y. Extraction and verification of coherent structures in near-wall turbulence. Chinese Physics B. 2013;**22**(7):074703

[23] Huang L, Kemao Q, Pan B, et al. Comparison of Fourier transform, windowed Fourier transform, and wavelet transform methods for phase extraction from a single fringe pattern in fringe projection profilometry. Optics and Lasers in Engineering. 2010;**48**(2):141-148

[24] Canal MR. Comparison of wavelet and short time Fourier transform methods in the analysis of EMG signals. Journal of Medical Systems. 2010;**34**(1): 91-94

[25] Du P, Wen J, Zhang Z, et al. Maintenance of air layer and drag reduction on superhydrophobic surface. Ocean Engineering. 2017;**130**:328-335

[26] Haibao H, Peng D, Feng Z, et al. Effect of hydrophobicity on turbulent boundary layer under water. Experimental Thermal and Fluid Science. 2015;**60**:148-156

[27] Sang YF. A review on the applications of wavelet transform in hydrology time series analysis. Atmospheric Research. 2013;**122**:8-15

Chapter 8

An Efficient Approach Based on the Near-Field Technique to Solve EMI Problems: Application to an AC/DC Flyback Converter

Bessem Zitouna and Jaleleddine Ben Hadj Slama

Abstract

Flyback converters have been widely used in low- and high-power applications because of their simplicity and low cost. However, they incur electromagnetic compatibility problems which are more difficult to control. The present chapter proposes an efficient modeling method based on the near-field technique to solve real-world radiation problems of the power electronics circuits. Firstly, for the characterization of an AC/DC flyback converter, several experimental measurements of the magnetic near field are performed in the time domain over the converter. Subsequently, we have applied the time domain electromagnetic inverse method based on the genetic algorithms on the measured signals to find the equivalent radiating sources of the studied circuit. The accuracy and the efficiency of the proposed approach have been demonstrated by the good agreement between cartographies of the near magnetic field components calculated using the developed model and those measured. Finally, the developed equivalent model has been used to predict cartographies of other components of the magnetic field which will be compared to measured cartographies. This confirms that the identified equivalent sources can represent real sources in the studied structure. The proposed method could be used for diagnosis and fault location in power electronics systems.

Keywords: electromagnetic compatibility (EMC), flyback converter, inverse method, near-field measurement, time-domain analysis, genetic algorithms

1. Introduction

To respond to the necessity and simplicity of marketed converter applications, innovation in power electronics is based on the growing constraints imposed by the exponential rise of our needs: better management of primary energy sources while offering increasingly sophisticated functions at reduced cost. This cost function can obviously take different forms depending on the context: weight, volume, efficiency, disturbances on the converter and its environment, technological cost, economic cost, protection and reliability, and lifetime of devices. No device can be excluded today from environmental constraints. At this stage, a lot of energy conversion structures are now very efficient. For example, the flyback converter is probably the most widely used structure in the electronics industry and is frequently utilized for various applications (battery chargers, energy saving lamps, photovoltaic systems, LCD monitors, DVD players, ...). Integration and coexistence in the same housing, as well as the increase in switching frequencies and carried powers, cause frequent and unwanted electromagnetic interference in the vicinity of these systems. These interferences present important sources of malfunction of the device itself and neighboring systems. For this reason, electro-magnetic compatibility (EMC) must be addressed from the starting process of design and manufacture of high-tech electronic devices. Indeed, the study of electromagnetic compatibility of a card gives quantitative tools to the power electronics to influence the radiated and conducted disturbances. It is essential to know the electromagnetic disturbances emitted by the equipment under test at different distances and to verify that they do not exceed a certain limit in order to avoid disturbing the neighboring equipment. Therefore, the EMC characterization tests have become an essential step in the various phases of the development of power electronics products. Unfortunately, these tests remain costly because we often need heavy, precise and very expensive equipment (anechoic chamber). To circumvent these limits, it is essential to develop radiating models that allow us to estimate the electromagnetic emissions of these systems before the prototype is realized (during the phase of virtual prototyping). The objective of this work is to elicit the electromagnetic inverse method in the time domain based on the near-field technique as an innovative and important solution that allows characterizing and modeling the radiation of the products of the power electronics. Thus, the added value of this chapter is to show the implementation of the inverse electromagnetic method in the time domain for the field of power electronics. In fact, the proposed approach will be of some use to people who make the development of power electronics systems. Actually, identifying all the sources of radiation in an electronic cartography and developing an equivalent radiation model that will allow us to estimate the electromagnetic emissions of these systems help solve the problems of interferences encountered in power electronics. The proposed method can be used for example as a method of analysis, fault detection and diagnosis of power electronic circuits. Indeed, the electromagnetic signature of a component could make it possible to verify its proper functioning. In order to find solutions related to the problems encountered in power electronics, the inverse electromagnetic method has been applied to different types of circuits.

In the literature, a lot of work has been already achieved on the modeling of electronic components [1–3]. The inverse method based on the elementary dipoles was used to extract the equivalent model from PCB circuits [4–6]. In frequency domain, the inverse method was also used in order to model electronics cards [7–9].

These various approaches have been developed in the frequency domain and have been utilized to characterize and to model the radiated emissions on only one frequency. It seems that there is no time. This supposes that the studied systems have had sinusoidal radiations that do not correspond to the reality of power electronic systems where the electromagnetic disturbances are very important over a broad band of frequencies. For this effect, modeling this kind of radiation by the frequency inverse method requires to repeating the identification of equivalent sources for each signal frequency. This causes a very high processing time. However, from the results found in the frequency domain, we cannot know at what time of the cycle of operation the radiating sources intervene, and we thus suppose that the radiations of the sources contribute simultaneously, which does not correspond to reality. Nevertheless, the switching in power electronics often presents offsets which will be found at the level of radiated emissions. The spectral distribution therefore evolves as a function of time and the components do not all have the same radiation frequencies. Consequently, the models obtained by the electromagnetic inverse method in the frequency domain have several limitations and remain inapplicable for power electronics systems which are excited by different types of nonsinusoidal signals and which consequently emit on one broad band of frequencies. To this end, the added value of our approach is to propose an efficient technique based on the inverse electromagnetic method in the time domain which takes into account the temporal offset at the levels of the various radiated emissions of the circuit, which permits the Identification of the contribution of each radiating source of the circuit over time.

Until now, few studies have been performed and published on the time-domain inverse method. The authors in some study tried to combine the frequency inverse method with the time-frequency computation method [10, 11]. However, the developed modeling method was limited because it always depended on the parameters of the time intervals that mainly depended on the selected frequency band, the considered initial frequency and the used computer performance. Other approaches have been performed [12–15]. These studies were dedicated to the development of new computational techniques and analysis of an electromagnetic near field in the time domain. To develop a resolution method in the time domain, enabled by passing this kind of problem, we put forward the development and implementation of the temporal inverse electromagnetic method based on elementary dipoles [16].

The methodology of the time-domain electromagnetic inverse method has been presented [16]. This method was applied to identify the equivalent radiation model in a fairly simple structure, which was unfortunately not representative enough for all power electronic circuits. To demonstrate again the robustness and efficiency of the electromagnetic inverse method developed in the time domain when applied to complicated real cards composed of several bulky components, where the radiating sources are usually very close to each other, we propose to study in this chapter a complete application case (PCB and power electronic components). Hence, we will focus much more on the application of the temporal inverse electromagnetic method to find an equivalent model of an industrial system that emits nonsinusoidal radiations. This will make it possible to calculate the field emitted by the studied system for various distances and to study the coupling with the neighboring systems.

In this chapter, the time domain electromagnetic inverse method is tested and used in an AC-DC flyback converter application. First, we describe the device under test. Then, we will present how the suggested approach is implemented and what these advantages can be. To do this, several works will be performed. We will firstly present the test bench of the near field in the time domain. Second, we will present the measurement results of the vertical component of the radiated magnetic near field (H_z) performed over an AC/DC converter, so as to model the radiation of this converter by the electromagnetic inverse method in the time domain. In the following part, the modeling methodology and its resolution based on the genetic algorithms are described. To validate the identified model using our suggested approach, a comparison is made between the tangential components (H_x) of the magnetic field, calculated using the optimized model parameters and the one measured over the studied converter.

2. Description of the studied flyback converter

The system studied in this chapter is an AC-DC converter based on the principle of switched-mode power supplies (**Figure 1**).

Switching power supplies are much smaller and lighter than linear power supplies, which explain their increasingly widespread use in various fields, particularly in those of embedded systems. Also, switched-mode power supplies have a good efficiency until 90%. Contrarily, they have regulatory problems which are more difficult to control [17–19]. Due to the rectangular signal to the switching frequency, these power supplies produce a relatively large noise. This problem makes them unsuitable for certain applications. To this end, it is essential to characterize and control the EMC behavior of this type of converters.

The studied converter in this chapter is of a flyback type of a low power (5 W). The basic schema of a studied converter is illustrated in **Figure 2**.

Figure 1.
Flyback AC/DC converter.

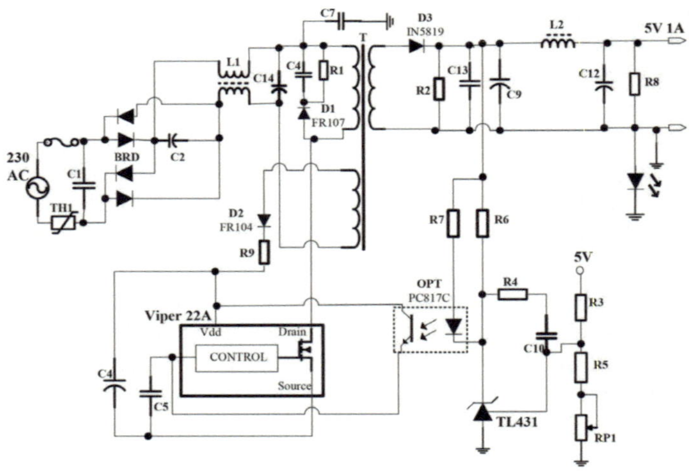

Figure 2.
Schematic of AC/DC flyback converter.

Type	Input voltage	Output voltage	Maximum current	Efficiency
Flyback	220 V AC	5 V DC	1 A	79%

Table 1.
Characteristics of studied converter.

The electrical characteristics of the studied flyback converter are illustrated in **Table 1**.

3. Description of magnetic near-field test bench in time domain

In our study, the measurement of the studied converter radiation is carried out in one single measurement for different radiation frequencies. This presents the benefits of a near field in the time domain compared to the frequency test bench.

Figure 3 presents the different parts of the near-field test bench in time domain.

The temporal measurement method uses a high-precision oscilloscope that presents a wide bandwidth. This oscilloscope is utilized for displaying and recording temporal signals picked up by the measurement of the magnetic field probe.

To sweep the probe above the studied structure, a plotting table is used. The displacement of the probe over the device under test is manually performed (**Figure 4**).

The displacement of the probe above the studied structure is manually performed. The displacement procedure of the probe from measurement point to another on the sweeping surface is described in **Figure 5**.

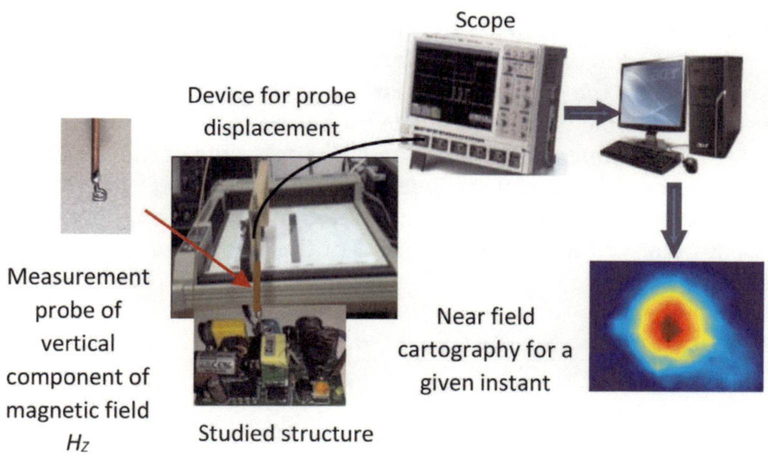

Figure 3.
Near-field test bench in time domain.

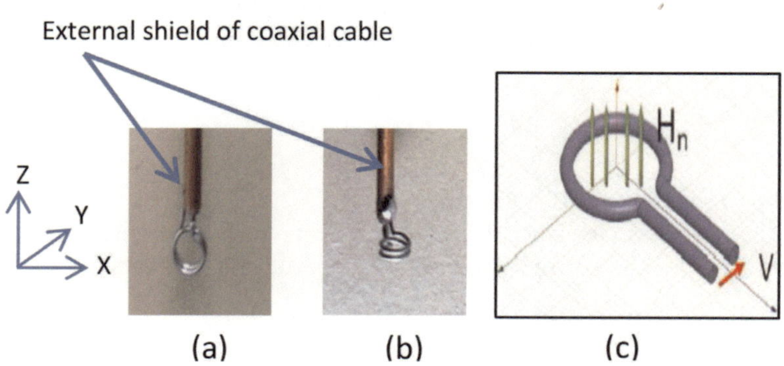

Figure 4.
Detailed structure of magnetic probes: (a) probe of tangential components H_x and H_y, (b) probe of vertical component, (c) measurement principle of electronic probe H_z.

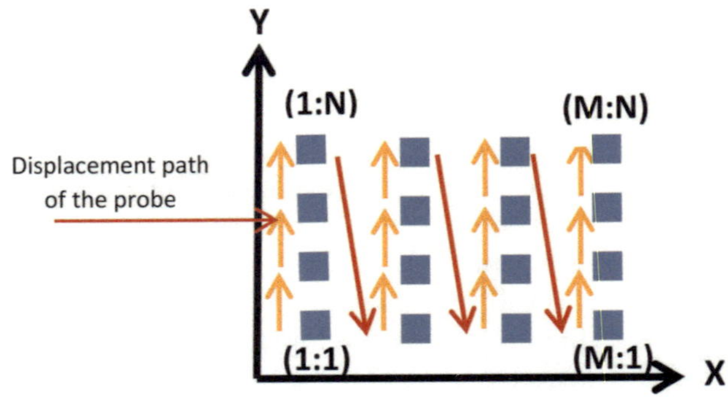

Figure 5.
Probe displacement in measurement surface.

In this study and according to our needs, we utilize two coil probes: one for measuring the normal component of the magnetic field (H_z) and the other for measuring the two tangential components (H_x and H_y). Each utilized probe is shielded. The shielding of the used probe is made by copper. It consists of a loop connected to the central conductor on one side and to the external shield of a coaxial cable on the other side, as shown in **Figure 4**. The probe is connected to the oscilloscope through a highly shielded coaxial cable.

To measure the magnetic fields around the components and systems, we use magnetic probes; and to capture the different components of the magnetic field H, it is necessary to place the normal to the surface of the collinearly loop of the desired component. It is possible to utilize a single probe and to orient it differently according to the component to be measured. The principle of the measurement protocol is based on the Faraday and Lenz law, which stipulates that if a variable magnetic field crosses through a closed circuit, then the resulting flux variation will cause an electromotive force at the terminals of the loop (**Figure 4c**). Accordingly, we have:

$$e(t) = -\frac{d\varphi(t)}{dt} \tag{1}$$

Finally, and through a transformation equation, we can deduce the magnetic field. The magnetic probe allows transforming the variable magnetic flux which crosses through it into a voltage at its terminals. Subsequently, we deduce the magnetic field at the center of the probe. Indeed, for a circular conductive loop of a radius R dived in a magnetic field B(t), the induced potential difference by the variable magnetic field is given by the following equation:

$$V(t) = -\oint \mu_0 \frac{\partial H(t)}{\partial t}\ \vec{\text{n}}\ dS \tag{2}$$

where $\vec{\text{n}}$ is the probe surface normal.

Since the probe surface is small enough, we can consider the magnetic field $H_z(t)$ constant over the entire loop area S. As a result, Eq. (5) becomes:

$$V(t) = -\mu_0 \times S\frac{\partial H(t)}{\partial t} \tag{3}$$

where $S = \pi \times r^2$ is the probe surface (r = 1.6 mm) and $\mu_0 = 4 \times \pi \times 10^{-7}$ H/m is the permeability in the free space.

In fact, extracting the magnetic field H(t) from the measured voltage at the probe terminals can be defined as follows:

$$H(t) = -\frac{1}{\mu_0 \times S}\int_0^t V(t)\ dt \tag{4}$$

4. Measurement of near field emitted by studied converter

This suggested approach is based on time domain measurements of the near field above the studied structure. The distribution of the near field on the chosen scanned surface is presented in the form of cartography. The cartography is a matrix representation of the amplitude and the phase of the measured near field at each point and at each instant over the studied system. It is characterized by the dimensions of the measurement surface (Xmin:Xmax; Ymin:Ymax), the distance between two measuring points (ΔX et ΔY), and the measuring height (Z) (**Figure 6**).

Figure 7b represents the chosen face used for the time domain measurements to identify the equivalent radiating sources. This face enables a good detection of the magnetic near field radiated by all components of the studied card.

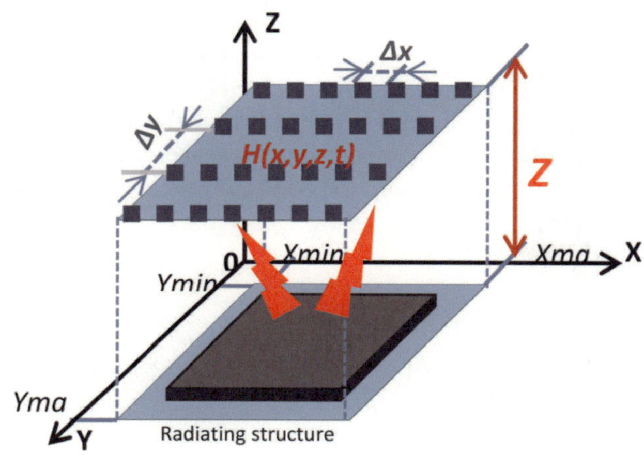

Figure 6.
Cartography parameters of near-field measurements.

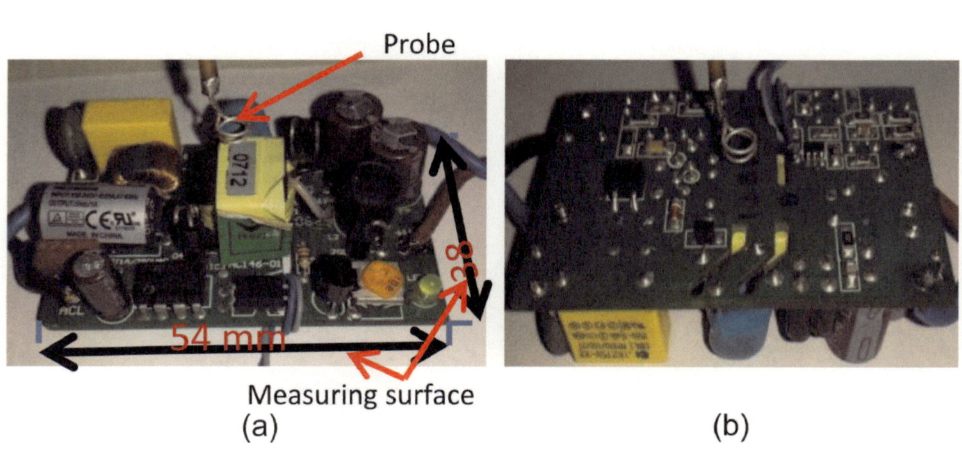

Figure 7.
(a) The studied card and (b) the selected studied card face for measuring the magnetic near field used to identify the model.

By analogy with the frequency inverse method, in this work, the identification of the equivalent radiating sources is based on the measurements of the magnetic near field [8, 9, 20]. This demonstrates its effectiveness in guaranteeing the uniqueness of the equivalent radiating model [9]. To bypass the complexities to measure the electrical near field, it is possible to extract the values of the electric field by exploiting the measurements of the magnetic field [21, 22].

5. Equivalent radiating model of studied flyback converter

In this study, the proposed temporal electromagnetic inverse method is based on the genetic algorithms. To apply our approach, a near-field measurements characterized by a very high signal-to-noise ratio are needed. The proposed method consists in identifying an equivalent model that emits the same radiation of the studied structure to be modeled.

The optimized equivalent model is based on a network of electric or magnetic dipoles (**Figure 8**).

The dipole may be represented by a d vector that comprises all the parameters: $d = (M_d, x_d, y_d, z_d, \theta_d, \varphi_d)$, where M_d is the magnetic moment of the dipole which varies against time. The x_d, y_d and z_d represent the dipole's position, and their orientations are represented by θ_d and φ_d. In the time domain, the components of the magnetic field emitted by the elementary electric and magnetic dipoles in an observation point M (x_o, y_o, z_o) can be deduced from the analytical expressions in the frequency domain using the frequency-time transformation operator. In the Cartesian coordinate system, the magnetic field components are expressed by the following equations [16]:

For the electric dipole:

$$\begin{bmatrix} H_x \\ H_y \\ H_z \end{bmatrix} = -\frac{\Delta l}{4\pi R^2} \times \left(\frac{1}{c}\frac{dI(t')}{dt} + \frac{1}{R}I(t')\right) \left(\begin{bmatrix} \sin\theta & \sin\phi \\ \sin\theta & \cos\phi \\ \cos\theta & \end{bmatrix} \cdot \begin{bmatrix} xd - x0 \\ yd - y0 \\ zd - z0 \end{bmatrix}\right) \wedge \begin{bmatrix} xd - x0 \\ yd - y0 \\ zd - z0 \end{bmatrix} \begin{pmatrix} \vec{i} \\ \vec{j} \\ \vec{k} \end{pmatrix} \tag{5}$$

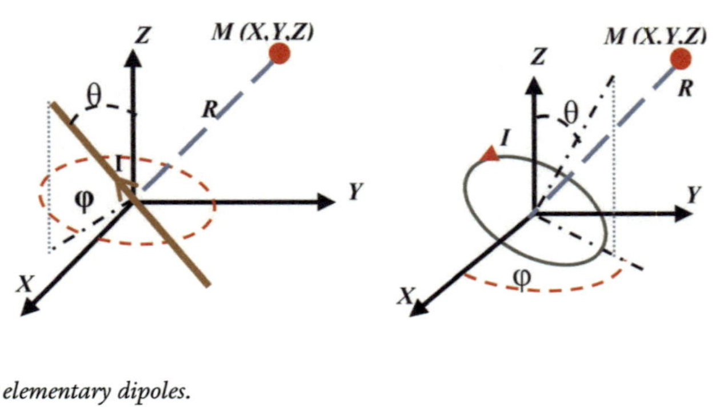

Figure 8.
Presentation of the elementary dipoles.

For the magnetic dipole:

$$\begin{bmatrix} H_x \\ H_y \\ H_z \end{bmatrix} = -\frac{r^2}{4R} \times \left[\left(\frac{1}{c^2} \frac{d^2 I(t')}{dt^2} + \frac{1}{Rc} \frac{dI(t')}{dt} + \frac{1}{R^2} I(t') \right) \right.$$
$$\begin{bmatrix} \sin\theta \ \sin\phi \\ \sin\theta \ \cos\phi \\ \cos\theta \end{bmatrix} - \frac{1}{R^2} \left(\frac{1}{c^2} \frac{d^2 I(t')}{dt^2} + \frac{3}{Rc} \frac{dI(t')}{dt} \right.$$
$$\left. + \frac{3}{R^2} I(t') \right) \left(\begin{bmatrix} \sin\theta \ \sin\phi \\ \sin\theta \ \cos\phi \\ \cos\theta \end{bmatrix} . \begin{bmatrix} xd - x0 \\ yd - y0 \\ zd - z0 \end{bmatrix} \right) \tag{6}$$
$$\wedge \begin{bmatrix} xd - x0 \\ yd - y0 \\ zd - z0 \end{bmatrix} \begin{pmatrix} \vec{i} \\ \vec{j} \\ \vec{k} \end{pmatrix}$$

where R $= \sqrt{\mathrm{tt'??}(\mathrm{Xd} - \mathrm{Xo})^2 + (\mathrm{Yd} - \mathrm{Yo})^2 + (\mathrm{Zd} - \mathrm{Zo})^2}$ t′ = t − (R/c) is the delay time variable, $R = \sqrt{(Xd - X0)^2 + (Yd - Y0)^2 + (Zd - Z0)^2}$.

As the temporal measured signals above the studied system are not sinusoidal well as the excitations currents are not unique. In this proposed method, it is not necessary to initially propose a number of elementary dipoles during the equivalent model identification. Thus, the proposed method consists in identifying at each time a single particular dipole, until the identification of all dipoles that corresponds the equivalent model. Because the measures are performed at a very close distance above the studied structure, a hypothesis is adopted; it is based on the linearity between the radiated magnetic field by an elementary dipole and the current flowing in this dipole. This assumption is adopted for guessing the currents forms on the various dipoles, and is very helpful when simplifying the resolution during the optimization phase of the equivalent model parameters by the genetic algorithms.

At this stage, the problem of identifying the source dipoles is processed. The identification procedure of the radiating sources is presented in the following flow-chart given in **Figure 9**.

In order to identify accurately the shape of the first dipole excitation signal, we will apply to the initially measured cartography a subprogram to seek the measured signal which has the maximum amplitude relative to other measured maximum temporal signals in this cartography. And on the basis of the measurement point that corresponds to the most intense radiation, we extract a limited part of the initial cartography and we propose a single elementary radiating dipole (electric or magnetic dipole) for the extracted cartography. In fact, the searched current form flowing in the first dipole to identify is well known; it is a normalized temporal signal relative to this measured maximum signal in this local cartography. Subsequently, an optimization method based on the genetic algorithms is applied to identify the parameters of the proposed dipole in this selected cartography. At each iteration, the genetic algorithms shall modify all the parameters of the dipole (a constant k which represents the amplitude of the excitation current circulating in

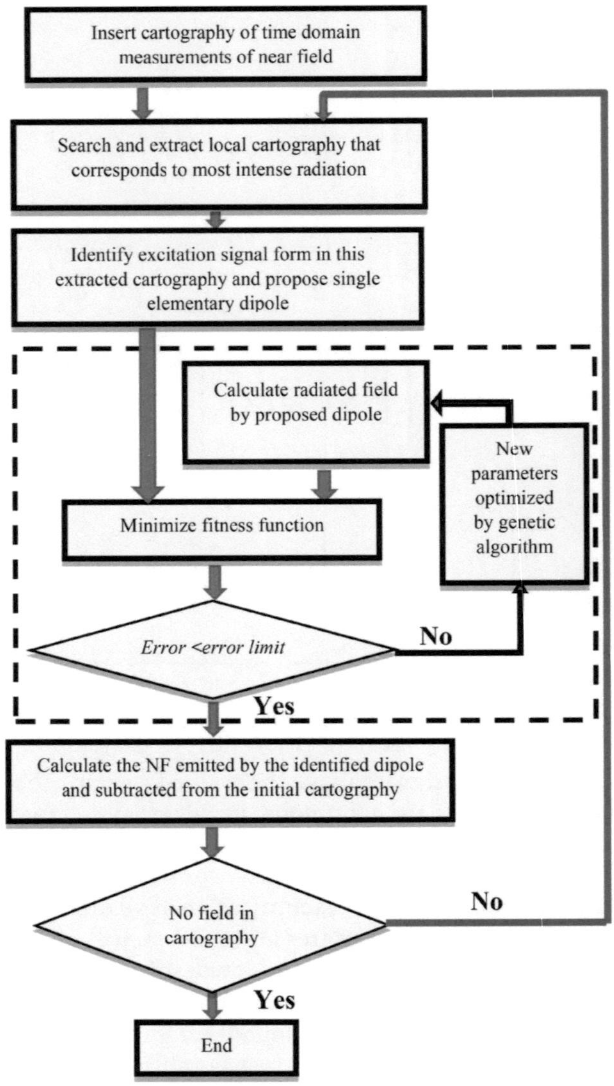

Figure 9.
Chart of proposed method based on optimization algorithm.

this proposed dipole, its geometry, its coordinates, and its orientations) in order to minimize the error calculated by the fitness function. If the error is unacceptable and the genetic algorithms cannot converge after a certain number of iterations, the optimization cycle repeats itself several times until obtaining a new composed generation of best solutions who is the calculated field coincides with the measured one on all points of the cartography and at all moments (even in the case of the small values of the measured field). Thus, the radiating dipole and its corresponding parameters are identified.

By using the analytical equations, the parameters of the first identified dipole are used to calculate the near magnetic field radiated in order to delete it from the initial measured cartography. This simplifies the resolution of the remaining cartography. The procedure is repeated until the scanning of all the measured cartography and the different dipole sources are identified.

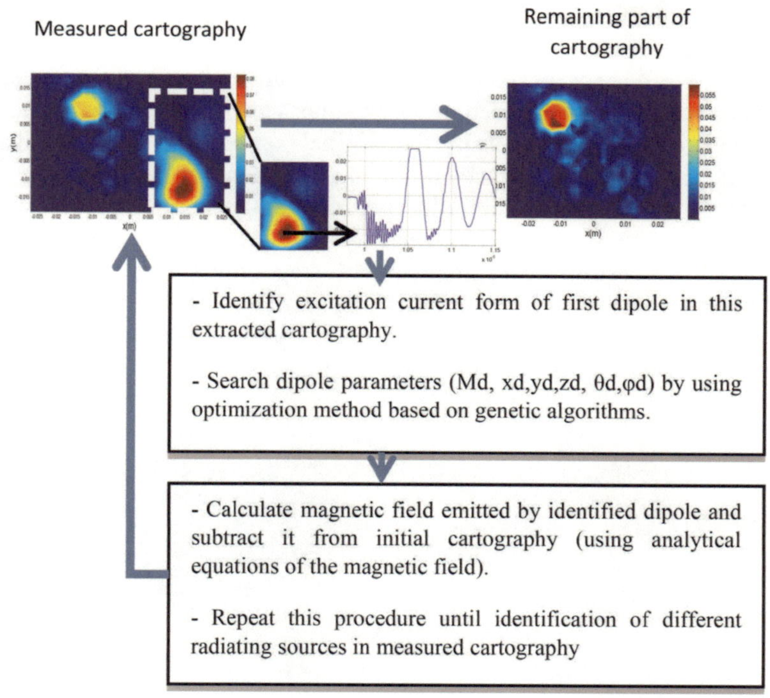

Figure 10.
Methodology of proposed electromagnetic inverse method in time domain.

Fitness function	$Error = \sum_{t_K=1}^{T} \sum_{i=1}^{M} \left| \frac{H_Z(i, t_K)\text{measured-}H_Z(i, t_K)\text{estimated}}{H_Z(i, t_K)\text{measured}} \right| \times 100$
Population size (N_p)	$N_p = 20 \times$ number of parameters of dipoles
Selection function	Roulette
Crossover rate	0.8

Table 2.
Optimum parameters of genetic algorithms.

A supplementary explanation of the proposed approach is illustrated in **Figure 10**. At each identification, this procedure will be repeated until the extraction of all radiating sources in this measured magnetic fields cartography.

The superposition method is applied in a near-field zone where it is assumed that in each area of the local cartography we identify a relatively intense field. The emission is mainly caused by a very close source and the contributions from the other relatively distant sources are very low compared with that of the intense source. Consequently, the search for the model is carried out dipole by dipole until identifying all radiating sources in the initially measured cartography. Indeed, the fitness function is used by the genetic algorithms for identifying the existing source in the each local cartography. Thus, the error of the global cartography is the sum of the errors of different local cartographies.

To guarantee and accelerate the convergence of the proposed temporal inverse method, we take into account the study of [23] to choose the optimal parameters of the genetic algorithms. These parameters are given in **Table 2**.

By applying the proposed method to identify the radiating sources, we have found seven magnetic dipoles as a number of sources. Despite the high density of components in the converter and knowing that the measurements of radiated disturbances are performed at a very close distance above these components, and on the basis of research work on the modeling of the radiation of electronic components and systems, we have carried out the analysis of the radiations of the studied converter. This permits us to identify the original components of the equivalent radiating dipoles. Unfortunately, the modeling of systems by the inverse method in the frequency domain has several limitations and remains not applicable for systems of power electronics operating over a wide frequency band and excited by different types of nonsinusoidal signals. At this stage, it is the interest of the temporal inverse method proposed in this chapter. Thus, without modeling of the radiated emissions for each frequency of the measured signals (which causes a very significant calculation time). The proposed approach has the advantage of finding

Figure 11.
Equivalent radiating source of transformer determined by proposed method.

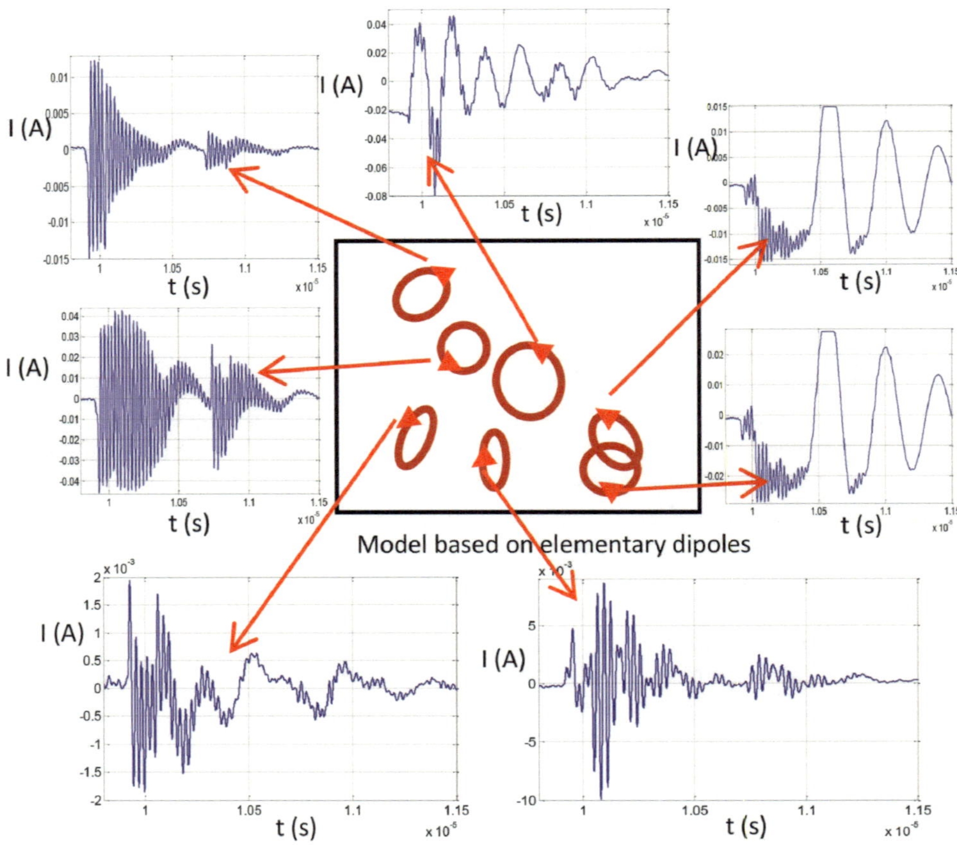

Figure 12.
Identified equivalent model of studied structure and forms of excitation signals.

in a reasonable processing time a single model of radiation valid over the whole band of frequencies in measured signal. From the results obtained by the inverse method proposed in the time domain, we can see that the first two identified magnetic dipoles represent the equivalent models of two diodes. The third identified source represents the equivalent radiation of the transformer. In fact, this last source has a center situated at coordinates X_d = 0.10 cm, Y_d = −0.21 cm and Z_d = −1.21 cm of the studied structure. It presents the coordinates of the transformer position in the studied card, as depicted in **Figure 11**.

Figure 12 gives a spatial representation of the equivalent dipoles identified by our proposed approach as well as the different shapes of the excitation currents of the source dipoles.

The parameters of the equivalent model obtained by the proposed method are shown in **Table 3**.

Hence, it presents the case where the emitted disturbances of the tracks are very low compared to that of the components. Finally, we notice that the components of the power electronics card represent the majority of the radiation of the studied structure as illustrated in **Figure 13**.

In order to study these electromagnetic disturbances, we present in **Figure 14** the measured magnetic near-field cartographies at different moments.

Identified dipoles	M_{di} (A m^2)	[X_{di} Y_{di} Z_{di}] (cm)	$\theta_i(0)$	$\varphi_i(0)$
#1	3.12 e − 7	1.46/−1.33/−0.645	0.57	7.45
#2	4.42 e − 7	1.42/−0.32/−0.79	58.47	−132.99
#3	1.12 e − 6	0.10/−0.21/−1.21	9.17	9.74
#4	2.96 e − 7	−0.96/0.20/−0.61	−11.46	−17.77
#5	3.86 e − 7	−1.34/1.19/−0.65	−43.56	128.98
#6	1.48 e − 7	−0.35/−1.08/−0.37	72.80	179.42
#7	1.90 e − 8	−1.36/−0.74/−0.62	83.12	8.85

Table 3.
Model parameters obtained by the proposed method.

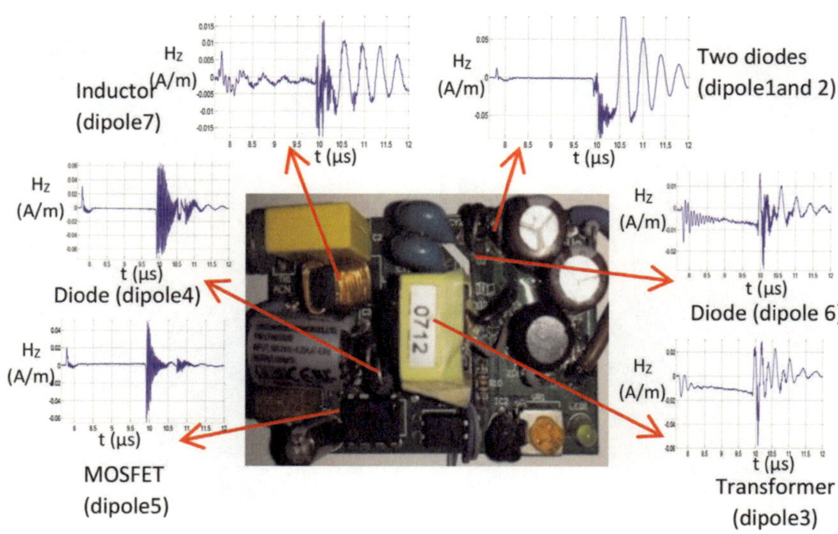

Figure 13.
Internal structure of studied converter and radiations emitted by different radiating components.

By analyzing **Figure 14**, we notice that the all sources do not appear at the same time. This is due to the time lag at the level of the electrical quantities passing through the different elements of the studied structure. This kind of transient phenomena is not easy to identify in the frequency analysis where the equivalent sources appear at the time such as presented in [8]. For a diagnostic study, where it is desired to control the good functioning of a sensitive element in a power electronics card, this type of time analysis becomes an effective alternative that enables

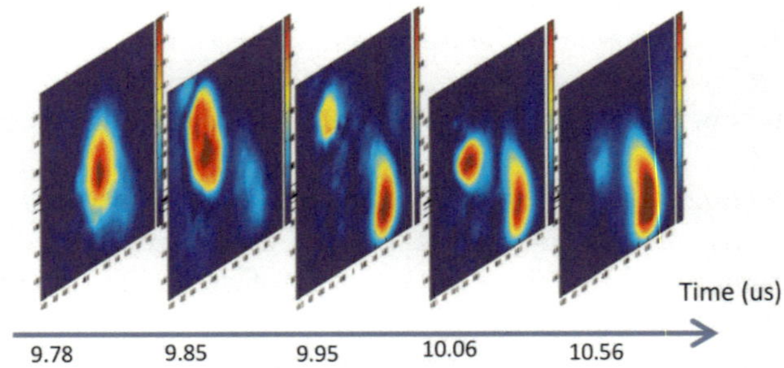

Figure 14.
Cartographies of the magnetic near field at various moments.

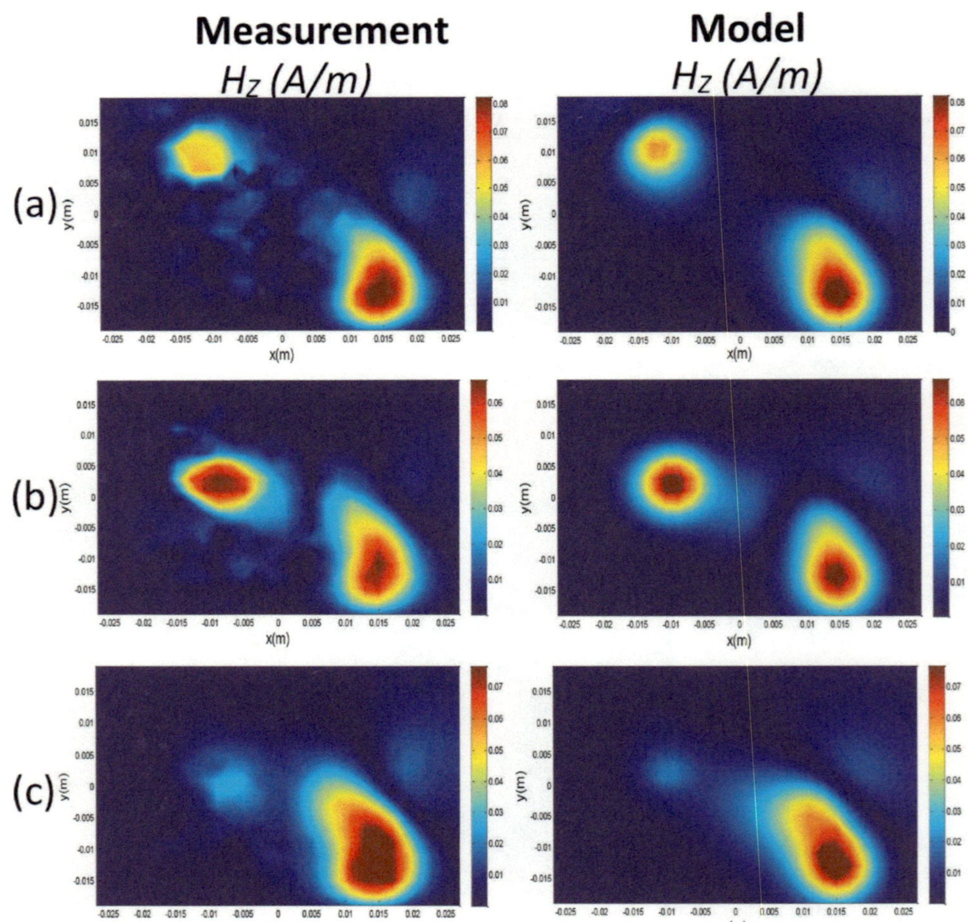

Figure 15.
Measured magnetic field and estimated one (a) t = 9.95 μs, (b) t = 10.06 μs, (c) t = 10.56 μs.

us to use the electromagnetic signature based on the temporal near field for the disgnosis of some components of the card. The electromagnetic inverse method in the time domain can therefore be used as a nonintrusive method of diagnosing and detecting defects in converter circuits. We cite for example the case of clamping-diode faults in a three-level NPC inverter circuit using the temporal analysis of the near magnetic field. Actually, the failure of a diode results in a modification during a delimited sequence at each period, from the temporal cartography of the magnetic field measured in a zone close to the circuit.

In **Figure 15**, we present at various moments a comparison between the measured cartographies of the normal magnetic field component (H_z) and the calculated cartographies using the parameters of the equivalent model obtained by the electromagnetic inverse method proposed in the time domain.

By examining the results got, we notice a good agreement between these cartographies. This demonstrates that the suggested method can identify with very good accuracy all radiating sources of the circuit.

6. Validation of identified equivalent model

In order to validate the found equivalent model, we measured the tangential component of the magnetic field (H_x measured) and subsequently we compared it with that is calculated (H_x estimated) by exploiting the optimized parameters of the

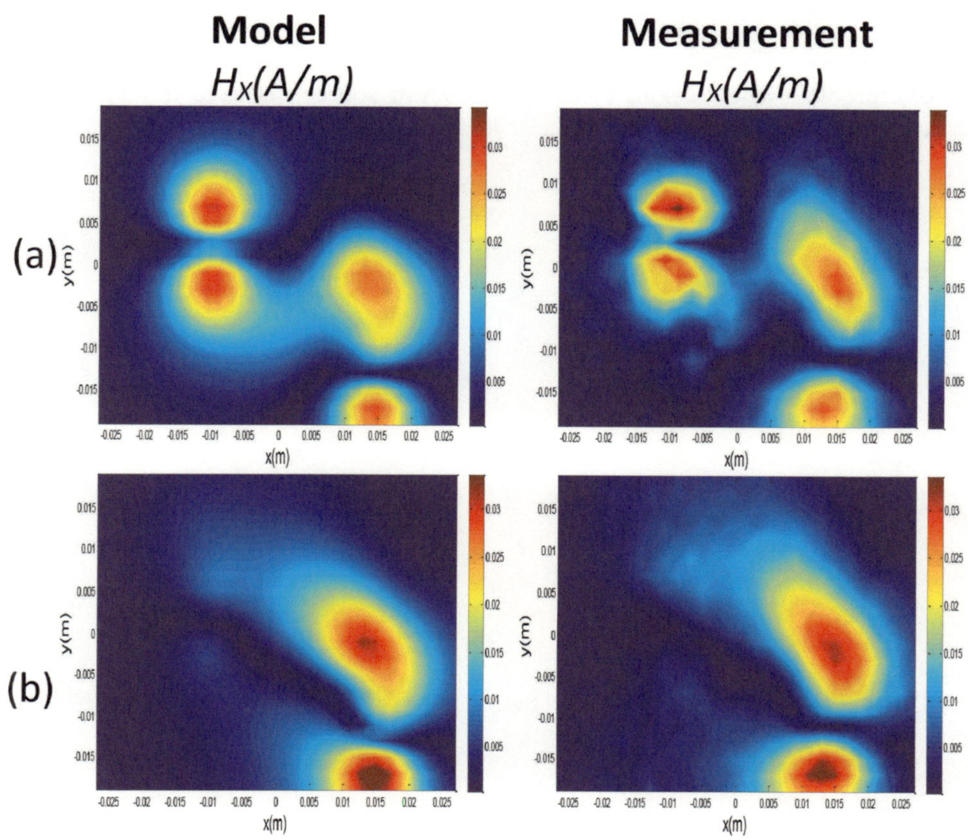

Figure 16.
Comparison of estimated near-field cartographies (H_x) to those measured at (a) t = 10.06 μs and (b) t = 10.47 μs.

equivalent radiating sources. In two distinct instants (t_1 = 10.06 μs and t_2 = 10.47 μs), a comparison between the measured and estimated of the near-field cartographies is presented in **Figure 16**.

According to the results presented in the previous figure, the magnetic near field calculated using the identified model parameters is in good agreement with the measured magnetic near field. These results confirm the existence of the equivalent sources network found by the electromagnetic inverse method in the time domain. Thus, the results showed that the proposed method guarantees the uniqueness of the solution. This confirms the effectiveness of the proposed approach for model the high-power structures where the radiated emissions are very high.

7. Conclusion

The frequency domain electromagnetic inverse method has several disadvantages when modeling radiation of power electronics systems. These disadvantages are mainly related to the radiation over a broad frequency band. To overcome these drawbacks, we have proposed in this chapter the use of the time domain electromagnetic inverse method. This novel method has been applied to identify the equivalent radiating sources of an AC-DC converter. The radiating sources are identified by exploiting the measurements of the vertical component (H_z) of the magnetic field performed over the studied converter. This equivalent model has been validated by using the measurements of the tangential component of the near magnetic field (H_x). The good agreement between the calculated results by using the optimized parameters of the equivalent model and the experimental results measured above the studied structure highlights the robustness of the suggested inverse problem when seeking equivalent radiating sources for industrial systems creating transient signals.

Author details

Bessem Zitouna* and Jaleleddine Ben Hadj Slama
Laboratory of Advanced Technology and Intelligent Systems (LATIS), National Engineering School of Sousse (ENISo), University of Sousse, Tunisia

*Address all correspondence to: bessem.zitouna@yahoo

References

[1] Saidi S, Ben Hadj Slama J. Analysis and modeling of power MOSFET radiation. Progress In Electromagnetics Research M. 2013;**31**:247-262

[2] Labiedh W, Ben Hadj Slama J. Analysis and modeling of the magnetic near fields emitted by an IGBT and by a power diode generic radiating model for active components. In: International Conference on Electrical Sciences and Technologies in Maghreb (CISTEM). 2014. pp. 1-6

[3] Levy P-E, Gautier C, Costa F, Revol B, Labarre C. Accurate modeling of radiated electromagnetic field by a coil with atoroidalferromagnetic core. IEEE Transactions on Electromagnetic Compatibility. 2013;**55**(5):825-833

[4] Shim HW, Hubing T. A closed-form expression for estimating radiated emissions from the power planes in a populated printed circuit board. IEEE Transactions on Electromagnetic Compatibility. 2006;**48**(1):74-81

[5] Tong X, Thomas DWP, Nothofer A, Sewell P, Christopoulos C. Modeling electromagnetic emissions from printed circuit boards in closed environments using equivalent dipoles. IEEE Transactions on Electromagnetic Compatibility. 2010;**52**(2):462-470

[6] Beghou L, Liu Y, Pichon L, Costa F. Synthesis of equivalent 3-D models from near field measurements application to the EMC of power printed circuits boards. IEEE Transactions on Magnetics. 2009;**45**(3):1650-1653

[7] Beghou L, Costa F, Pichon L. Detection of electromagnetic radiations sources at the switching time scale using an inverse problem-based resolution method—Application to power electronic circuits. IEEE Transactions on Electromagnetic Compatibility. 2015; **57**(1)

[8] Saidi S, Ben Hadj Slama J. A near-field technique based on PZMI, GA, and ANN: Application to power electronics systems. IEEE Transactions on Electromagnetic Compatibility. 2014; **56**(4):784-791

[9] Benyoubi F, Pichon L, Bensetti M, Le Bihan Y, Feliach M. An efficient method for modeling the magnetic field emissions of power electronic equipment from magnetic near field measurements. IEEE Transactions on Electromagnetic Compatibility. 2017; **59**(2):609-617

[10] Liu Y, Ravelo B, Fernandez-Lopez P. Modeling of magnetic near-field radiated by electronic devices disturbed by transient signals with complex form. Applied Physics Research. 2012;**4**(1): 3-18

[11] Liu Y, Ravelo B. Application of near-field emission processing for microwave circuits under ultra-short duration perturbations. Advanced Electromagnetics. 2012;**1**(3)

[12] Liu Y, Ravelo B. Fully time-domain scanning of EM near-field radiated by RF circuits. Progress In Electromagnetics Research B. 2014;**57**: 21-46

[13] Rioult J, Seethramdoo D, Heddebaut M. Novel electromagnetic field measuring instrument with real-time visualization. Proc IEEE Int. Symp. EMC, Austin, Texas, USA. 2009:133-138

[14] Ravelo B, Liu Y, Slama JBH. Time-domain planar near-field/near-field transform with PWS operations. The European Physical Journal Applied Physics. 2011;**53**(03):1-8

[15] Liu Y, Ravelo B, Jastrzebski AK, Hadj Slama JB. Calculation of the time domain z-component of the EM-near-field from the x- and y-components. In:

41st European Microwave Conference. 2011

[16] Zitouna B, Ben Hadj Slama J. Enhancement of time-domain electromagnetic inverse method for modeling circuits radiations. IEEE Transactions on Electromagnetic Compatibility. 2016;**58**(2):534-542

[17] Kim Y-H, Jang J-W, Shin S-C, Chung-Yuen W. Weighted-efficiency enhancement control for a photovoltaic AC module interleaved flyback inverter using a synchronous rectifier. IEEE Transactions on Power Electronics. 2014;**29**(12)

[18] Chen Y, Chang C, Yang P. A novel primary-side controlled universal-input AC-DC LED driver based on a source-driving control scheme. IEEE Transactions on Power Electronics. 2015;**30**(8)

[19] Zhu Z, Wu Q, Wang Z. Self-compensating OCP control scheme for primary-side controlled flyback AC/DC converters. IEEE Transactions on Power Electronics. 2017;**32**(5)

[20] Gao X, Fan J, Zhang Y, Kajbaf H, Pommerenke D. Far-field prediction using only magnetic near-field scanning for EMI test. IEEE Transactions on Electromagnetic Compatibility. 2014; **56**(6):1335-1343

[21] Ravelo B. E-field extraction from H-near-field in time-domain by using PWS method. Progress In Electromagnetics Research B. 2010;**25**:171-189

[22] Liu Y, Ravelo B, Jastrzebski AK. Calculation of time-domain near field $E_{x,y,z}(t)$ from $H_{x,y}(t)$ with PWS and FFT transforms. In: Proc. Int. Symp. Electromagn. Compat.; 17-20 September 2012; Roma, Italy. 2012. pp. 1-6

[23] Saidi S, Slama JBH. Effect of genetic algorithm parameters on convergence of the electromagnetic inverse method. In: 8th International Multi-Conference on Systems, Signals & Devices (SSD); 22-25 March 2011; Sousse, Tunisia. 2011. pp. 1-5

Chapter 9

Mathematical Fundamentals of a Diagnostic Method by Long Nonlinear Waves for the Structured Media

Vyacheslav Vakhnenko, Dmitri Vengrovich and Alexandre Michtchenko

Abstract

We have proven that the long wave with finite amplitude responds to the structure of the medium. The heterogeneity in a medium structure always introduces additional nonlinearity in comparison with the homogeneous medium. At the same time, a question appears on the inverse problem, namely, is there sufficient information in the wave field to reconstruct the structure of the medium? It turns out that the knowledge on the evolution of nonlinear waves enables us to form the theoretical fundamentals of the diagnostic method to define the characteristics of a heterogeneous medium using the long waves of finite amplitudes (inverse problem). The mass contents of the particular components can be denoted with specified accuracy by this diagnostic method.

Keywords: diagnostics, nonlinear waves, inverse problem, asymptotic model, structured medium

1. Introduction

Natural media, in the general case, should not be treated as structureless. The experiments have shown that the intrinsic structure of a medium influences the wave motions [1–8]. Existing inhomogeneities complicate the problem and, at the same time, are fully manifested under the propagation of nonlinear waves. The principal part of the problem is associated with the phenomena caused by the nonlinear behavior of natural media, in particular, more substantial increase of nonlinear effects in structured media than that in homogeneous ones [1–5, 7].

2. The model notion of the medium with structure

The wave processes in heterogeneous media are usually described in terms of more or less complicated models. Under the conditions of local equilibrium, the media are traditionally modelled irrespective of their structure. In the framework of continuum mechanics, the known idealization of a real medium as a homogeneous one has been relatively successful in the description of wave processes (see, e.g., [9–11]). The continuum models are commonly applied to the mixtures whose dispersive dissipative properties are treated with regard to the interactions between the components [12–15]. On this level, the media are modelled in the framework of a homogeneous elastic, viscous elastic, and elastic-plastic media. In this case, the features of the medium structure are taken into account indirectly through the kinetic parameters (relaxation time, viscous coefficients, etc.) [4–6, 10, 12–15].

The model of multi-velocity interpenetratable continua was developed in terms of classical continuum mechanics [16] and statistical physics in order to describe the dynamical behavior of multicomponent media. A fundamental assumption in the theory of mixtures [15] reproduces the assumption in the model of multi-velocity interpenetratable continua [16], namely, that the particles of the existing components occupy each microvolume. The equations of motion for each component involve the terms describing the mass, force, and energy interactions between the components. The problem is complicated by the necessity to employ, in the general case, the experimental data for establishing theoretical relations between the macro parameters at the component interaction level. Moreover, if the component interaction is determined, then these models would be indispensable in the theory of multicomponent media.

In all the models mentioned, the formalism of continuum mechanics is based on the principle of local action as well as on the generalization of the mechanics laws relating the point mass to the continuum [11].

When going from the integral equations to differential balance equations, the existence of a differentially small microvolume dv is assumed. On the one hand, this volume is so small that the mechanics laws of the point can be extended to the whole microvolume. On the other hand, the volume contains so many structural elements of the medium that, in this sense, it can be regarded as macroscopic one despite its smallness as compared to the entire volume occupied by the medium. So, the passage to the differential balance equations is based on the assumption that microstructural scales ε are small as compared to the characteristic macroscopic scale of the λ and the passage should be made to the limiting case $\varepsilon/\lambda \to 0$. Contraction of the volume dv to the point is in the general case correct for continuous functions [11, 15]. This means that all points within the differentially small volume are equivalent. Hence, for the case of a mixture, the equivalence of the points implies that field characteristics should be averaged over dv. Hence, it is assumed that the equations of motion can be written in terms of average density, mass velocity, and pressure of each component. We note that these models do not contain the exact sizes of components.

The application of the models of a homogeneous medium to the description of the dynamical wave processes in a structured natural medium is associated with specific fundamental difficulties [3, 4, 6, 8]. In what follows, we treat the medium structure at the macrolevel. We abandon the assumption that the differentially small volume dv contains all the components of the medium. Nevertheless, we consider the long-wave approach with the wavelength λ much higher than the characteristic length of the medium structure ε. We consider a structured medium (**Figure 1**) in which separated components are considered as a homogeneous medium (the differentially small volume dv is much smaller than the characteristic size of a particular component ε).

Within continuum mechanics [17], the known idealization of a real medium as homogeneous is widely used for modelling their dynamic behavior. In these models, the effect of heterogeneity is taken into account indirectly throughout the kinetic parameters such as a viscous coefficient and relaxation time. The inner processes, in this case, are manifested through dispersive dissipative properties of a medium.

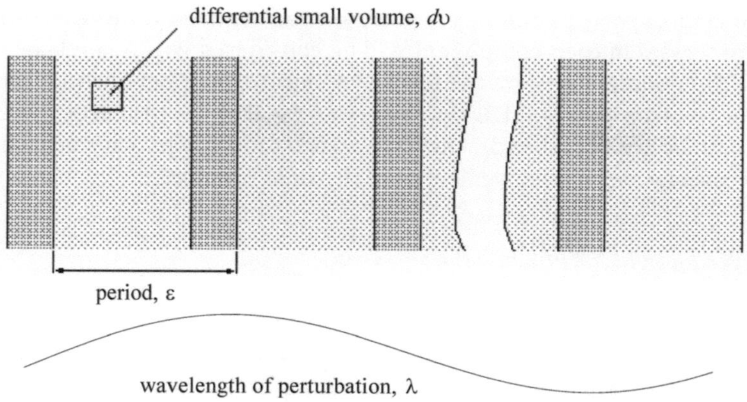

Figure 1.
Model of the layered medium with two homogeneous components in the period.

Traditionally, it was considered that in heterogeneous media with wavelength appreciably exceeding the size of the structural heterogeneities, the perturbations propagate in the same way as inhomogeneous media [9, 10, 15]. However, this statement should be proven, and we shall show that this approximation is not universally correct. In general case, the wave propagation cannot be described in terms of the average characteristics (continuum model).

The properties of a medium deviate from the equilibrium state under the propagation of intensive waves. Moreover, an unperturbed medium can be in one of the unstable stationary states. So, a geophysical medium, within a current physical concept, is an open thermodynamic system, which substantially influences the exchanges of energy and mass. Thus, a description of open systems should take into account the peculiarities of their inner structure, dynamical processes occurring on the level of structural elements. What is more, the state of media under the action of high-frequency wave perturbations departs from equilibrium, and, thus, the behavior of media cannot be described in the framework of equilibrium thermodynamics. Consequently, there is a necessity to develop new mathematical models to take into account the nonlinear wave perturbations and irreversible inner exchange processes.

3. Asymptotic averaged model for structured medium

We describe the wave processes in nonequilibrium heterogeneous media in terms of an asymptotic averaged model [18–22]. The obtained integral differential system of equations cannot be reduced to the average terms (pressure, mass velocity, specific volume) and contains the terms with characteristic sizes of individual components.

3.1 Background and initial equations

The most straightforward heterogeneous media for which the effect of the structure can be analyzed are media with a regular structure. Features of the propagation of long-wave perturbations will be investigated by using, as an example, a periodic medium under conditions of equality of stresses and mass velocities on the boundaries of neighboring components. It is supposed that the microstructure elements of medium dv (see **Figure 1**) are large enough that it is possible to submit to the laws of classical continuum mechanics for each component. At the same time, the inner processes in each component will be considered within a relaxation approach. The notions based on the relaxation nature of a phenomenon are regarded to be promising and fruitful. We consider that the properties of the medium, such as density, sound velocity, and relaxation time, vary periodically (although this assumption is unessential in the final result).

3.1.1 Motion equations for individual component

The analysis of wave motions is based on the hydrodynamic approach. This restriction can be imposed for the modelling of nonlinear waves in water-saturated soils, bubble media, aerosols, etc. [13]. The set of acceptable media could be extended to solid media where the powerful loads are studied in the condition that the strength and plasticity of the material can be neglected [23]. In the hydrodynamic approach, we have considered the media without tangential stresses, while there are equalities of the stresses as well as of mass velocities on boundaries of neighboring components. Also, we assume that the medium is barotropic. The individual components of the medium are considered to be described by the classical equations of hydrodynamics. In the Lagrangian coordinate system (l, t), the equations of one-dimensional motion for each component have the form

$$\begin{gathered} \frac{\partial r^{\nu}}{\partial l^{\nu}} = \frac{V}{V_0}, \quad u = \frac{\partial r}{\partial t}, \\ \frac{\partial u}{\partial t} + V_0 \left(\frac{r}{l}\right)^{\nu-1} \frac{\partial p}{\partial l} = 0. \end{gathered} \tag{1}$$

The equation of continuity can also be used in the alternative form

$$\frac{\partial V}{\partial t} - \nu V_0 \frac{\partial r^{\nu-1} u}{\partial l^{\nu}} = 0. \tag{2}$$

Here $V = \rho^{-1}$ is the specific volume; ν is a parameter of symmetry, where $\nu = 1$ is planar symmetry, $\nu = 2$ is cylindrical one, and $\nu = 3$ is spherical one; and index 0 relates to the initial state. The other notations are those that are generally accepted.

Conditions for matching are the equality of mass velocities and pressures on the boundaries of the components:

$$[u] = 0, \qquad [p] = 0. \tag{3}$$

3.1.2 Dynamic state equation

Considering the models of a relaxing medium as more general than the equilibrium models for describing the evolution of high-gradient waves, we will take into account the relaxing processes for each component. Thermodynamic equilibrium is disturbed owing to the propagation of fast perturbations in a medium. There are processes of the interaction that tend to return the equilibrium. The parameters characterizing this interaction are referred to as the inner variables, unlike the macro parameters such as the pressure p, mass velocity u, and density ρ. In essence, the change of macro parameters caused by the changes of inner parameters is a relaxation process. From the nonequilibrium thermodynamics standpoint, the models of a relaxing medium are more general than the equilibrium models for describing the wave propagation.

An equilibrium state equation of a barotropic medium is one-parameter equation. As a result of relaxation, an additional variable ξ (inner parameter) appears in the state equation. It defines the completeness of the relaxation process:

$$p = p(\rho, \xi). \tag{4}$$

There are two limiting cases:

i. The lack of relaxation (inner interaction processes are frozen) $\xi = 1$,

$$p = p(\rho, 1) = p_f(\rho). \tag{5}$$

ii. The relaxation complete (there is the local thermodynamic equilibrium) $\xi = 0$,

$$p = p(\rho, 0) = p_e(\rho). \tag{6}$$

The equations of state (5) and (6) are considered to be known. These relationships enable us to introduce the sound velocities for fast processes:

$$c_f^2 = dp_f/d\rho \tag{7}$$

and for slow processes

$$c_e^2 = dp_e/d\rho. \tag{8}$$

The slow and fast processes are compared, utilizing relaxation time τ_p. The dynamic state equation is written down in the form of the first-order differential equation:

$$\tau_p\left(\frac{d\rho}{dt} - c_f^{-2}\frac{dp}{dt}\right) + (\rho - \rho_e) = 0. \tag{9}$$

The equilibrium equations of state are considered to be known:

$$\rho_e - \rho_0 = \int_{p_0}^{p} c_e^{-2} dp. \tag{10}$$

Clearly, for the fast processes $(\omega\tau_p \gg 1)$, we have the relation (5), and for the slow ones $(\omega\tau_p \ll 1)$, we obtain (6).

The substantiation of Eq. (9) within the framework of the thermodynamics of irreversible processes has been given in [17, 24–26]. As far as we know, the first work in this field was paper by Mandelshtam and Leontovich (see Section 81 in [17]). We note that the mechanisms of the exchange processes are not explicitly defined when deriving Eq. (9), and the thermodynamic and kinetic parameters appear only in this equation. These characteristics can be found experimentally.

The phenomenological approach for describing the relaxation processes in hydrodynamics has been developed in many publications [13, 17, 26]. The dynamic equation of state was used (a) for describing the propagation of sound waves in a relaxing medium [17], (b) for taking into account the exchange processes within media (gas-solid particles) [26], and (c) for studying wave fields in gas-liquid media and in soil [13]. In most works, the equation of state has been derived from the concept of precise mechanism for the inner process. Within the context of mixture theory, Biot [12] attempted to account for the nonequilibrium in velocities between components directly in the equations of motion in the form of dissipative terms.

We assume that the relaxation time and sound velocities do not depend on time, but they are functions of pressure and the individual properties of the components. This means that in the process of a relaxation interaction, we can take into account the exchange of moment and heat but not that of mass. The dynamic equation of state determines the features of the intrastructural interaction for each component.

The equations of motion (1) have been written in the Lagrangian coordinate system. The necessity of such a description stems from the fact that the dynamic equation of state (9) has been written to the mass element of a medium. Besides, the use of the Lagrangian coordinates is essential for the application of the method of asymptotic averaging, since in these coordinates, the structure is independent of a wave process.

3.2 Asymptotic averaged system of equations

A regularity of structure and a nonlinearity of long-wave processes investigated here specify the choice of mathematical methods. One way of studying this heterogeneous medium is based on a method of asymptotic averaging of equations with high-oscillating coefficients [20, 27–30]. The essence of this method consists in the application of a multiscale method in combination with a space averaging. In accordance with this method, the mass space coordinate $m = l^\nu / V_0$ is divided into two independent coordinates: slow coordinate s and fast one ξ, wherein

$$m = s + \varepsilon\xi, \qquad \frac{\partial}{\partial m} = \frac{\partial}{\partial s} + \varepsilon^{-1}\frac{\partial}{\partial \xi}. \tag{11}$$

The slow coordinate s corresponds to a global change of the wave field and s is a constant value during a period, while the fast coordinate ξ traces the variations of a field in the structure period. The dependent functions are presented as a degree series over the structure period ε

$$\begin{aligned} V(m,t) &= V^{(0)}(s,t,\xi) + \varepsilon V^{(1)}(s,t,\xi) + \varepsilon^2 V^{(2)}(s,t,\xi) + \dots \\ p(m,t) &= p^{(0)}(s,t,\xi) + \varepsilon p^{(1)}(s,t,\xi) + \varepsilon^2 p^{(2)}(s,t,\xi) + \dots \\ u(m,t) &= u^{(0)}(s,t,\xi) + \varepsilon u^{(1)}(s,t,\xi) + \varepsilon^2 u^{(2)}(s,t,\xi) + \dots \; . \\ r^\nu(m,t) &= (r^\nu)^{(0)}(s,t,\xi) + \varepsilon (r^\nu)^{(1)}(s,t,\xi) + \varepsilon^2 (r^\nu)^{(2)}(s,t,\xi) + \dots \end{aligned} \tag{12}$$

where $p^{(i)}$, $u^{(i)}$, $V^{(i)}$, and $r^{(i)}$ are defined as the one-period functions of ξ. In the Lagrangian mass coordinates the period is a constant which allows the averaging procedure to be performed.

We now will prove that $p^{(0)} = p^{(0)}(s,t)$, $p^{(1)} = p^{(1)}(s,t)$, $u^{(0)} = u^{(0)}(s,t)$, and $(r^\nu)^{(0)} = (r^\nu)^{(0)}(s,t)$ are independent of the fast variable ξ. Indeed, after substitution of Eqs. (11) and (12) into the initial equations of motion, we obtain

$$
\begin{aligned}
&-\varepsilon^{-1}\frac{\partial (r^{\nu})^{(0)}}{\partial \xi}+\varepsilon^{0}\left(\frac{\partial (r^{\nu})^{(0)}}{\partial s}-\frac{\partial (r^{\nu})^{(1)}}{\partial \xi}-V^{(0)}\right)+\ldots=0,\\
&\varepsilon^{0}\left(u^{(0)}-\frac{\partial r^{(0)}}{\partial t}\right)+\ldots=0,\\
&-\varepsilon^{-1}\nu(r^{\nu-1})^{(0)}\frac{\partial p^{(0)}}{\partial \xi}+\varepsilon^{0}\left(\frac{\partial u^{(0)}}{\partial t}+\nu\left(r^{\nu-1}\right)^{(0)}\frac{\partial p^{(0)}}{\partial s}+\nu\left(r^{\nu-1}\right)^{(1)}\frac{\partial p^{(0)}}{\partial \xi}+\nu\left(r^{\nu-1}\right)^{(0)}\frac{\partial p^{(1)}}{\partial \xi}\right)+\ldots=0,\\
&-\varepsilon^{-1}\nu\frac{\partial (r^{\nu-1})^{(0)}u^{(0)}}{\partial \xi}+\varepsilon^{0}\left(\frac{\partial V^{(0)}}{\partial t}+\nu\frac{\partial (r^{\nu-1})^{(0)}u^{(0)}}{\partial s}-\nu\frac{\partial (r^{\nu-1})^{(1)}u^{(0)}}{\partial \xi}-\nu\frac{\partial (r^{\nu-1})^{(0)}u^{(1)}}{\partial \xi}\right)+\ldots=0,
\end{aligned}
\tag{13}
$$

According to the general theory of the asymptotic method, the terms of equal powers of ε should vanish independently of each other. Thus, $\partial p^{(0)}/\partial\xi = 0$, $\partial u^{(0)}/\partial\xi = 0$, and $\partial(r^{\nu-1})^{(0)}/\partial\xi = 0$, i.e., $p^{(0)} = p^{(0)}(s,t)$, $u^{(0)} = u^{(0)}(s,t)$, and $r^{(0)} = r^{(0)}(s,t)$, are independent of ξ. Furthermore

$$
\begin{aligned}
&\frac{\partial (r^{\nu})^{(0)}}{\partial s}+\frac{\partial (r^{\nu})^{(1)}}{\partial \xi}=V^{(0)},\\
&u^{(0)}=\frac{\partial r^{(0)}}{\partial t},\\
&\frac{\partial u^{(0)}}{\partial t}+\nu\left(r^{\nu-1}\right)^{(0)}\frac{\partial p^{(0)}}{\partial s}+\nu\left(r^{\nu-1}\right)^{(0)}\frac{\partial p^{(1)}}{\partial \xi}=0,\\
&\frac{\partial V^{(0)}}{\partial t}-\nu\frac{\partial (r^{\nu-1})^{(0)}u^{(0)}}{\partial s}-\nu\frac{\partial (r^{\nu-1})^{(1)}u^{(0)}}{\partial \xi}-\nu\frac{\partial (r^{\nu-1})^{(0)}u^{(1)}}{\partial \xi}=0.
\end{aligned}
\tag{14}
$$

Thus, we can average the equations during the period ξ. We define $\langle\cdot\rangle = \int_0^1(\cdot)d\xi$ and perform the normalization $\int_0^1 d\xi = 1$. Since $p^{(1)}$, $u^{(1)}$, and $r^{(1)}$ are periodic, the integrals can be calculated as $\langle\partial p^{(1)}/\partial\xi\rangle = 0$, $\langle\partial u^{(1)}/\partial\xi\rangle = 0$, and $\langle\partial r^{(1)}/\partial\xi\rangle = 0$. Moreover, as $\langle u^{(0)}\rangle = u^{(0)}$, $\langle p^{(0)}\rangle = p^{(0)}$ than $\partial p^{(1)}/\partial\xi = 0$. This means that $p^{(1)}$ does not also depend on ξ. After integrating over the structure period the equations containing the value of zero order of ε, we obtain the averaged system

$$
\begin{aligned}
&\frac{\partial (r^{\nu})^{(0)}}{\partial s}=\left\langle V^{(0)}\right\rangle,\\
&u^{(0)}=\frac{\partial r^{(0)}}{\partial t},\\
&\frac{\partial u^{(0)}}{\partial t}+\nu\left(r^{\nu-1}\right)^{(0)}\frac{\partial p^{(0)}}{\partial s}=0,\\
&\frac{\partial \left\langle V^{(0)}\right\rangle}{\partial t}-\nu\frac{\partial (r^{\nu-1})^{(0)}u^{(0)}}{\partial s}=0
\end{aligned}
\tag{15}
$$

with the averaged equation of state

$$
d\left\langle V^{(0)}\right\rangle=-\left\langle\frac{\left(V^{(0)}\right)^{2}}{c_{f}^{2}}\right\rangle dp-\left\langle\frac{V^{(0)}}{\tau_{p}V_{e}(p^{(0)})}\left(V^{(0)}-V_{e}\left(p^{(0)}\right)\right)\right\rangle dt. \tag{16}
$$

Unlike the values $u^{(0)}, p^{(0)}, p^{(1)}$, and $r^{(0)}$, the specific volume $V^{(0)}$ is a function of ξ. Hereafter, we will consider only the zero approximation of the equations, and, therefore, the upper index 0 is omitted. Choosing the wavelength λ to be large enough, we can always reduce the effect to zero from other approximation terms.

The averaged system of Eqs. (15) and (16) is an integrodifferential one and, in the general case, is not reduced to the averaged variables p, u, and $\langle V^{(0)} \rangle$. The derivation of Eqs. (15) and (16) relates to a rigorous periodic medium. However, it may be shown that Eqs. (15) and (16) are also relevant to media with a quasiperiodic structure. Indeed, the pressure p and the mass velocity u are independent of the fast variable ξ. Hence on a microscale ξ, the action is statically uniform (waveless) over the whole period of the medium structure, while on the slow scale s, the action of perturbation is manifested by the wave motion of the medium. On a microlevel, the behavior of medium adheres only to the thermodynamic laws. There is a mechanical equilibrium. On a macrolevel, the motion of the medium is described by the wave dynamics laws for averaged variables. Mathematically, in the zero-order case of ε, the size of the period is infinitesimal ($\varepsilon \to 0$). This signifies that the location of particular components in the period is irrelevant. Eqs. (15) and (16) do not change their form if the components are broken and/or change their location in an elementary cell. This means that Eqs. (15) and (16) describe the motion of any quasiperiodic (statistical heterogeneous) medium which has a constant mass content of components on the microlevel and the location of these components within the cell is not important.

In the case of nonlinear wave propagation, the individual components suffer different compressions. The structure of the medium is changed, with the result that the averaged specific volume $\langle V \rangle$ is changed. This change differs from the change of the specific volume for homogeneous medium under the same loading. Thus, the structure of medium is manifested in the wave motion, despite the fact that the equations of motion (15) (but not the equation of state) are written down for the averaged values u, p, and $\langle V \rangle$ only.

3.3 System of equations in Eulerian coordinates

In certain cases of theoretical analysis, it is more convenient to use the Eulerian coordinate system. The immediate employment of a method of the asymptotic averaging in Eulerian variables is impossible because of the variability of the microstructure sizes. However, from the zero approximation in the equations of motion (11), which are presented by the averaged values p, u, and $\langle V \rangle$, the equations can be rewritten in the Eulerian system of coordinates (r, t_E) utilizing a transformation from the Lagrangian system (s, t) [18–22]:

$$r = r(s,t), \quad t_E = t. \tag{17}$$

There is an essential presumption that the velocity of the particle in the zero approximation is constant throughout of the structure, and, consequently, we can describe an averaged trajectory for the particle:

$$\left(\frac{\partial r(s,t)}{\partial t} \right)_s = u(s,t). \tag{18}$$

From the physical point of view, it is clear that the position of the particle is unambiguously defined by its coordinate and time:

$$dr^{\nu} = Ads + \nu r^{\nu-1} u dt, \qquad t_E = t. \tag{19}$$

From the mathematical point of view, this means that in the transformation (19) the value dr^ν is a total differential. Therefore, we must have

$$\frac{\partial A}{\partial t} = \frac{\partial \nu r^{\nu-1} u}{\partial s}. \tag{20}$$

This condition is satisfied if $A = \langle V \rangle$, because the equation converts into the continuity Eq. (15). We obtain the following transformation between Lagrangian and Eulerian systems of coordinates:

$$dr^\nu = \langle V \rangle ds + \nu r^{\nu-1} u dt, \qquad t_E = t. \tag{21}$$

It is reasonable to define the slow Lagrangian coordinate (non-mass one) as

$$R^\nu = s \langle V \rangle. \tag{22}$$

Eq. (15) in the Eulerian system of coordinates then take the form

$$\begin{aligned} &\frac{\partial \langle V \rangle^{-1}}{\partial t_E} + \frac{\partial r^{\nu-1} u \langle V \rangle^{-1}}{\partial r} = 0, \\ &\frac{\partial u}{\partial t_E} + u \frac{\partial u}{\partial r} + \langle V \rangle \frac{\partial p}{\partial r} = 0. \end{aligned} \tag{23}$$

It is convenient to determine the fast Eulerian coordinate ζ as

$$\left(\frac{\partial \zeta}{\partial \xi} \right)_t = \frac{\tilde{\rho}}{\rho(\xi)}. \tag{24}$$

It should be noted that the average density $\tilde{\rho}$ in the Eulerian coordinates is a value usually used for density. A chain of identities

$$\langle V \rangle = \int_0^1 V(\xi) d\xi = \int_0^1 V \frac{\rho}{\tilde{\rho}} d\zeta = \tilde{\rho}^{-1} \tag{25}$$

proves that $\langle V \rangle^{-1}$ is the average density of the medium in the Eulerian coordinates. Note that $\tilde{\rho} \neq \langle \rho \rangle$. The value $\tilde{\rho}$ is a real density. The value $\langle V \rangle$ is the specific volume averaged in units of mass over the period, and it is expressed as the ratio of the volume to the mass inside this volume. This value can be determined experimentally. At the same time, the averaged values p and u coincide in both Lagrangian and Eulerian systems of coordinates. Now the equations of motion (23) can be written in the usual form of the averaged density $\tilde{\rho}$.

The notation of the equations of motion in the averaged values enables us to suggest the method of the computer solution for the system of equations, where the integration step is restricted by the perturbation wavelength and not by the period of the structure [22]. Then the main computational problem associated with the smallness of the integration step can be avoided, and the equations of motion can be solved at a significant distance of wave propagation within a reasonable time.

3.4 Nonlinear waves

We will analyze the propagation of nonlinear waves in a structured medium. To make the results more clear, we will restrict our consideration to a nonrelaxation media $(c = c_f = c_e)$. The averaged equation of state in this case is simplified to the form

$$d\langle V\rangle = -\left\langle\frac{V^2}{c^2}\right\rangle dp, \tag{26}$$

and we can introduce an effective sound velocity by the formula

$$c_{\text{eff}} = \sqrt{\langle V\rangle^2 / \left\langle\frac{V^2}{c^2}\right\rangle}. \tag{27}$$

We obtain a traditional representation of the system of Eqs. (15) and (26).

The system of the equations is concerned in the hyperbolic type of a system. Now we restrict ourselves to the plane symmetry $(\nu = 1)$. Substituting the equation of state (26) into the equation of the continuity (the last equation in (15)), we get

$$\left\langle\frac{V^2}{c^2}\right\rangle \frac{\partial p}{\partial t} + \frac{\partial u}{\partial s} = 0. \tag{28}$$

The combination of this equation with the third equation in (15) $(\nu = 1)$ leads to the relationships

$$\left(\frac{\partial u}{\partial t} \pm \left\langle\frac{V^2}{c^2}\right\rangle^{1/2} \frac{\partial p}{\partial t}\right) \pm \left\langle\frac{V^2}{c^2}\right\rangle^{-1/2} \left(\frac{\partial u}{\partial s} \pm \left\langle\frac{V^2}{c^2}\right\rangle^{1/2} \frac{\partial p}{\partial s}\right) = 0. \tag{29}$$

From this relationship, it is seen that the averaged system of the equations pertains to the hyperbolic system. The equations for the characteristic in Lagrangian coordinates (mass space coordinate) have the forms

$$\frac{ds}{dt} = \pm\left\langle\frac{V^2}{c^2}\right\rangle^{-1/2}. \tag{30}$$

In characteristic, the relations are the following:

$$I_{\pm} = u \pm \int \left\langle\frac{V^2}{c^2}\right\rangle^{1/2} dp. \tag{31}$$

Analogously to the homogeneous medium, we call these relations as the Riemann invariants. The value (30) has the physical meaning, namely, it is the averaged velocity of the wave propagation in the Lagrangian coordinates. This velocity depends on pressure and integrally on a structure. Note the particular case. It is known that in vacuum the wave does not propagate. This result also follows formally from Eq. (30). The hyperbolism of a system points up that this system can describe the shock wave. The equations for the characteristic (30) and the Riemann invariants (31) are the integrodifferential equations, since they retain the variable $\langle V^2/c^2\rangle$, which depends on the properties of the structural elements in medium.

It should be noted that c_{eff} is not an averaged value, i.e., $c_{\text{eff}}^2 \neq \langle c^2\rangle$. Evidently, the structure of the medium introduces a certain contribution to the nonlinearity. In fact, even if $c_f \neq f(p)$, then in the general case, the value of c_{eff} is a function of pressure.

The system of Eq. (15) is hyperbolic ones, and this specifies the breaking solutions, which are shock waves. For the analysis of such solutions, it is necessary to present Eq. (15) in the form of integral conservation laws:

$$\oint[\langle V\rangle ds + udt] = 0, \quad \oint[uds - pdt] = 0. \tag{32}$$

Now we can quickly formulate the conditions on the shock front, when there is conservation of the fluxes of mass and impulse through the shock front:

$$(\langle V_1\rangle - \langle V_0\rangle)D + u_1 - u_0 = 0, \quad (u_1 - u_0)D - p_1 + p_0 = 0, \tag{33}$$

where indexes 0 and 1 relate to the parameters of the flow before and after the front, respectively. Hence, the formula for the averaged velocity of the shock front in terms of the Lagrangian variable D (dimension $[D]$ is kg/s) and the mass velocity u follow from the following relations:

$$\begin{aligned} D &= \sqrt{(p_1 - p_0)/(\langle V_0\rangle - \langle V_1\rangle)}, \\ u_1 - u_0 &= \sqrt{(p_1 - p_0)(\langle V_0\rangle - \langle V_1\rangle)}. \end{aligned} \tag{34}$$

These systems are not expressed in the average hydrodynamical terms; hence the dynamical behavior of the medium cannot be modelled by a homogeneous medium even for long waves, if they are nonlinear. The structure of the medium influences the nonlinear wave propagation.

In the next section, it will be proven that the heterogeneity of the medium structure always introduces additional nonlinearity that does not arise in a homogeneous medium. This effect makes it possible to formulate the theoretical grounds of a new diagnostic method that determines the characteristics of a heterogeneous medium with the use of finite-amplitude long waves (inverse problem). This diagnostic method can also be employed to find the mass contents of individual components.

4. Diagnostics of a medium by long nonlinear waves

In the previous section, we proved that the long wave with finite amplitude responds to the structure of medium. At the same time, a question appears, namely, is there sufficient information in the wave field to reconstruct the structure of medium? It turns out that the knowledge on the evolution of nonlinear waves enables one to define with certain accuracy the concentrations of medium components.

4.1 The increase of nonlinearity in medium with structure

In this section, we shall prove the statement that the structure of medium always exalts the nonlinear effects under the propagation of long waves. At first, let us consider the sound velocity in homogeneous c_{hom} and heterogeneous c_{eff} media. Now we will show that in the general case with pressure increase the velocity of the sound becomes higher in a structured medium than in a homogeneous one:

$$c_{\text{eff}} \geq c_{\text{hom}}. \tag{35}$$

For the sake of clarity, we consider a medium in which the sound velocities of individual components are independent of the pressure:

$$c \neq f(p), \quad dc/dp = 0. \tag{36}$$

The equality sign is fulfilled (a) for an initial pressure, by virtue of the normalization, and also (b) for a special structured medium in which the relation $V(\xi)/c^2(\xi)$ is not a function on the fast variable ξ. We must prove which case results in equality and which gives the inequality.

Let us write the relations (36) for homogeneous medium consisting only one component:

$$c_{\text{hom}} \neq f(p), \quad dc_{\text{hom}}/dp = 0. \tag{37}$$

For multicomponent medium, the derivative dc_{eff}/dp is defined from the relationship

$$\frac{dc_{\text{eff}}}{dp} = \frac{2\langle V\rangle}{\langle V^2/c^2\rangle}\left(\langle V\rangle\left\langle\frac{V^3}{c^4}\right\rangle - \left\langle\frac{V^2}{c^2}\right\rangle^2\right) \geq 0. \tag{38}$$

This last inequality follows from the well-known Cauchy-Schwarz inequality (see, e.g., [31]). Therefore, with the increase of pressure, the sound velocity c_{eff} increases. Consequently, we have the inequality (35) at $p \geq p_0$.

Moreover, at $p > p_0$ the shock adiabatic curve for the medium with a structure always lies above that for the homogeneous medium (they touch only at the initial point $p = p_0$):

$$\frac{d^2p}{d\langle V\rangle^2} \geq \left(\frac{d^2p}{dV^2}\right)_{\text{hom}}. \tag{39}$$

Indeed, a ratio of these derivatives is equal to

$$\begin{aligned} \frac{d^2p}{d\langle V\rangle^2} \Big/ \left(\frac{d^2p}{dV^2}\right)_{\text{hom}} &= \frac{\langle V^3/c^4\rangle\langle V^2/c^2\rangle^{-3}}{c_{\text{hom}}^2\langle V\rangle^3} \\ &= \frac{\langle V^3/c^4\rangle\langle V\rangle c_{\text{eff}}^2}{c_{\text{hom}}^2\langle V^2/c^2\rangle^2} \geq \frac{\langle V^3/c^4\rangle\langle V\rangle}{\langle V^2/c^2\rangle^2} \geq 1. \end{aligned} \tag{40}$$

Hence, a long wave with a finite amplitude responds to the structure of the medium, and the nonlinear effects increase as compared with those in the homogeneous medium. The nonlinearity takes place even if individual components are described by the linear evolution equation (i.e., at condition (36)).

The exception, as it was noted already, is a medium with the properties of structure $V(\xi)/c^2(\xi) \neq f(\xi)$. For this medium, only the equality sign is correct in the inequalities (35) and (39). Particular elements of the structure respond to the pressure variations, but the relative structure does not change, i.e., the ratio $V(\xi,p)/V(\xi,p_0)$ does not depend on ξ. In this case, the value $c_{\text{eff}} = \sqrt{\langle c^2\rangle}$ is an averaged characteristic (see Eq. (27)). Therefore, the system of equations may be presented using the averaged variables p, u, $\langle V\rangle$, and $c_{\text{eff}} = \sqrt{\langle c^2\rangle}$. Heterogeneity does not introduce an additional nonlinearity for this medium, and the structure of medium does not affect the wave motion.

In addition to the analysis of the sound velocity in homogeneous and heterogeneous media, we consider now the evolution equations with the nonlinear term and compare the coefficients of nonlinearity in these media. Let us derive the evolution equation with weak nonlinearity. First of all, we have to note that the mass velocity u is related to the pressure p by means of [22]

$$u = \int_{p_o}^{p} \sqrt{\langle V^2/c^2 \rangle} dp. \tag{41}$$

Functional dependence of an average specific value on the pressure increment $p' = p - p_0$ with the accuracy $O(p'2)$ can be presented as a series:

$$\langle V \rangle(p) = \langle V \rangle_0 + \left.\frac{d\langle V \rangle}{dp}\right|_{p=p_0} p' + \left.\frac{1}{2}\frac{d^2\langle V \rangle}{dp^2}\right|_{p=p_0} p'^2. \tag{42}$$

In this case, the system of Eq. (23) for planar symmetry $\nu = 1$ can be written as

$$\langle V \rangle_0 \frac{\partial u}{\partial x} + \left\langle \frac{V^2}{c^2} \right\rangle_0 \frac{\partial p'}{\partial t} - \left.\frac{1}{2}\frac{d^2\langle V \rangle}{dp^2}\right|_{p=p_0} \frac{\partial p'^2}{\partial t} = 0, \tag{43}$$

$$\frac{\partial u}{\partial t} + \langle V \rangle_0 \frac{\partial p'}{\partial x} = 0. \tag{44}$$

The relationship $u \frac{\partial p'}{\partial x} = p' \frac{\partial u}{\partial x}$ follows from Eq. (41) with the assumed accuracy $O\left(p'^2\right)$ and was used for derivation of the first equation. The evolution equation for one variable assumes the form

$$\langle V \rangle_0^2 \frac{\partial^2 p'}{\partial x^2} - \left\langle \frac{V^2}{c^2} \right\rangle_0 \frac{\partial^2 p'}{\partial t^2} + \left.\frac{1}{2}\frac{d^2\langle V \rangle}{dp^2}\right|_{p=p_0} \frac{\partial^2 p'^2}{\partial t^2} = 0. \tag{45}$$

Now let us consider the waves propagating in one direction, and then with the indicated accuracy, we can write (hereinafter index 0 is omitted):

$$-\frac{\sqrt{\langle V^2/c^2 \rangle}}{\langle V \rangle}\frac{\partial}{\partial t} + \frac{\partial}{\partial x} \to 2\frac{\partial}{\partial x} \tag{46}$$

(see, e.g., Section 93 in Ref. [17]). Thus, after factorization of Eq. (45) we get

$$\frac{\partial p'}{\partial t} + c_{\mathit{eff}} \frac{\partial p'}{\partial x} + \frac{1}{2}\langle V \rangle \left\langle \frac{V^2}{c^2} \right\rangle^{-3/2} \frac{d^2\langle V \rangle}{dp^2} p' \frac{\partial p'}{\partial x} = 0. \tag{47}$$

The coefficient of nonlinearity α_p for the structured medium, when the sound velocities in the individual components are independent of the pressure $c \neq f(p)$, can be presented as

$$\alpha_p \equiv \frac{1}{2}\langle V \rangle \left\langle \frac{V^2}{c^2} \right\rangle^{-3/2} \frac{d^2\langle V \rangle}{dp^2} = \frac{d(u + c_{\text{eff}})}{dp} = \langle V \rangle \left\langle \frac{V^3}{c^4} \right\rangle \left\langle \frac{V^2}{c^2} \right\rangle^{-3/2}. \tag{48}$$

For all cases we take $\alpha_p > 0$. For a homogeneous medium with $dc/dp = 0$, we have $\alpha_{p\,\mathrm{hom}} = V/c$.

In certain media the value V/c^2 does not change within the period. The individual elements of the structure respond to the pressure variations so that a relative structure does not change, i.e., the ratio $V(\xi, p)/V(\xi, p_0)$ does not depend on ξ. In this case, the value $c_{\mathrm{eff}} = \sqrt{\langle c^2 \rangle}$ derived from Eq. (27) is the averaged characteristic. Consequently, the system of equations may be presented in the averaged variables p, u, $\langle V \rangle$, and $c_{\mathrm{eff}} = \sqrt{\langle c^2 \rangle}$. Heterogeneity does not introduce the additional nonlinearity for these media. Such media behave like the homogeneous media under the action of the nonlinear wave perturbations.

For media, when the sound velocity is independent of the pressure ($c \neq f(p)$), it is possible to show that heterogeneity of the medium, in the general case, introduces the additional nonlinearity. Let us consider the ratio of the nonlinearity coefficients for heterogeneous and homogeneous media. In the space of dimensionless normalized variables, this implies that at $p = p_0$ we have $\langle V \rangle_0 = 1$ as well as $\langle V^2/c^2 \rangle_0 = 1$ for the compared media.

Using the conditions (27) we can obtain

$$\frac{\alpha_p}{\alpha_{p\,\mathrm{hom}}} = \langle V \rangle \left\langle \frac{V^3}{c^4} \right\rangle \left\langle \frac{V^2}{c^2} \right\rangle^{-2} \geq 1. \tag{49}$$

This inequality is the well-known Cauchy-Schwarz inequality (see formula (15.2-3) in Ref. [31]). Since $\langle V \rangle \geq 0$ and $\langle V/c^2 \rangle \geq 0$, we prove

$$\begin{aligned} \langle V \rangle \langle V^3/c^4 \rangle &\equiv \int_{-\infty}^{\infty} V d\xi \cdot \int_{-\infty}^{\infty} \frac{V^3}{c^4} d\xi = \int_{-\infty}^{\infty} \frac{V^2}{c^2} \left(\frac{V}{c^2} \right)^{-1} d\xi \cdot \int_{-\infty}^{\infty} \frac{V^2}{c^2} \frac{V}{c^2} d\xi \\ &\geq \left(\int_{-\infty}^{\infty} \sqrt{\frac{V^2}{c^2} \left(\frac{V}{c^2} \right)^{-1}} \cdot \sqrt{\frac{V^2}{c^2} \frac{V}{c^2}} d\xi \right)^2 \\ &= \left(\int_{-\infty}^{\infty} \frac{V^2}{c^2} d\xi \right)^2 \equiv \langle V^2/c^2 \rangle^2. \end{aligned} \tag{50}$$

It only remains to find the condition for the equality sign in (49). For this purpose, we apply the Cauchy-Schwarz inequality in vector form (see formula (15.2-5) in Ref. [31]):

$$\left| \left(\vec{a}, \vec{b} \right) \right|^2 \leq \left(\vec{a}, \vec{a} \right) \left(\vec{b}, \vec{b} \right). \tag{51}$$

However, the equality sign is realized if and only if the vectors $\vec{a}$ and $\vec{b}$ are linearly dependent, i.e., $\vec{a} = k\vec{b}$ ($k = \mathrm{const}$). By designating $\left(\vec{a}, \vec{a} \right) \equiv V/c^2$ and $\left(\vec{b}, \vec{b} \right) \equiv V^2/c^2$, it is easy to notice that the equality sign is realized if and only if

$$\sqrt{\frac{V^2}{c^2} \left(\frac{V}{c^2} \right)^{-1}} \Bigg/ \sqrt{\frac{V^2}{c^2} \frac{V}{c^2}} = \mathrm{const}. \tag{52}$$

(see sections 14.2-6 in Ref. [31]), i.e., when the value $V/c^2 = \text{const}$ does not vary within the period $\left(V(\xi)/(c(\xi))^2 \neq f(\xi)\right)$. This heterogeneous medium has been considered above. For all other heterogeneous media for which the value V/c^2 changes within period, the inequality is realized in Eq. (49). So, in a heterogeneous medium, the value α_p is always greater than $\alpha_{p\,\text{hom}}$ in a homogeneous medium. Thus, it is proved that, in the general case, the heterogeneities in a medium introduce the additional nonlinearity. This effect provides the basis for a new method of diagnostics to define the properties of multicomponent media using the propagation of long nonlinear waves in such media.

4.2 Fundamentals of new diagnostic method

The structure of the medium affects the wave field. There are different methods which allow the detection of gas bubbles and/or cracks in liquid [32], concrete [33], and ice cover [34] employing the nonlinear effects.

In this section, we describe our new diagnostic method for the properties of the medium. The features of the motion of finite-amplitude long waves and the effect of the increase of nonlinearity in the heterogeneous medium in comparison with homogeneous medium form the basis for the development of theoretical fundamentals of the diagnostic method. In this method, the properties of individual components are defined by long waves of finite amplitudes; more specifically, the dependence $V/c^2 = V/c^2(\zeta)$ on the fast Eulerian coordinate ζ (see Eq. (24)) is defined.

Thus, the nonlinear wave evolution allows one to obtain the structure of the medium with an inherent accuracy. As a final result, the mass concentrations of the individual components can be found using this method.

It should be kept in mind that the period of the structure of medium is infinitely small in the long-wave model, so it is not always possible to indicate the location of the structure elements inside the period reliably. Hence, the media with the different structures plotted in **Figure 2**, for example, affect identically on wave fields. These two media are indistinguishable in the framework of the suggested method. Taking into account this indefiniteness, we consider the function $V/c^2 = V/c^2(\zeta)$ that is to be the decreasing, integrable, mutually one-valued function on the interval $\zeta \in [0, 1]$, and equal to zero outside of this interval.

Now we represent the theoretical fundamentals for new method of diagnostics of medium by means of the long nonlinear waves. Let us prove the principal relation which enables us to obtain the inverse function $\zeta = \zeta(V/c^2)$ for the desired function $V/c^2 = V/c^2(\zeta)$ through the inverse Fourier transformation [19, 35–37]:

$$\zeta\left(Vc^{-2}\right) = F^{-1}\left[\sum_{n=0}^{\infty} \frac{\left\langle V\left(Vc^{-2}\right)^{n+1}\right\rangle}{(n+1)!\langle V\rangle} \mathrm{i}^n q^n\right]\left(Vc^{-2}\right). \tag{53}$$

It is known from theory of probability that the distribution function $f(x)$ (any one-valued, integrable, positive function) can be expressed by its central moments:

$$\alpha_n = \int_{-\infty}^{\infty} x^n f(x) dx. \tag{54}$$

Indeed, by using the characteristic function

$$\chi(q) = F[f(x)](q), \tag{55}$$

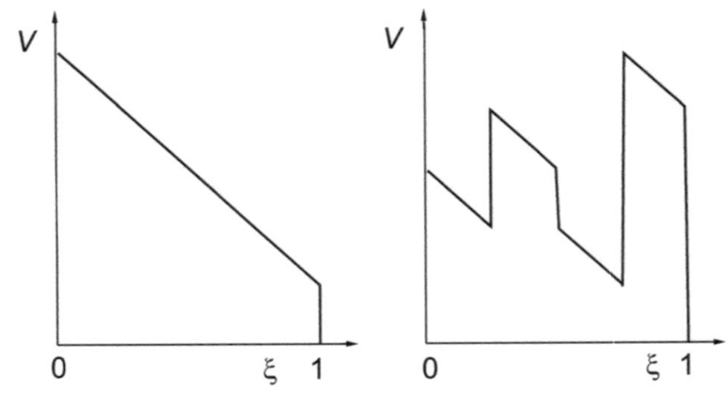

Figure 2.
The equivalent distributions of the specific volume in elementary sell for diagnostic method.

any positive integrable function $f(x)$ can be written as follows:

$$f(x) = F^{-1}[\chi(q)](x), \tag{56}$$

where $F[\cdot]$ is the Fourier transformation and $F^{-1}[\cdot]$ is the inverse Fourier transformation.

We take into account the important fact from the theory of probability: the characteristic function $\chi(q)$ is uniquely determined by the central moments α_n:

$$\chi(q) = \sum_{n=0}^{\infty} \alpha_n \mathrm{i}^n \frac{q^n}{n!}. \tag{57}$$

Hence, the function $f(x)$ can be found by means of the inverse Fourier transform:

$$f(x) = F^{-1}\left[\sum_{n=0}^{\infty} \alpha_n \mathrm{i}^n \frac{q^n}{n!}\right](x), \tag{58}$$

if series $\sum_{n=0}^{\infty}|\alpha_n|(s^n/n!)$ converges absolutely for some value $s > 0$ (see Section 18.3.7 in Ref. [31]).

These facts from the theory of probability are used to prove such a statement: if $V/c^2 = V/c^2(\zeta)$ is a decreasing positive integrable function on the interval $\zeta \in [0, 1]$ and equals to zero outside of it, then the inverse function $\zeta = \zeta(V/c^2)$ for the required function $V/c^2 = V/c^2(\zeta)$ can be written as (53) in the averaged values

$$\langle V(V/c^2)^n \rangle \equiv \int_{-\infty}^{\infty} V(V/c^2)^n d\xi. \tag{59}$$

Indeed, for the monotonic one-valued function $V/c^2 = V/c^2(\zeta)$, we find the integral in (59) by integrating the inverse function $\zeta = \zeta(V/c^2)$, since the transformation Jacobian is not equal to zero. We have the chain of identifies

$$\begin{aligned} \langle V(V/c^2)^n \rangle &= \int_0^1 V(\xi)\left(\frac{V}{c^2}\right)^n d\xi = \langle V \rangle \int_0^1 V\left(\frac{V}{c^2}\right)^n \rho d\zeta \\ &= \langle V \rangle \int_{-\infty}^{\infty} \left(\frac{V}{c^2}\right)^n \frac{d\zeta}{d(V/c^2)} d(V/c^2). \end{aligned} \tag{60}$$

In the geometric sense, this relation signifies that the integral (in our case, it is an area between the curve $V/c^2 = V/c^2(\zeta)$ and axes $O\zeta$ and $O(V/c^2)$) can be calculated either over ζ or over V/c^2 (see **Figure 2**). Whereas, the inequality is realized for the monotonic decreasing function $V/c^2 = V/c^2(\zeta)$.

For a function defined on a finite interval, if this function is positive and bounded above, we have

$$\begin{aligned}\left\langle V\left(V/c^2\right)^n\right\rangle &= \langle V\rangle \int_{-\infty}^{\infty} \left(\frac{V}{c^2}\right)^n \frac{d\zeta}{\left(dV/c^2\right)} d\left(V/c^2\right) \\ &= -n\langle V\rangle \int_{-\infty}^{\infty} \left(\frac{V}{c^2}\right)^{n-1} \zeta d\left(V/c^2\right).\end{aligned} \tag{61}$$

This relation provides the connection between the central moment α_n and the value $\left\langle V\left(V/c^2\right)^n\right\rangle$

$$\left\langle V\left(V/c^2\right)^n\right\rangle = -n\langle V\rangle\alpha_{n-1}. \tag{62}$$

Then the characteristic function $\chi(q)$ for the inverse function $\zeta = \zeta(V/c^2)$ is expressed through $\left\langle V\left(V/c^2\right)^n\right\rangle$. By applying the inverse Fourier transformation, finally, we find the required relationship (53).

The physical value Vc^{-2} is bounded by some constant M, hence

$$\alpha_n = \int_{-\infty}^{\infty} \left(Vc^{-2}\right)^{n-1}\zeta d\left(V/c^2\right) \leq \int_{0}^{M} \left(Vc^{-2}\right)^n d\left(V/c^2\right) = \frac{M^{n+1}}{n+1}. \tag{63}$$

The series $\sum_{n=0}^{\infty}|\alpha_n|(s^n/n!) \leq \sum_{n=0}^{\infty}M^{n+1}s^n/(n+1)!$ converge at $s < M^{-1}$. Consequently, the power series (53) also converges.

The coefficients $\left\langle V\left(V/c^2\right)^n\right\rangle$ $(n = 3, 4, \ldots)$ in Eq. (53) can be easily calculated, if we know the functional dependence $\langle V\rangle(p)$ or $\left\langle V^2/c^2\right\rangle(p)$. Indeed, they can be successively defined by the recurrence relation

$$\frac{d\left\langle V\left(Vc^{-2}\right)^n\right\rangle}{dp} = -(n+1)\left\langle V\left(Vc^{-2}\right)^{n+1}\right\rangle, \tag{64}$$

that follows directly from the equation of state. With mentioned accuracy, it is possible to diagnose the structural properties of the medium.

We have proven the principal relation (53) for the method of diagnostics that allows one to find the properties of the individual components in structured media by means of the long nonlinear waves.

4.3 Approximation of diagnosed medium by layer medium

Diagnostics of the structured medium properties by the long nonlinear waves is connected with the definition of values $\left\langle V\left(V/c^2\right)^n\right\rangle$. As indicated above, there is a problem related to the accuracy of the description of the structure by finite series (53).

Now, we shall show that the partial sum of series (53) is a step-function and approximates the desired function $\zeta = \zeta(V/c^2)$ with certain accuracy, namely, the diagnosed medium can be approximated by a layer medium. Let us write down the chain of the identities for any integrable function:

$$\begin{aligned} 2\pi f(-x) &= F[F[f(x)](q)](x) = F\left[\sum_{n=0}^{\infty} \frac{\mathrm{i}^n q^n}{n!} \alpha_n\right] \\ &= \sum_{n=0}^{\infty} \frac{\mathrm{i}^n \alpha_n}{n!} 2\pi(-\mathrm{i})^n \delta^{(n)}(x). \end{aligned} \tag{65}$$

Here we used the known relationships for the Fourier transform [31]):

$$F[F[f(x)](q)](x) = 2\pi f(-x), \tag{66}$$

$$F[q^n](x) = 2\pi(-\mathrm{i})^n \delta^{(n)}(x). \tag{67}$$

Hence, any integrable function can be represented by a series:

$$f(-x) = \sum_{n=0}^{\infty} \frac{\alpha_n}{n!} \delta^{(n)}(x). \tag{68}$$

We will prove that the finite series (53) approximates the desired function $f(x)$ by step-function. Consider the step-function $f_1(x)$ consisting of N steps:

$$f_1(x) = \begin{cases} \varphi_1, & 0 < x \leq b_1, \\ \varphi_2, & b_1 < x \leq b_2, \\ \vdots & \vdots \\ \varphi_N, & b_{N-1} < x \leq b_N \end{cases} \tag{69}$$

in order to approximate the desired function $f(x)$. The relation (69) can be written down through the Heavyside functions as follows:

$$\begin{aligned} f_1(x) &= \varphi_1[\Theta(x) - \Theta(x - b_1)] + \varphi_2[\Theta(x - b_1) - \Theta(x - b_2)] + \ldots \\ &\quad + \varphi_N[\Theta(x - b_{N-1}) - \Theta(x - b_N)], \end{aligned} \tag{70}$$

Evidently, by increasing the number of steps N and choosing the values φ_i and b_i, any integrable function $f(x)$ can be approximated by the step-function $f_1(x)$. It is convenient to use a notation

$$\begin{aligned} f_1(-x) &= \varphi_1[\Theta(x + b_1) - \Theta(x)] + \varphi_2[\Theta(x + b_2) - \Theta(x + b_1)] + \ldots \\ &\quad + \varphi_N[\Theta(x + b_N) - \Theta(x + b_{N-1})], \end{aligned} \tag{71}$$

that follows immediately from (70) after substitution:

$$\Theta(x) = 1 - \Theta(-x). \tag{72}$$

The Heavyside function $\Theta(x + b)$ can be expanded into a Taylor series in the neighborhood of point x:

$$\Theta(x + b) = \Theta(x) + \sum_{n=1}^{\infty} \frac{b^n}{n!} \Theta^{(n)}(x). \tag{73}$$

It is well-known that the derivative of Heavyside function $\Theta(x)$ is $\delta(x)$-function, then $\Theta^{(n+1)}(x) = \delta^{(n)}(x)$. We equate functions (68) and (71) and consider that the number of steps for function $f_1(x)$ is infinitely larger, and in this case we obtain

$$\begin{aligned} &\varphi_1 \sum_{n=0}^{\infty} \frac{b_1^{n+1}}{(n+1)!} \delta^{(n)}(x) + \varphi_2 \sum_{n=0}^{\infty} \frac{b_2^{n+1} - b_1^{n+1}}{(n+1)!} \delta^{(n)}(x) + \ldots + \\ &+ \varphi_N \sum_{n=0}^{\infty} \frac{b_N^{n+1} - b_{N-1}^{n+1}}{(n+1)!} \delta^{(n)}(x) + \ldots = \sum_{n=0}^{\infty} \frac{\alpha_n}{n!} \delta^{(n)}(x). \end{aligned} \tag{74}$$

This relationship shows that when we use the partial sum of series on the right-hand side of Eq. (74) $\sum_{n=0}^{2N-1} \frac{\alpha_n}{n!} \delta^{(n)}(x)$ and also the N leading terms on the left-hand side, then the desired function $f(x)$ is approximated by the step-function $f_1(x)$ with N steps. In other words, if it is necessary to restore the structure of medium by means of N periodic repeated layers, then we need to know the $2N - 1$ moments α_n, i.e., the values $\langle V(Vc^{-2})^n \rangle$.

For the sake of convenience, we write down the relation (74) in the expanded form. For this purpose, we multiply it by x^n and integrate over x. We obtain the nonlinear system of the equations in the unknowns $b_1, b_2, \ldots, b_N, \varphi_2, \varphi_3$, and $\ldots, \varphi_N$ (variable $\varphi_1 = 1$ owing to normalization):

$$\begin{aligned} &\varphi_1 b_1 + \varphi_2(b_2 - b_1) + \varphi_3(b_3 - b_2) + \ldots + \varphi_N(b_N - b_{N-1}) = \alpha_0, \\ &\varphi_1 b_1^2 + \varphi_2(b_2^2 - b_1^2) + \varphi_3(b_3^2 - b_2^2) + \ldots + \varphi_N(b_N^2 - b_{N-1}^2) = 2\alpha_1, \\ &\cdots \\ &\varphi_1 b_1^{2N-1} + \varphi_2(b_2^{2N-1} - b_1^{2N-1}) + \varphi_3(b_3^{2N-1} - b_2^{2N-1}) + \ldots + \\ &\quad + \varphi_N(b_N^{2N-1} - b_{N-1}^{2N-1}) = (2N-1)\alpha_{2N-2}. \end{aligned} \tag{75}$$

Now, if b_i implies the partition of $(V/c^2)_i$ and φ_i implies the partition of ζ_i, we can obtain the system of Eq. (75) to define the structure of medium. Solution of these equations gives the information about the component properties of the medium, namely, the value V/c^2 on the structure period $\zeta \in [0, 1]$ is found in the form of the step-function.

Let us note the special case of a periodic medium for which the value V/c^2 is constant within the period. This medium, as we already know, does not differ from a homogeneous one for the propagation of the long nonlinear waves. The same result follows from a system (75). Indeed, for homogeneous media the moments α_n are equal to

$$\alpha_n = \frac{\left\langle V(Vc^{-2})^{n+1} \right\rangle}{(n+1)\langle V \rangle} = \frac{b^{n+1}}{n+1}. \tag{76}$$

Here, the conditions of normalization $\langle V^2/c^2 \rangle_0 = (V^2/c^2)_0 = 1$ and $\langle V \rangle_0 = V_0 = 1$ have been used as before. Therefore, the values in the right-hand side of Eq. (75) are equal to $b \equiv Vc^{-2} = \text{const}$. It is easy to see that the solution of system is $b_1 = b_2 = \ldots = b_N = b = 1$ and $\varphi_1 = 1$ (where φ_i is any value for $i \geq 2$). This corresponds to the layer medium, for which $V/c^2 \neq f(\zeta)$, in particular, this medium can be a homogeneous one.

According to the asymptotic averaged model of a structured medium, the period of the structure is infinitely small, and this diagnostic method cannot give the exact

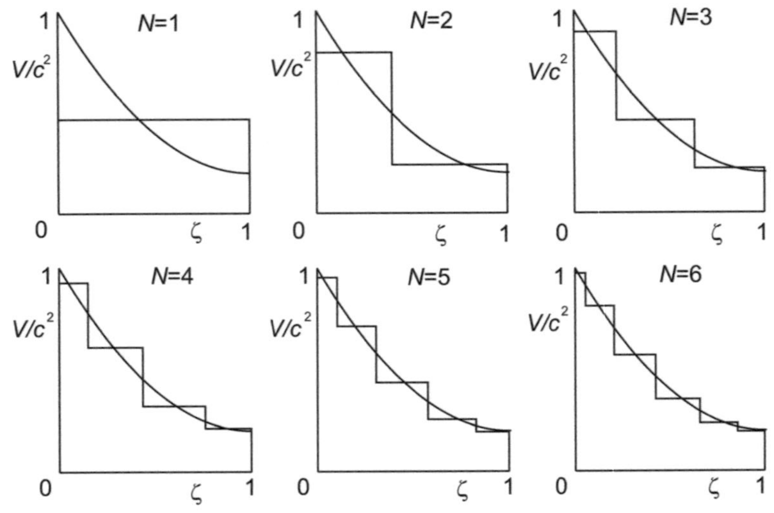

Figure 3.
Approximation of the diagnosed medium $V/c^2 = 0.2 + 0.8(1 - \zeta)^2$ *by N-component medium.*

location of the structure elements inside the period. Hence, using this method, only the mass contents of the particular components can be determined.

We present, as an example, the results of the calculation to define the structure of layer media, which can properly approximate the diagnosed medium. The structure of the diagnosed medium is $V/c^2 = 0.2 + 0.8(1 - \zeta)^2$ in **Figure 3**. In order to approximate the diagnosed medium by layer periodic medium, which has N layers within the period, it is necessary to know $2N - 1$ values $\langle V(Vc^{-2})^n \rangle$ for finite series (53). If we regard that the $2N - 1$ averaged characteristics $\langle V(Vc^{-2})^n \rangle$ coincide for the diagnosed medium and the layer medium, these averaged values at $n \leq 2N - 1$ can be calculated from the known distributions $V/c^2 = 0.2 + 0.8(1 - \zeta)^2$. At $n > 2N - 1$ the values $\langle V(Vc^{-2})^n \rangle$ for diagnosed medium and for approximated layer medium are different. The distributions of $V/c^2(\zeta)$ within the period for diagnosed medium and for approximated media with N components are shown in **Figure 3**. On the one hand, the calculated distributions for layered media are the best approximation for the medium we test. On the other hand, we have illustrated the accuracy of the approximation of the diagnosed medium by the finite series (53).

Thus, the new method for the diagnostics of the medium characteristics by long nonlinear waves is suggested on the basis of the asymptotic averaged model of the structured medium. The mass contents of the particular components can be denoted by the abovementioned diagnostic method.

5. Conclusion

The asymptotic averaged model is suggested for the description of the wave processes in nonequilibrium heterogeneous media. The obtained integral differential system of equations cannot be reduced to the average terms (pressure, mass velocity, specific volume) and contains the terms with characteristic sizes of individual components.

On the microstructure level of the medium, the dynamical behavior is governed only by the laws of thermodynamics. On the macrolevel, the motion of the medium can be described by the wave-dynamical laws for the averaged variables with the integrodifferential equation of state containing the characteristics of the medium microstructure. A rigorous mathematical proof is given to show that finite-amplitude long waves respond to the structure of the medium in such a way that the homogeneous medium model is insufficient for the description of the behavior of the structured medium. An important result that follows from this model is that, for a finite-amplitude wave, the medium structure (in particular, existence of microcracks) produces nonlinear effects even if the individual components of the medium are described by a linear law. Finding the wave fields in the structured medium is the direct problem, on the one hand.

On the other hand, the system analyzed here is not expressed in the average hydrodynamical terms; hence the dynamical behavior of the medium cannot be modelled by a homogeneous medium even for long waves, if they are nonlinear. The heterogeneity of the medium structure always introduces additional nonlinearity that does not arise in a homogeneous medium. This effect enabled one to formulate the theoretical grounds of a new diagnostic method that determines the characteristics of a heterogeneous medium with the use of finite-amplitude long waves (inverse problem). This diagnostic method can also be employed to find the mass contents of individual components.

Additional information

Physics and Astronomy Classification Scheme (PACS): 43.25.Zx, 43.25.Ba, 43.25.Ed, 43.25.Gf

Author details

Vyacheslav Vakhnenko[1*], Dmitri Vengrovich[1] and Alexandre Michtchenko[2]

1 Institute of Geophysics, Ukrainian Academy of Sciences, Kyiv, Ukraine

2 Instituto Politécnico Nacional, SEPI-ESIME-Zacatenco, Ciudad de México, México

*Address all correspondence to: vakhnenko@ukr.net

References

[1] Bereznev I, Nikolaev A. Experimental investigations of nonlinear seismic effects. Physics of the Earth and Planetary Interiors. 1988;**50**: 83-87. DOI: 10.1016/0031-9201(88) 90096-9

[2] Bonner B, Wanamaker B. Acoustic nonlinearities produced by a single macroscopic fracture in granite. In: Thompson D, Chimenti D, editors. Review of Progress in Quantitative Nondestructive Evaluation. Vol. 10B. Boston, MA: Springer; 1991. pp. 1861-1867. DOI: 10.1007/978-1-4615-3742-7_94

[3] Guyer R, Johnson P. Nonlinear Mesoscopic Elasticity: The Complex Behaviour of Rocks, Soil, Concrete. Weinheim: Wiley-VCH Verlag GmbH and Co. KgaA; 2009. p. 395. ISBN: 978-3-527-40703-3

[4] Johnson P, McCall K. Observation and implications of nonlinear elastic wave response in rock. Geophysical Research Letters. 1994;**21**:165-168. DOI: 10.1029/93GL03162

[5] Johnson P, Shankland T, O'Connell R, Albright J. Nonlinear generation of elastic waves in crystalline rock. Journal of Geophysical Research. 1987;**92**:3597-3602. DOI: 10.1029/JB092iB05p03597

[6] Nesterenko V. Dynamics of Heterogeneous Materials. New York: Springer-Verlag; 2001. p. 510. ISBN: 978-1-4757-3524-6

[7] Ostrovsky L. Wave processes in media with strong acoustic nonlinearity. The Journal of the Acoustical Society of America. 1991;**90**:3332-3337. DOI: 10.1121/1.401444

[8] Sadovsky M, Pisarenko G. Seismic Process in Block Medium. Moscow: Nauka; 1991. p. 95 (in Russian). ISBN: 5-02-000776-5

[9] Achenbach J. Wave Propagation in Plastic Solids. Amsterdam: North-Holland; 1973. p. 440. ISBN: 9780720403251

[10] Aki K, Richards P. Quantitative Seismology: Theory and Methods. Vol. I and II. San Francisco: W.H. Freeman and Co.; 1980. DOI: 10.1002/gj.3350160110

[11] Truesdell C. Rational Thermodynamics. New York: Springer-Verlag; 1984. p. 578. ISBN: 978-1-4612-5206-1

[12] Biot M. Theory of propagation of elastic waves in a fluid-saturated solid. I. Low-frequency range. The Journal of the Acoustical Society of America. 1956; **28**:168-178. DOI: 10.1121/1.1908239

[13] Lyakhov G. Waves in Soils and Porous Multicomponent Media. Moscow: Nauka; 1982. p. 286. Available from: http://elib.pstu.ru/vufind/Record/RUPSTUbooks151687

[14] Raats P. Applications of the theory of mixtures in soil physics. In: Truesdell C, editor. Rational Thermodynamics. New York: Springer-Verlag; 1984. pp. 326-343. ISBN: 978-1-4612-5206-1

[15] Rajagopal K, Tao L. Mechanics of Mixtures. Singapore: World Scientific Publishing; 1995. p. 195. ISBN-10: 9810215851

[16] Nigmatulin R. Dynamics of Multiphase Media. Vols. 1 and 2. Boca Raton, Florida: CRC Press; 1990. p. 878. ISBN-10: 1560322071

[17] Landau L, Lifshitz E. Fluids Mechanics. New York: Pergamon Press; 1987. p. 554. ISBN: 9781483161044

[18] Vakhnenko V, Danilenko V, Michtchenko A. An asymptotic averaged model of nonlinear long waves propagation in media with a regular structure. International Journal of Non-Linear Mechanics. 1999;**34**: 643-654. DOI: 10.1016/S0020-7462(98) 00014-6

[19] Vakhnenko V, Danilenko V, Michtchenko A. Diagnostics of the medium structure by long wave of finite amplitude. International Journal of Non-Linear Mechanics. 2000;**35**: 1105-1113. DOI: 10.1016/S0020-7462 (99)00082-7

[20] Vakhnenko V. Blast waves in multi-component medium with thermal relaxation. Natural Science. 2014;**6**: 1055-1092. DOI: 10.4236/ ns.2014.612096

[21] Vakhnenko V, Danilenko V, Kulich V. Averaged description of shock-wave processes in periodic media. Soviet Journal of Chemical Physics. 1994;**12**(3):534-546. ISSN: 0733-2831

[22] Vakhnenko V, Kulich V. Long-wave processes in periodic media. Journal of Applied Mechanics and Technical Physics. 1992;**32**:814-820. DOI: 10.1007/ BF00851969

[23] Lavrentiev M, Chabat B. Effets hydrodynamiques et modéles mathématiques. Moscow: Éditions Mir; 1980. p. 365. OCLC Number: 301487224

[24] Clarke J. Lectures on plane waves in reacting gases. Annales de Physique. 1984;**9**:211-306. DOI: 10.1051/anphys: 0198400902021100

[25] Danylenko V, Sorokina V, Vladimirov V. On the governing equations in relaxing models and self-similar quasiperiodic solutions. Journal of Physics A: Mathematical and General. 1993;**26**:7125-7135. DOI: 10.1088/ 0305-4470/26/23/047

[26] Yasnikov G, Belousov V. Effective thermodynamic functions of a gas with solid particles. Journal of Engineering Physics. 1978;**34**:734-737. DOI: 10.1007/ BF00860421

[27] Bakhvalov N, Panasenko G. Homogenisation: Averaging Processes in Periodic Media. Boston: Kluwer Academic Publishers; 1989. p. 366. DOI: 10.1007/978-94-009-2247-1. ISBN: 978-0-7923-0049-6

[28] Bakhvalov N, Eglit M. Processes in periodic media not described in terms of averaged characteristics. Doklady Akademii Nauk SSSR (transi, as Soviet Math. Dokl.). 1983;**268**:836-840. Available from: http://mi.mathnet.ru/e ng/dan/v268/i4/p836

[29] Berdichevsky V. Variational Principles of Continuum Mechanics. Berlin-Heidelberg: Springer-Verlag; 2010. p. 900. ISBN: 978-3-540-88465-1

[30] Sanchez-Palencia E. Non-Homogeneous Media and Vibration Theory. Berlin, New York: Springer-Verlag; 1980. p. 398. ISBN: 978-3-540-10000-3

[31] Korn G, Korn T. Mathematical Handbook for Scientists and Engineers. New York, San Francisco, Toronto, London, Sydney: McGraw-Hill Book Company; 1968. p. 720. DOI: 10.1002/ zamm.19690490921

[32] Fenlon F, Wonn J. On the amplification of modulated acoustic waves in gas-liquid mixtures. In: Lauterborn W, editor. Cavitation and Inhomogeneities in Underwater Acoustics. Berlin, Heidelberg: Springer; 1980. pp. 141-150. DOI: 10.1007/ 978-3-642-51070-0. ISBN: 978-3-642-51072-4

[33] Schkolnik I. Nondestructive testing of concretes: New aspects. Nondestructive Testing and Evaluation.

1993;**10**:351-358. DOI: 10.1080/10589759308952807

[34] Ekimov A, Lebedev A, Ostrovskii L, Sutin A. Nonlinear acoustic effects due to cracks in ice cover. Acoustical Physics. 1996;**42**:51-54. ISSN: 10637710

[35] Vakhnenko V, Danilenko V. Nonlinear waves as a technical tool for diagnostics of the medium structure. In: Proceedings of 10th International Congress on Sound and Vibration. Stockholm: International Institute of Acoustics and Vibration; 2003. pp. 3549-3556. Available from: http://www.igph.kiev.ua/vakhnenko/vakhnenko.html (N 31)

[36] Vakhnenko V. Diagnosis of the properties of a structurized medium by long nonlinear waves. Journal of Applied Mechanics and Technical Physics. 1996;**37**(N5):643-649. ISSN: 0021-8944

[37] Vakhnenko V, Danilenko V. An asymptotic model of non-linear waves in natural multi-component media. Geophysical Journal. 1997;**16**:674-685. ISSN: 02759128